CHARLOTTE CANNING

BY THE SAME AUTHOR

Dante Gabriel Rossetti: The Paintings & Drawings
A Catalogue Raisonné, 2 Vols. (*Clarendon Press 1971*)

Sublime and Instructive
Letters from John Ruskin. (*Michael Joseph 1972*)

CHARLOTTE CANNING

Lady-in-Waiting to Queen Victoria
and Wife of the first Viceroy of India
1817–1861

VIRGINIA SURTEES

JOHN MURRAY

Printed in Great Britain by
W & J Mackay Limited, Chatham
0 7195 3230 2

To my sister
Evangeline Bruce

Simplified family tree showing most o

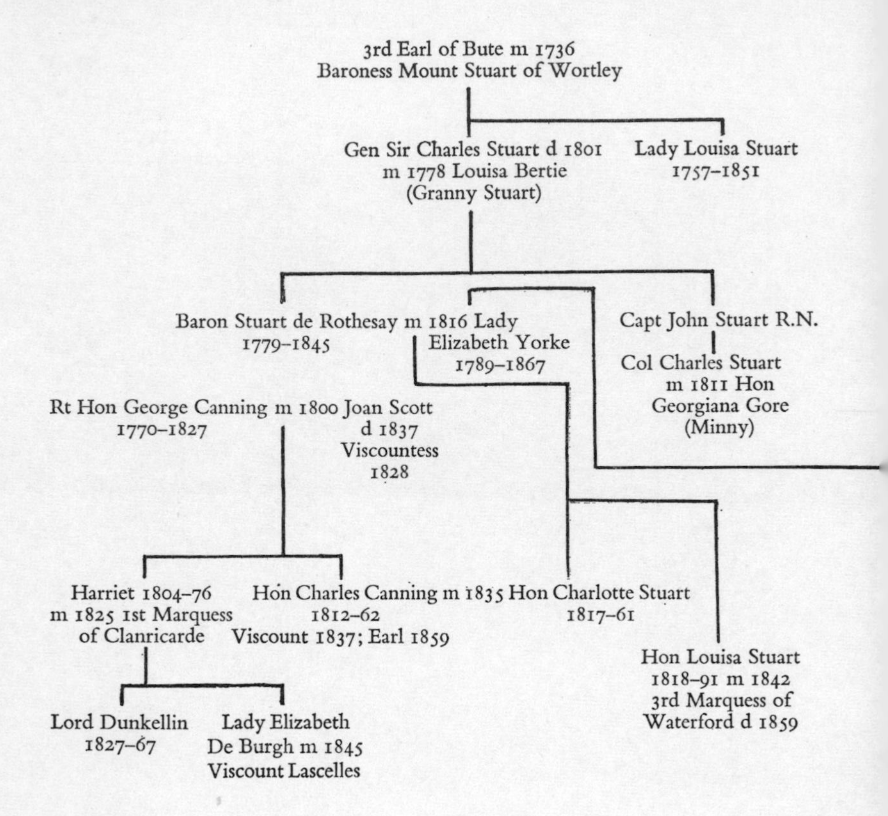

harlotte's relations mentioned in the text

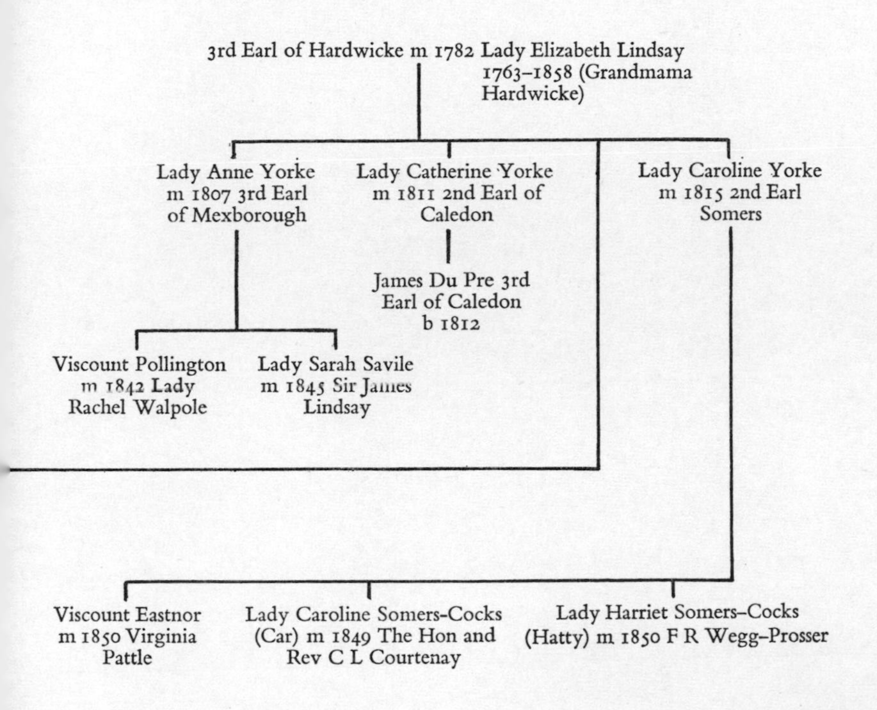

Viscount Eastnor m 1850 Virginia Pattle

Lady Caroline Somers-Cocks (Car) m 1849 The Hon and Rev C L Courtenay

Lady Harriet Somers-Cocks (Hatty) m 1850 F R Wegg-Prosser

Contents

Illustrations

Illustrations

Acknowledgments

To Her Majesty the Queen for Gracious Permission to quote from, and to publish, material in the Royal Archives, Windsor Castle, as well as letters from Queen Victoria; and to reproduce certain pictures from the Royal Collection.

My debt to the Earl of Harewood is very considerable. This book is based almost entirely on the great quantity of Lady Canning's papers belonging to him—including Queen Victoria's letters—deposited at Sheepscar Library, Leeds City Archives. Without imposing any restrictions whatsoever, he has accorded me copyright permission and leave to make use of such material as I required, much of which is unpublished; at the same time enabling me to reproduce several water-colour drawings by Lady Canning from the large number at Harewood House, as well as the portraits of Lord and Lady Canning. I am deeply obliged to him for so much consideration. To this debt of thanks I add the name of Mr Neville A. Ussher, Agent to the Earl of Harewood, whose inexhaustible kindness and patience have been severely, though never demonstrably, tried.

To Mr Robert Mackworth-Young, Her Majesty's Librarian, I offer my grateful thanks for advice and help; and also to Miss Jennifer Sherwood, Curator of the Print Room, Windsor Castle. To Miss Jane Langton, Registrar of the Royal Archives, and Miss Elizabeth Cuthbert, who have willingly replied to my questions from their great range of information—no trifling enquiry being beyond their capacity—and for their kindness to me, I wish to record my sincere thanks. I am also indebted to Sir Oliver Millar, Surveyor of the Queen's Pictures, and to Mr Geoffrey de Bellaigue, Surveyor of the Queen's Works of Art.

At Leeds, Mr J. M. Collinson of the Sheepscar Library Archives, and his staff afforded me every assistance during the many occasions when I have worked under their friendly eye, and I take this opportunity of thanking them.

Although Lord Canning's role in the first part of this book is a shadowy one, I have nevertheless from the beginning turned to '*Clemency*' *Canning*, by Mr Michael Maclagan who has given me generously of his time, advice, and judgement. For the Cannings' period in India it is this book which has been the background to my own. Further debts are manifold, and in particular I wish to inscribe the names of the Hon. Betty Askwith, and Miss Mary Lutyens, who have repeatedly advised and encouraged me; also that of Lord Harris.

For help in various ways I should like to thank Dr Freiherr von Andrian-Werburg, Registrar of the Coburg Archives, Mrs M. Bowen, Mrs Anthony Butler, Mr Nicholas Cox, Princesse Claire de Croÿ, Lady Sarah Cumming-Bruce, Mr Donald Fazarkerley, Mr John Gere, Fräulein Eva Gritsch, Miss Pauline Harrold, the Hon. Mrs Hervey-Bathurst, Mr and Mrs Victor Kennett, the Marquess of Lansdowne and the Earl of Shelburne, the Reverend Prebendary Harold Loasby, Lt-Colonel Charles Micklewright, Mr Richard Ormond, Dr Stephen Pasmore, Captain George Pretyman, Miss Sophia Ryde, Sir John Summerson, Mr Christopher Tower, Mrs P. A. Tritton, Mr Bertram Unné, Mr David Yorke. I acknowledge with thanks permission granted me by the British Museum to quote from letters to the Marchioness of Clanricarde from Countess Canning; by Sir William Gladstone, Bart. to quote from the Gladstone and Newcastle Mss. at St Deiniol's Library, Hawarden and the Hon. Archivist of the Flintshire Record Office for placing this material at my disposal; by the India Office Library and Records to quote from their material and to reproduce several photographs; by A. D. Peters & Company to reprint from *The Stanleys of Alderley* by Nancy Mitford; by the Controller of Her Majesty's Stationery Office to quote from Crown-Copyright records in the Public Record Office; and I thank the staff of the London Library for the benefit of their assistance.

Acknowledgments

In India my obligation to His Excellency Mr A. L. Dias, Governor of Bengal, for allowing me to see over Government House, Calcutta, and for extending to me every facility is great, as is also my gratitude to Mr P. K. Sarkar, Secretary to the Governor, for accompanying me to Barrackpore and for being himself an indefatigable guide there and at Calcutta. Encouraged by Miss Mollie Panter-Downes to visit Ooty, and with the unfaltering patience and wide local knowledge of Mr Lynn Townsend, I was privileged to accompany him and his wife in their jeep along every path and turning at Ootacamund and Coonoor which Lady Canning must have covered. Finally I take this opportunity of thanking the unknown Indian fellow passenger at Calcutta airport for pointing out to me that the sweetmeat with which we were indulged, of curdled milk, flour, and sugar, rolled into a ball and fried in syrup, was the legendary 'ledikeni' (Lady Canning), for which perhaps she showed some predeliction, over a hundred years ago.

Foreword

The pattern of Charlotte Canning's life falls naturally into two definable parts. Although superficially Lady Canning's upbringing and married life in England and her duties as Lady of the Bedchamber to Queen Victoria, suggest a requisite training for her subsequent position as Viceroy's wife, nothing that she had experienced had been a preparation for the horrors of the Indian Mutiny, nor can her leisurely travels on her husband's yacht in early marriage have acquainted her with the rigours of a journey such as she undertook to the borders of Tibet in 1860. Her journey to India in 1855 at the age of thirty-eight as wife of the new Governor-General (later India's first Viceroy) formed the bridge between a habit of life (such as was familiar to her contemporaries) and the unknown world of the East, where the diversity of customs, religions, and tongues was strange to her, and where during one of the gravest periods in the history of British India her courage and steadfastness sustained her husband, though the havoc it wrought on her own constitution doomed her to an early grave.

The contrast of these two parts forms the basis of this book: the trivia of daily life, family events, high mortality, and the abounding concern with Victorian ailments take their measured place, while the Indian canvas is brushed in with the same enquiring mind and observant eye, but on a wider scale. Linking the whole, and interwoven into this narrative from 1842 until the curtain falls at Barrackpore, is Char's very sincere devotion to the Queen whom she served for thirteen years. Her affection for the Royal Children is also evident; of her sympathy for Prince Albert one might be wrong to conjecture.

The first section deals principally with human beings and

relationships. Perhaps, because these had been her background since infancy, politics enter very little into her letters or journals, and though married to a prominent statesman he of all her family remains remote. While the Aunthood, Countess of Mexborough, Countess of Caledon, Countess Somers, and Grandmama Hardwicke, people the letters to her mother or to her sister 'fat Lou', Marchioness of Waterford, Canning remains in the shadows. Char loved him deeply and constantly; if there was infidelity on his part—and there is a suggestion of a name amongst the married ladies of society—the heavy blanket of Victorian discretion silences any rumours from the past, and Lady Canning herself never referred to it. Only in India where, by his comprehension of the meaning of justice he finally emerges in these pages, 'Clemency' Canning lit by the blaze of controversy from home, assumes the place accorded to him by history.

The last scene is one of poignancy. In 1855 when Viscount Canning's appointment to India hung in the balance, Char had written to her sister that she was ready to 'follow like a dog', though the protracted exile from home oppressed her. Now, after the long absence in India, and with her health impaired, she was almost in sight of the loving family she had left six years earlier—her mother, her widowed sister, both most particularly dear; the aunts, cousins, friends, Tyttenhanger and Highcliffe, all that had made up her earlier life. The Queen had offered Canning the Ranger's house at Blackheath and she was busy entertaining plans for their future establishment: a poultry yard, a cow, and a dairy stocked with bamboo milk buckets from Burma. One senses the piercing joy of the thought of home. Yet it was not an earthly home to which she journeyed. So deep and abiding was her faith that she had once said to her cousin Lady Caroline Somers-Cocks, how strange it was 'that *such* a blessing as death' should cause misery. 'Car', she had said, 'I sometimes think I ought to *fear* death more. My last prayer at night is that I may be *ready*.' Struck down suddenly by jungle-fever contracted on a journey from Darjeeling she lingered a very few days and died in Calcutta. Her husband buried her in the garden at Barrackpore by the side of the holy waters of the Hooghly River in the pale light of the setting moon, while the first rays of the sun pierced the sky. After her death the same cousin wrote of her as pavilioned in 'the bright Home she had so yearned for'.

In preparing this book much of the selected material has had to be omitted for lack of space and, for this same reason, points of omission in Lady Canning's letters have not been indicated, nor in those few from Lord Canning and Lady Stuart de Rothesay (all at Leeds City Archives). Topics omitted include descriptive passages, weather, vegetation, small family concerns not directly relevant, or when, as in the case of the journals written up while abroad or in the Highlands with Queen Victoria, the sightseeing and enthusiasm of onlookers sound a repetitive note. Concerning the Cannings' wide circle of friends the choice of what to discard has been taken with hesitation and reluctance. At Eton and Oxford Canning's set included Lord Harris, Lord de Tabley, Lord Lincoln, Gladstone, Lord Malmesbury, and other names of distinction which recur in Lady Canning's letters; of her own contemporaries she scribbled down irresistible snatches of gossip, but these, with accounts of visits to the great country houses, have had to be abandoned. Nevertheless many incidents of inconsequence have been retained since trivialities constitute the stuff of life and add a fragment to our knowledge of the past.

Most of the material is unpublished—the letters from and to Queen Victoria entirely so, as well as Lady Canning's journals written while travelling with the Queen—but where it appears already in *The Story of Two Noble Lives*, by Augustus Hare, the wording or dating may not be found to correspond for Hare was still bound by certain conventions, nor had he access to all Lady Canning's papers; his dating is also sometimes at fault. Where no source is given, material is taken from Lady Canning's papers; capitals and ampersands have not been modified and original spelling has been preserved. Among Lady Canning's papers are the rough drafts of her letters to Queen Victoria from India, in many cases badly burnt at the edges as a result of fire in her tent during a camp journey; draft copies of her letters to Lord Granville (then Lord President) during the Indian Mutiny have suffered likewise. In general her accounts of the Mutiny are a model of clarity—Queen Victoria remarked on their being 'the *best* which are received from India'—but they are set down from information she received at the time and may not conform to the judgement of history, which lies outside the scope of this book.

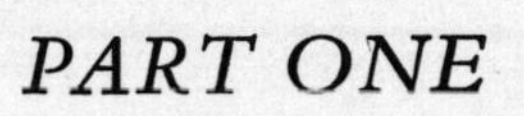

PART ONE

I

Charlotte Stuart

From birth the gracious eye of Majesty fell upon Charlotte. In Paris her parents had not been backward in submitting a petition for their child, so that thirteen days after the birth of the baby, Princess Elizabeth acting as her mother's scribe, availed herself of one of the 'plain sheets of cheap paper which all the Royal Family at Windsor used',[1] and took up her pen at Queen Charlotte's behest.

April 13th 1817

The Queen commands me to desire you will write to Mr Disbrowe* & assure him She will with pleasure accept of being God Mother to Sir Charles & Lady Elizabeth's little Girl, & no kind of objection that the name Elizabeth should be joined to that of Charlotte, thinking it may be agreeable to Sir Charles the child's having its Mother's name.

The Queen orders me to add that She thinks it will be a civility either You or Mr Disbrowe should write to Lady Mansfield to be Her proxy, with a civil message from Her.

Yours sincerely E

The ceremony itself evoked some derision which Lady Granville,† on a visit to Paris at the end of the Napoleonic wars, recounted in a letter home.

June 1817

We went to Sir Charles Stuart's christening party, and ball. Lady Mansfield stood proxy for the Queen and I never saw anything so

* Vice-Chamberlain to Queen Charlotte; Countess Mansfield was her lady-in-waiting.

† Lady Harriet Cavendish (Haryo), second daughter of the 5th Duke of Devonshire and the beautiful Duchess, had married her aunt's lover Lord Granville Leveson-Gower in 1809. In 1815 he had been raised to the peerage.

ridiculous as her entry with two little pages in Highland costume holding up her train. It was very grand and very dull.[2]

The little girl who had been ushered so ceremoniously into Christian society was born on March 31st 1817 at the British Embassy, the first child of Sir Charles and Lady Elizabeth Stuart. Sir Charles (he had not yet been granted a peerage), now approaching forty, had taken the step to matrimony the previous year, and deciding to choose a wife had set about it in his customary forthright manner. From all accounts he was not a sympathetic man although an able and eccentric one—characteristics inherited from his grandfather, the 3rd Earl of Bute (Prime Minister for a few months in the early reign of George III) who had married the only daughter of Lady Mary Wortley-Montagu. Lady Louisa Stuart, his aunt, whose well-informed mind and intellectual tastes marked her as an outstanding woman of her time, and his father, General Sir Charles Stuart who had served the army with distinction and had numbered Nelson and Sir John Moore among his friends, helped to provide a formidable heritage. Stuart, educated at Eton and Christ Church, Oxford, entered the Diplomatic service, proceeding to Vienna in 1801 (the year of his father's death) and there spent his first years as Secretary of Legation. At St Petersburg in 1804 he held the same position under Lord Granville Leveson-Gower, the distinguished diplomatist, later Viscount and Earl Granville, who told a friend that he and 'Silence', their nickname for Charles Stuart, were on an agreeable footing.

In Lisbon, as Minister during the Peninsular campaign, Stuart won the Duke of Wellington's esteem by his zeal and tact in the management of the Spanish and Portuguese Juntas, no easy task, and one for which he was invested with the Civil Knight Grand Cross of the Bath. For two months in 1814, after the abdication of Napoleon Bonaparte, he held the appointment of Minister Plenipotentiary *ad interim* in Paris, and on making way for the Great Duke, proceeded almost immediately to The Hague.

It was now that Sir Charles began his courtship of Lady Elizabeth Yorke, the third of four daughters of the 3rd Earl of Hardwicke; her elder sisters had been married some years and the younger married in 1815. Sir Charles shortly returned to Paris as Ambassador, and to Lady Elizabeth, no longer young, conversant with the ways of society, perfect in French, there could have been little cause for hesitation, though she could not have failed to have heard of Sir Charles's propensity for the *coulisses* of the Paris Opera, and for the charms of its *corps de ballet*. The theatre too had its enticements. But no doubt she surveyed the marriage in much the same light as did her suitor—as one of convenience. Her lack of even conventional good looks was compensated by a happy disposition, dignity, and a zest for life. She had grown up at Wimpole Hall in Cambridgeshire, the seat of the Earls of Hardwicke, and at Tyttenhanger, nearer London, in an age when marriages were formed with an eye to expediency, and if, as in this case, love was in short supply, neither party would have felt the deficiency. Mary and Agnes Berry (the 'Berrino' as they were affectionately known), devoted friends of the Countess of Hardwicke, distinguished for their salon and the affection bestowed upon them by Horace Walpole, were eager to promote a match which conformed with the proprieties of the day. Their hopes were realized when in February 1816 the bride, at the age of thirty, entered the Paris Embassy on the arm of the Ambassador and immediately made a position for herself amongst the French.

The Misses Berry were always her champion: 'I saw Elizabeth *chez moi* ... at her return from court, in all her *beaux atours*, and remarkably well she looked ... Her success here among the French is, I assure you, great, and she has already more acquaintances than I dare be sworn any Ambassadress has had.'[3] 'Were I now to turn from the *lace and fringe* of life, and talk to you of her excellent stuff of both head and heart on which they are applied, I should tell you nothing new.'[4] The entertaining was done in ample style. 'We were at a *Grand Bal Paré* at the Ambassador's ... given in honor of the Duke of Cambridge ... The Supper was very splendid, and must have cost Sir Charles a *pretty penny*.'[5] Lady Granville's tone was a shade less enthusiastic: 'Lady Elizabeth Stuart is very agreeable and amiable, and by dint of rouge and an auburn wig looks only not pretty, but nothing worse. Sir

Charles praised her to me with enthusiasm, and as she does not seem to mind his theatrical career, I am sure I do not know who should . . . They are both very agreeable, and, though there is no sentimentality between them, they seem the best friends possible, and I believe half his bad behaviour is put on.'[6] 'Sir Charles stays almost always behind the scenes [at the Opera] and winks and nods are going on all the time between him and the actresses. Lady Elizabeth is not more romantic than is to be wished, so that I do not think anybody has a right to object to anything but *le genre* of his infidelities, which I think deplorable.'[7] Their nature must have been known all over Paris. 'Sir Charles is all graciousness and very entertaining, *le moins mari que possible*, *affichéing* the worst company and lowest connections, but I understand has *des égards* for Lady Elizabeth, with which she is perfectly satisfied.'[8] With a stroke of the pen Lady Granville hands down the Ambassador and his lady to posterity: 'Lady Elizabeth [follows] . . . after him to prompt civilities, which he performs like a pug-dog just going to snap.'[9]

The year after Char's birth a second daughter was born; this was beneficial to the older child. 'I think Charlotte is less of a Princess than she was', her mother wrote in 1818, 'she has less homage of late as people have been busy— & she has had fewer opportunities of being gracious. She is a very delightful little thing with pretty ways, but don't tell Lady Stuart [her mother-in-law] I do *not* think she will be very pretty, she is as like her as possible, but with the advantage of dark eyes'. Both children grew up to be beautiful, an astonishing feat with such ill-favoured parents, and one that Lady Stuart de Rothesay was the first to recognize, for it amused her to recount how at a ball a guest gazing at her daughters was overheard to say: 'How beautiful they are', and, looking at her, added 'isnt it strange, *considering*?'[10] Charlotte became an accepted beauty, while Louisa was noted for her outstanding good looks and graceful carriage.

By the end of 1824 George Canning, the new Foreign Secretary, announced a change in Paris and Sir Charles, who was followed by Lord Granville as Ambassador, was sent on a special mission to

Brazil and Portugal lasting a year; though successful he felt that Canning had underated his performance and had secured the priase to himself. The two men were incompatible, but with Canning's death three years later (by then Prime Minister) opportunities of a welcome nature arose. The Duke of Wellington was at the head of the Government, and remembering his past soundness and loyalty in Lisbon suggested that Sir Charles should take the Foreign Office. This he refused but asked for a return to the Paris Embassy, thus obliging the Granvilles to pack up and make way for the 'diligent young Lord' (leaving Lord Aberdeen, the new Foreign Secretary, no time in which to acquaint them with their successor's appointment) and himself wrote 'to say he shall be here in a fortnight'.[11]

The 'young Lord' now rising fifty, had been enobled by his Sovereign at the beginning of the year (1828) against opposition from some of the Ministers on political grounds, and if Charles Greville is to be believed, he was 'personally obnoxious to the King and universally disliked'.[12] On hearing of Lord Stuart de Rothesay's choice of title, George IV remarked: 'Ah, a sly fellow, he has stolen one of my titles',[13] for since 1398 the Dukedom of Rothsay had been vested in the eldest son of the Monarch, but Lord Stuart, descending from the Butes, had selected it as the name of the Island's chief town.

For a further few years the family settled down in the rue du Faubourg St Honoré, the parents to a life familiar to them and Char and Lou ready to absorb something of the manners and fashion of the women, and to perfect their French which in later years they continued to turn to for certain modes of expression.

But once again the Stuarts were obliged to make way for the Granvilles. The Duke of Wellington's government fell and with no employment in view Lord Stuart de Rothesay was reluctant to leave Paris and dawdled there after the arrival of his successor. For an impression of the circumstance wherein two Ambassadresses under the same roof surmounted the embarrassment of the situation—each before now in the position of the other—no description could be more spirited than that afforded by Lady

Granville—while the conduct of Lady Stuart de Rothesay is wholly disarming.

Paris Jan, 14th 1831. The *housses* are on: the room, the green beauty, looks just like its old self, with the sun broiling upon it . . . Yesterday I took Betty to the Opera with me. She is good, sensible, has behaved perfectly well in a difficult situation, but she talks too much, too loud, is too absent, too busy—huffy, with notions of all kinds about civilities and ceremonies. . . . She even likes a nod and a smile occasionally, in the midst of the things, and, in short, would like to enact with me ex-Queen and *régnante*.[14]

Feb. 21st I cannot let my thoughts dwell on Betty . . . I shall be sorry when she goes; to lose a very pleased, happy person, miss her in my society, she being a most efficient talking, animated member of society. Always glad to come early, stay late, talk without ceasing. *Bon jours* and how-d'ye-does all the visitors much more audibly and busily than I do myself. She is esteemed and popular, and whatever was amiss in the doing here was, and is known to have been, singly and wholly his work . . . Nobody feels the least *gêné* at finding her always sitting near me, and all her toads toad on because they see that I toad to her too. Mexborough* is ravished and sits with her mouth wide open.[15]

Feb. 28th. I like Betty much better as we go on. Her faults of manner, or at least the impression they make, wear off, and she is become happy, easy. She is constantly here, and sometimes very droll, always shrewd and clever. People have left off looking surprised at seeing her here in the evening, when they drop in with their best speeches, which is a great comfort to her and to me.[16]

The return to England was a happy occasion for Charlotte and Louisa. There was their father's modern house in London at 4 Carlton [House] Terrace to explore. In 1826 when it was known that Nash was to build a terrace of new houses on the north of the Mall, Lord Stuart had been one of the three dozen persons to apply to the Commissioners of Woods and Forests and Land Revenue for a plot of ground. His application was approved and

* The Countess of Mexborough, Char's eldest maternal aunt, was inordinately extravagant. She spent recklessly on rebuilding and enlarging Methley Park, the Mexborough house in Yorkshire, bringing the family near to bankruptcy at her death.

the following year he was offered and accepted the ground in the centre of the 'Western Terrace where conjointly with my Brother-in-law Lord Caledon,* I propose to build'. Nash was then desired by the Commissioners to furnish a copy 'of the Elevations, and of several Drawings for the external Entablatures, Capitals, Window Dressing and other Architectural Decorations which it is understood on the part of Sir Charles Stuart are to be uniform throughout'. In reply Nash advised the Commissioners that he had prepared and bound in a book 'the Elevation of Lord Caledon's and Sir Charles Stuart's houses to the north, which being under one and the same line are intended to form one uniform front'.[17]

The houses were begun in 1827; the next year Lord Stuart de Rothesay took up his appointment as Ambassador to France and the owner of No 1, Mr W. E. Tomline, son of Bishop Tomline one time tutor to the younger Pitt, and himself a Member of Parliament for Truro, reported to Paris on the progress of the building. No 2 was owned by Lord Kensington, No 3 by Lord de Clifford, and as has been seen No 5 (now the Turf Club) belonged to the Earl of Caledon. The siting of the stables afforded a good deal of complaint; Lord Caledon contended that he and his brother-in-law should have 'priority of choice as being the parties who first engaged to take out leases'.[18]

Meanwhile Mr Tomline had grievances of his own: from the terms of his lease he was not aware of his responsibility for the repair of 'the ornamental garden in front of his house'; the unfinished state of Lord Kensington's house adjoining his own warranted immediate legal measure to be taken 'to compel Lord Kensington to complete his house forthwith or give up possession of his ground'.[19] Here Lord de Clifford at No 3 subjoined his complaints at the dilatoriness of Lord Kensington in completing his house, and the Commissioners were obliged to send a stern

* The 2nd Earl of Caledon, 'that plain matter of fact man', first Governor of the Cape of Good Hope after its transfer to Great Britain, had married Char's favourite maternal aunt. A member of the Dilettante Society, he was known as a man of taste.

note to the effect that Lord Kensington would be held to his contract. Simultaneously Mr Tomline was writing to Paris: '*April 3 1829.* Lord Caledon sent me yesterday a memorial he had drawn up to the Treasury . . . for a communication with Pall Mall. He has signed it for you. Your house is totally inaccessible in a carriage.' '*April 17.* They are beginning to rail off the garden in front of our houses, and from the plan it will not be a wide one. I hear you have been giving a most splendid entertainment to sixty people, and displayed a very magnificent Plate.' '*May 29.* Nothing new here except that the Queen of Portugal tumbled on her nose dancing at the King's Ball last night, and the Royal blood flowed freely. Your house goes on slowly; the plaster is not yet on the dining-room ceiling.'[20] The next year Mr Tomline was further outraged and reported to the Commissioners 'that when the King went to the Houses of Parliament Carlton House Terrace was so crowded by Persons who had no right . . . that the owners of the Houses were wholly unable to view from the Terrace. Not only many people got over the railing but a ladder was placed by which very great numbers ascended on to the Terrace'.[21]

Very little of the original structure of No 4 now remains other than the north and south elevations. Decimus Burton who was responsible for the interior would find it hard to recognize his original plan, for damage inflicted from bombs in the Second World War has obscured for ever the finely proportioned rooms the Stuarts knew. Alone the fenestration is unaltered, as is also the handsome wrought-iron staircase which led the visitor from the lofty hallway to the elegance of the floors above.

Besides the town house there was the welcome of Tyttenhanger. Lord Stuart de Rothesay was a loved parent but it was essentially their mother whom the daughters prized most. To Grandmama Hardwicke and the maternal aunts they were devoted—more so one feels than to Lady Stuart, their father's mother, though they were sufficiently attached to her to spend visits of some length at Whitehall Yard, and at Thatched Lodge, Richmond, granted by the Crown to her husband in 1785. But it was Tyttenhanger Park, near St Albans, still a rural countryside, which they looked on as their home and where they spent the greater part of their time. Though Lord Hardwicke had made it over to his second daughter, the Countess of Caledon, as her marriage portion, the house continued to be used by all the relations, and at his death in 1834 his widow, the Dowager Countess, leased it from her daughter so that the spacious, friendly house continued as a focus for the whole family. It had been built in the reign of Queen Anne in warm red brick, balanced and formal, the roof surmounted by a clocktower, and the beautifully proportioned rooms, many lined with linenfold panelling, opened into each other or on to the long corridor which ran through the house. Bickering flourished among the aunts, and a story is recounted in the family of how the Earl of Mexborough passing Covent Garden while driving through London one day with Viscount Pollington, his eldest son, was witness to two brawling women leaning forward belligerently conducting a slanging-match. 'Doesn't that remind you of Tyttenhanger?', remarked Lord Mexborough impassively as they drove on.[22]

But yet another house was to form their background. A crippling tax on their father's finances was his obsession with Highcliffe Castle. He had known the original house well as a boy. His grandfather had owned Kenwood, and the house in Berkeley Square which later generations came to know as Lansdowne House. These Lord Bute sold, reserving only Luton for his successor, and engaged Robert Adam to build him a house on the fringe of the New Forest in Hampshire, for the great sweep of Christchurch Bay had captivated him. The situation was certainly an exceptional one. Standing on a cliff facing south and overlooking an expanse of peaceful shore stretching from east to west, the house commanded a view of the English Channel and, on a fine day, of the massive chalk Needles; far over on the right unimpeded by buildings, the eye could pick out the beautiful Priory church of Christchurch. After Lord Bute's death in 1792 it was pulled down but throughout his years of service abroad Lord Stuart de Rothesay dreamed extravagant dreams of the castle he would raise in its place. On his return from Paris the time seemed opportune, and in the face of grave warnings against building on the edge of a cliff where the earth crumbled and the sea tore at its very foundations, ambition prevailed where caution counselled and Highcliffe Castle rose phoenix-like in a Gothic mould from the ruins of his grandfather Bute's house.

The cost was monumental and the result romantic and curious. From time to time Lady Stuart de Rothesay arriving from London or Tyttenhanger and finding additional scaffolding and further immoderate planning, would denounce the heavy expenditure, for her husband had not been content to build with English stone. Without telling her he had imported from Normandy part of an old Manoir with a great oriel window; also delicately carved stonework. The house he conceived was Gothic in style, turreted and decorated with mouldings and gargoyles, stained glass in the windows, and the imposing entrance closer in design to an abbey. 'When I think it is for *this* we are *ruined*,' exclaimed Lady Stuart, '. . . it was no joke to deceive me as you did.' Yet even today, in its lamentable state the house casts its spell, and seen on a late spring morning with the sun slanting through the damaged rooms it is easy to recapture its magic from the past.

After five years the builders at last departed, and Lady Stuart was able to create ilex groves and sheltered walks; an anecdote is told that in order to withstand the onslaught of erosion she would 'pass her time in throwing stones and handfuls of gravel over the cliff to try and stop it up and preserve it from the encroachments of the sea'.[23] Writing in 1838 from Bournemouth, Count d'Orsay* must have voiced something of her own fears: '. . . *notre pauvre ami Stuart qui, a force d'avoir été fin diplomate est tombé dans l'idiotisme! La position de son manoir en est la preuve anticipée, car dans 60 ans, d'après les calculs mathématiques et topographiques, son manoir sera avalé par la mer!*'[24]

During these years the two sisters were growing up. Already their great-aunt, Lady Louisa Stuart, commented on the 'two fine girls now quite women, tho' but 16 and 15'. The first family

* Artist, and man of fashion.

death, that of their maternal grandfather at Wimpole, brought forth a letter—the first of many on a similar theme.

Nov 20th 1834

My dearest Mama. Your letter was a very great shock to us as we had no idea how much worse our dearest Grandpapa had become; it is a very great affliction to us all but it is a great comfort to think he was so composed and that he suffered no pain at the last. It must be a happiness to you to have seen him once more though only for those few days. I hope our dear Grandmama will not be made more ill by her very great sorrow.

Your most affecte daughter
Charlotte E Stuart

Pray let dearest Grandmama know how unhappy we are at the loss of our dear Grandpapa but I scarcely know what to say to *her* as her grief must be so very much more deep.

Charlotte had come out this year and was finding her balls and routs delightful, and having grown up in the aristocratic society of her day she was perfectly familiar with the great houses into which her family had married and intermarried. A miniature by Sir William Ross made a few years later displays the perfect oval of her face and the gentle but amused expression with which she looks out from large dark blue, heavy-lidded eyes. In a portrait made by Winterhalter for Queen Victoria in 1849, the same amused expression predominates though now matched with one of intelligence, and the heavy brows lend force to the features which, when seen in profile, denote an underlying strength. Probably more intelligent than her sister, and certainly with a wider outlook, Char's powers of enjoyment were more developed. Throughout her life she was sustained by her religion though she seldom referred to it, but her humility and compassion, springing from a deeply held faith, are manifest in her letters and journals. She excelled in drawing landscape and buildings which was to prove essential while photography was still in its infancy, for Queen Victoria required a degree of excellence from her Ladies, and much of Char's duty lay in recording 'views' of places she visited with the Queen. Later, amidst the abundance of exotic vegetation she became skilled in her flower painting but it was particularly in her records of the Indian scene that she showed an accomplishment of the highest order.

At eighteen, with high spirits and perfect manners, it could not be long before an advantageous offer of marriage presented itself. The man to whom she gave her heart was the Hon. Charles Canning, son of the great statesman towards whom Lord Stuart de Rothesay had felt only hostility and bitterness. Of all men, this was the suitor for his daughter's hand to whom he would be the most violently opposed.

Charles John Canning (Carlo to his family and intimates) had recently come down from Oxford where he had left behind a high reputation for scholarship; his prospects for a political career lay ahead. Two elder brothers had not survived, but his mother, created Viscountess Canning at the time of his father's death, was still living. She and her sister (married to the 4th Duke of Portland) were co-heiresses of a wealthy father. Much of her fortune had already been dissipated through the exigencies of political life, but Canning drew a pension of £3000 a year derived from a grant from Parliament to the family which had been attached to the youngest son. An elder sister, Harriet, had married the 1st Marquess of Clanricarde in 1825, and Lady Granville noted that 'The girl charms us all with being the reverse of what she looks. She is remarkably frank and open in manner, without the slightest pretension, all good humour and readiness to please. Her beauty is not to be denied, but it has singularly little charm . . . She is clever and though less brilliant than I expected, she is not pert or overpowering.'[25]

As a husband Charles Canning had everything to recommend him: a handsome appearance, high principles, an assured future and a distinguished name—though the name proved an almost insuperable obstacle to Charlotte's happiness, for her father remained implacable. Her grandmother, the Dowager Lady Hardwicke, was, as will be seen at the time of Lou's courtship, a fervent match-maker, and championed Char's right to choose for herself. At last, in the face of his daughter's determination and aware of the unhappiness he was causing—it was said that the only glimpse she could catch of Canning was from the terrace of their house where she would run out to watch him as he rode along the Mall—he yielded to the family's entreaties (to which the Berrys mingled their own) and consented to the marriage. Once the decision was made he capitulated to Canning's excellent qualities and set about providing for his elder daughter. He turned to his brother-in-law to stand as adviser and wrote to Viscountess Canning accordingly.

Carlton Terrace, July 31st 1835

Dear Lady Canning, Our common object being the happiness & comfort of our Children, I am very desirous that their interests should be taken care of by arrangements suitable to all parties; & as it is not usual for principals to treat together, & solicitors are not always animated by the Friendly Spirit which I always wish to exist in, where you are concerned, I think we should do well, if two of our private Friends met together, & drew up the threads of the necessary Instructions for the guidance of our men of business—if this is agreeable to you, Ld Caledon would meet any person you will choose to name for that purpose, on Tuesday at three o'clock.

Believe me, with every kind feeling, yours sincerely,

Stuart de Rothesay

In a vivid little pencil sketch Louisa recorded the wedding ceremony at St Martin-in-the-Fields on September 5th, 1835; the bride aged eighteen is kneeling at the altar beside the twenty-two-year-old bridegroom. For the first part of their honeymoon they stayed at Lady Stuart's Thatched Lodge, Richmond, and the remainder was spent at Highcliffe which was now ready to receive the newly wedded pair.

2

Death and Ague

Following the London season of 1836 in which Lady Stuart de Rothesay had brought out her younger daughter, she and her husband prepared to set off with Louisa for Italy to afford her the benefit of studying the great Italian masters; but shortly before their departure Lord Stuart de Rothesay, always incalculable, had suddenly, and without previous warning, sailed off to Iceland at dead of night, unconcernedly explaining his absence a week later by letter. Accustomed to such inconsiderate habits his family were not unduly provoked but calmly awaited his return, and the party subsequently embarked for Italy at the end of the summer.

Meanwhile, in August of this year Charles Canning was elected Conservative Member of Parliament for Warwick, but this was of short duration for on inheriting his mother's title at her death the following spring, he took his seat in the House of Lords. The Cannings had a yacht but no London house; his duties called him to Warwick, and there were Tyttenhanger, Highcliffe, and Carlton House Terrace where they were always welcome, but since there was no autumn session they sailed for the west of Scotland for some leisurely weeks of country-house visiting and sport. At St Mary's Isle, Kirkcudbrightshire, the seat of the Earl of Selkirk, a ball was held in their honour. 'We danced reels in the servants hall . . . Carlo's dancing almost equalled Lord Douglas'.'* This was directed at Lou, for as well as being a remarkably handsome man and renowned for his dancing, he had been a suitor for her hand.

* The Marquess of Douglas and Clydesdale, eldest son of the 10th Duke of Hamilton.

By Christmas the Cannings were in the Dukeries staying at Welbeck Abbey, Nottinghamshire, with the Duchess of Portland (Canning's maternal aunt) and the 'goodnatured old Duke'. From there it was an easy drive to the Duke of Newcastle at Clumber.

Saturday, Jan 21st

We went yesterday to Clumber; as we could only stay one night I went early in the day to see as much as I could of Lady Lincoln,* & Carlo did the same, for the purpose of getting the day's shooting at Clumber instead of here. I think it much the most formal place I ever was at; of eight sons & daughters who were there—except Ly Lincoln—none said a word as long as their Father was within hearing.† He himself was very affable to us. Poor Ly Lincoln is very ill; she walks about the house & doesn't take so much care of herself as she used as it has all been to no purpose. I think Clumber a very fine but dull place. The poor Ldy Clintons are really nice girls & one is very handsome; if they were nicely dressed & not so 'painfully shy' they would really be very much prettier than many beauties—as it is they seemed doomed to live all their lives at Clumber. Give my love to dear Papa & Lou.

Yours very affec Charlotte

While Lady Stuart de Rothesay and Louisa lingered in Rome Lord Stuart prepared to return, making plans for his nephew Charles Stuart (son of his younger brother) to go out to Italy and chaperone the ladies back to England.

Welbeck

My dearest Mama. It is a great comfort to think that you have now reached the furthest point of your travels. I suppose if Papa returns now he will have to go some of the way by sea to avoid the mountains or

* Granddaughter of William Beckford of Fonthill Abbey, and the sister of Lord Douglas, she had married the Earl of Lincoln, son and heir of the Duke of Newcastle, in 1832, but owing to her wayward disposition and poor health accentuated by laudanum, the marriage was not a happy one. In 1842 she abandoned her husband and children for a lover in the Isle of Wight,[1] and though later Lord Lincoln sanctioned her return, a more serious crisis in which she eloped with Lord Walpole and was found by Gladstone 'far advanced in pregnancy' at Como, brought about a divorce.[2]

† Of the three absent sons, Lord Edward Pelham-Clinton was at sea with the Royal Navy, and the twins Lord Charles and Lord Thomas were suffering from bad colds in London.

does the Corniche remain open all the year? Is it true that Charles Stuart is going to meet you and act courier?

I must give you both Carlo's thanks and mine for your project of installing us in Carlton Terrace till yr return. I should have liked it very much for the sake of having so much more of Papa's company—but we have long ago promised to go & visit Ly Canning* till we get a house and establishment & as she writes us to stay a good while with her it will be our most economical plan. She has been searching for a house for us and writes to me of one she has discovered in Tilney St looking into the Park which I think sounds very tempting. We have given up all thoughts of London which I am a little sorry for but it's a great way off, and difficult to get to from here— & besides that now that we have waited so long to see Harriet [Clanricarde], Carlo wants to stay & enjoy her society a little longer. She has been to see Lady Lincoln several times, she is in such beauty & spirits that it's almost impossible to believe that every night she has those terrible spasms for *two hours* & the remedy of leeches which cured her last year for several months now only stops her pain for two nights.

The balls that they attended at Leamington and at Warwick (where Canning had been returned Member of Parliament the previous year) did not quite come up to their London counterpart in Charlotte's estimation though Weippart's band (Quadrille Band master and 'harpist &c. to the Queen' with premises at 21 Soho Square) had been engaged. However the visit to Leamington afforded her the chance of seeing the Eastnors at Victoria Cottage, for Viscount Eastnor was Member for Leamington until the death of his father Earl Somers in 1841, and his wife was the youngest of Char's maternal aunts: '*Lady Eastnor,*† *soeur de Lady Stuart de Rothesay, laide comme on l'est dans sa famille, est bien élevée, comme le sont toutes les filles de Lady Hardwicke*; *Lord Eastnor, grand chasseur, grand mangeur, grand buveur* . . .'[3] Some of their children were of the party, Car (Lady Caroline Somers-Cocks), perhaps Char's favourite first cousin, and her younger sister Hatty (Lady

* Viscountess Canning lived at 10 Grosvenor Square which Canning inherited at her death.

† To avoid confusion, this aunt and family will be referred to henceforth as though the earldom of Somers had already devolved upon her husband.

Harriet Somers-Cocks) who seems to have been an invalid during all her early years but eventually married, and, as will be seen, showed alarming signs of 'going over' to Rome.

Leamington, Jan 26th 1837

My dearest Lou. I was very sorry indeed to go away from Welbeck & to leave Lady Clanricarde whom I like better & better the more I know her; she *égayé*'d the family party immensely & so did Ld Clan. who came a few days after with that darling little Dunkellin* whom Carlo takes the greatest delight in tormenting & is always telling him 'Why don't you open it wider, boy?' at which Dunkellin stares more than ever.

We had a long day's journey to get here & only arrived at ten o'clock. The ball I believe was considered very good; it was very full & in a very large room & Weippart's band was had—there were plenty of absurd looking people at it, & not many constituents. Car seemed quite considered the belle though there were some very pretty girls; all Car's partners, I mean the Leamington people, looked to me terribly scrubby. When we first got to this ball poor Carlo was like an old chaperon Mama trying in vain to get me off his hands—nobody would ask me to dance, & then I danced with all my might 6 quadrilles—but only one was a civility as in all the rest my partners were old friends or London people.

The ball at Warwick could not be counted a success for all the party had colds, and 'Carlo, what with his cold & three days hunting, got by some means a very strange lameness in both his legs, a contraction of the muscles at the back of them & he could hardly stand or walk', but a hasty return to London by coach and a visit to the surgeon quickly effected a cure. Back at her mother-in-law's house in Grosvenor Square, Charlotte had further cases of illness to communicate to Louisa, for the Berrys had had quite dreadful influenza, and although Canning's first cousin had had it slightly its lingering effect on her was surprising, for on coming to call 'in the middle of her visit, Lady Canning's out of livery servant came in, and she got up & walked to him with the kindest "how do you do" upon which the man rushed out of the room &

* His eldest son aged ten, who twenty years later became Canning's Military Secretary in India during the Mutiny.

she confessed she took him for Carlo'. Char's account of the perplexities of deciding on a furnished house for the season while at the same time choosing another to rent on long lease as their eventual home, was one with which every young married woman was familiar.

We have been house hunting every day since I came, we have now to decide between two, one in Berkeley Sqr *very dirty*, & one in Dover St Perfectly clean, only just done up & very large. The latter is the cheapest but it's possible that we might get the other for the same price; it's very difficult to choose whether it's best for one's rooms to be cheerful inside or to have a cheerful view. The Dover St house [No. 46] belongs to Ld Valletort who has just had it done up for himself & is now too ill to come to town. Besides these we have been looking for a house to take on lease; Ly Canning has discovered one which I think will suit us very well if we can get it. It is in Tilney St, very near Hyde Park; it wld want a great deal to be done to it but even then wld be much cheaper than taking a house every year for a few months & would save us all the bother of moving.

Give my best love to dearest Mama. Carlo sends his to you both, Goodbye fat Lou. Yr affec Little Char.

Within the space of a few weeks there was a different story to tell for, while not conferring the same degree of affection on her mother-in-law as upon the members of her immediate family, Charlotte was nevertheless devoted to Viscountess Canning whose confidence and heart she had won, and was therefore genuinely able to share in her husband's grief at his mother's death. In the established custom of the time Charlotte furnished her absent mother with the minutiae of the final hours.

Grosv Sqre, March 17th 1837

My dearest Mama. I have not had the heart to write to you before to announce you the bitter sorrow that has befallen us. I think you may have heard that my dearest Lady Canning was ill of influenza on Tuesday. She has received a shock by sitting at the bed side of Poor Aunt Fanny the Wednesday before; the night had brought other melancholy events to her mind & on leaving the hot room in the evening she complained of having caught cold. The next day & the next her cold & cough increased very much, & at last consented to see the Physician whom she had met at Aunt Fanny's. He prescribed what is generally given in influenza & the next morning she seemed a little better, but determined not to get up. We had promised to go to Tyttenhanger after church, but I thought her so unwell that I hardly liked to leave her, but as Carlo thought she would be sorry to keep me away I went. Harriet [Clanricarde] & Eliza Canning* remained there with Carlo all the evening. She had opium & James's powders† given her at night—but never slept & grew very ill & towards morning became dreadfully sick & could keep nothing on her stomach. Carlo when he saw her grew frightened & sent an express for me. The next day there was no worse symptom but she was very weak & uneasy. She saw me in the middle of the day & said to me at once 'You were sent for', I said to her that it was the day I should return. She shook her head & told me I was very right to come & she was very glad to see me. At different times she said to Carlo & Eliza that she was no better & that a stupor might come like in the case of Aunt Fanny. On Tuesday night she saw Nevinson & Morrison, they thought the illness would last long & that we must try & keep up her strength.‡ We sat by her bed side till half past twelve when she entreated us all to go to bed; she had pressed Carlo very much to go to the House of Commons which he did at eleven. Harriet staid till one & gave her broth & medicine & a few drops of morphine. She slept a good deal & several times took jelly & at seven o'clock took food and then seemed so quietly asleep that Carlo waited in the next room: then Harriet took his place & he went down to breakfast at 1/2 past ten. In a little while she came & begged us to go & listen at the door for she no longer heard her breathe. We went in; Harriet took hold of her hand which was cold, I ran for a candle, & we found her quite dead, her eyes were quite shut & her countenance was beautiful & looked perfectly happy. She was quite prepared for death & wished for it, which is a comforting thought

* Second wife of Sir Stratford Canning (Viscount Stratford de Redcliffe, 1852) whom she married in 1825. Her father, James Alexander, was a first cousin of Char's Uncle Caledon and owned No 9 Carlton House Terrace. Sir Stratford Canning had been George Canning's first cousin, and was for many years a distinguished Ambassador to Turkey.

† Medicine to diminish fever, first made by Dr Robert James in the eighteenth century.

‡ These physicians practised at Montagu Square and Cavendish Square respectively.

for us. I cannot describe the grief we all felt. Carlo & Harriet both are calmer now. I feel I never told you half how very much I loved her or what her kindness & indulgence to me. I know she was very very fond of me. This year she had been so calm & cheerful that one could see that her mind was at peace with itself. It was sleep from an accumulation of phlegm in the air vessels the chest being very narrow from the curvature of the spine.

I hope I shall see my dearest Papa before long. Goodbye my dearest Mama. Give my love to Lou—I cannot write to her just yet. God bless you. Your affec daughter

Charlotte Canning

I'm afraid this is a confused account but I cannot read it over.

The following month the Cannings went for a change of air to Southend and Char, aware of her father's love of the sea, would not have been surprised to see him pass the end of the pier in a steamboat or smack. But there was to be no escape from illness, and Char's account of sickness and inept diagnosis has all the ingredients of burlesque.

Southend, April 6th 1837

My dearest Lou.

Our expedition to Southend has not answered to any of the party but me & Carlo. I have liked it very much as it is very quiet & I have had plenty of sea air but I must own that all the rest have good cause of complaint. The Stratfords came here two days before us & as soon as they arrived their boy became very ill & was all over covered with a rash.* The nurse also was taken extremely ill & had to be very much bled & the old doctor of the place would only say that he thought the boy must have got measles or scarlet fever but he didn't know which. In the midst of all this we & the Clanricardes & 3 little ones arrived. We were not allowed to go near Eliza for fear of infection & she was half killed with watching her child day & night with no one to help her. After four or five days he got better & it was pronounced that the illness had only been a very bad fever without a name & they all bundled back to London. We were meanwhile out boating and sailing

* George, the only son and now close on five years old had contracted an illness as a very young child and remained an invalid all his life, predeceasing his father; there were as well two daughters at this time.

all day & every day, the children often ill but nothing very bad till yesterday we were dreadfully frightened by poor little Elizabeth* suddenly having the most dreadful spasms in her stomach & head, screaming with agony. It turned out that she had been eating periwinkles at tea which had poisoned her & added to that had caught cold after having a rash. We have come to the conclusion that we could not have pitched upon a more unhealthy spot. Ague abounds here & I only hope that we may none of us catch it.

Clanricarde, Carlo & I amuse ourselves by sailing out on the rough days. I think Mama would have screamed had she seen us yesterday in a cockleshell of a boat with a sail set & the hurricane of wind driving us along at a railroad pace, one side of the boat under water. As it was not more than 3 foot deep the danger was not great. I hope there's some chance of seeing you really by the middle of May for I hope a fortnight at Paris will be enough for you. I think we shall not stay *very* long in London this year which is one reason why I want you to come back so much.

Goodbye give my love to Mama. Yr very affec Char

Unconfirmed gossip of an intriguing kind had reached England and Char wrote again in some haste to her mother.

I hear on every side that Mr Tomline† is to be *beaufrère* to me & I at last write to ask, not if it's true but how much is true. Has he been making up to Lou? We think it a little suspicious that his name has not even been mentioned in your letters or hers! Poor Granny [Stuart] is distracted about it & I rather think believes it because Ld. Bute told it her. What has become of Papa? I expect to see him walk in unawares at any moment.

I hope you will be here in May, Lou musn't loose all the London—Goodbye dearest Mama give loves to Lou, if I hear any thing of Papa at Granny's I shall reopen this.

Yrs affec C C

Aunt Caledon has arrived at Tytten. The Mexboro's are there and I believe the Eastnors also.

* Lady Elizabeth De Burgh, the Clanricardes eldest daughter.

† George Tomline, whose father had been the occupier of No 1 Carlton House Terrace, entered the army and became a Member of Parliament for Shrewsbury, a constituency he shared with Disraeli, and later for Great Grimsby. He died unmarried in 1889.

In fact Lord Stuart de Rothesay was almost home. A letter to his wife in Italy, written from Jersey in April, affords some indication of the provocations passengers were forced to undergo on a sea journey, for the quarantine regulations for a ship unloading cargo or passengers were fairly strictly enforced; travellers were obliged to stay at a lazaret during the period of quarantine, in varying degrees of discomfort.

Meanwhile in Paris Lady Granville was again active with her pen. 'Letters from Rome say that Miss Stuart is going to marry Mr Tomline, 25,000£ a year, handsome, agreeable, young, but that Lady Betty opposes. It is the girl's doing, but *la madre* wants rank, especially Lord Duoro.'[4] Writing from Grosvenor Square Char begged for further information. 'I long to hear what the report about Lou is founded upon for there is always *some* kind of foundation', and added news of aunts and cousins.

I believe none of the cousinhood intend to begin the world yet though there is a good deal going on; the 1st drawing room was yesterday. Lou had better make haste back or she will look old & faded by the number of new beauties that were presented. All 6 of Harriet's have been dangerously ill, the boy at school has alone escaped. 2 have had inflammation of the chest, 1 smallpox, 1 nearly whooping cough & then a fit, another a fever & 1 other cough & cold & fever. She has had a horrid time of it for every child has had at least two relapses. Carlo is suffering with toothache.

Here ends my paper so goodbye dearest Mama, give loves to Lou. Pray come home soon. Yr affec C C

A few days later Char herself succumbed and joined the lengthening list of invalids, but hers must have been a modified form of smallpox where the risk to life was insignificant.

Aware how fortunate she had been in getting off so lightly, though 'now that its over I'm not sorry I've had it', Char went on to explain that she had had 'a good many spots but not thick together. I have but two or three under my hair which are at all likely to mark, all the others have nearly disappeared off my face—I mean in regions where I scratched a good many traces still remain. Carlo was inoculated & has not feared me'. And the scabs were soon forgotten in the excitement of summer plans. Six weeks of spa waters and baths, three at Ems and three at Spa had been recommended for her, so she hoped her mother and Lou would be home before her departure. After that a share in a moor would take the Cannings to Scotland till October.

A few days later Char wrote to Paris, where festivities were going forward on the occasion of the marriage of the Duc d'Orléans, eldest son of the French King, to Princess Helena Mecklenburg-Schwerin. Contemporary biographers invested her with 'dignity, grace, modesty', with everything but beauty. Lady Granville detected that 'her teeth are little black stumps, the foot very big', but allowed her a '*parfaite obligeance*'.[5] Lord Malmesbury* was told that 'her dressmaker has been ordered to make her gown different from any that have been worn, and has accordingly invented one'.[6] Small wonder that Lady Stuart chose to prolong her stay. On three occasions she was at the British Embassy and Lady Granville reported that 'Lady Stuart and her girl Louisa called on me. I think the latter beautiful and exceedingly improved'. 'Lady Stuart came to see me to-day with her daughter, looking less well than usual and rather stormy. Betty, too, in a fuss. Lord Stuart won't come. They both want to stay to see the opening at Versailles.'[7]

Tyttenhanger, May 18th 1837

My dearest Mama, Tomorrow I hope for a Paris letter and then we shall soon begin to expect you, that is to say if the fêtes do not seduce you to outstay the fortnight. I think the programme in to-day's papers have rather made us think with Papa that you will stay, for Fontainebleau & Versailles sound very tempting. I don't think it would at all do for us to go to Paris on our way to Germany. We shall see you far more comfortably in London. We could not go to any gay doings, & you & Lou would; so solitary evenings in an Hotel would not be worth going to Paris for, & in the mornings you must have such heaps of things to do.

Will you get for me at Paris a doz. of pocket handfs. fine but not worked, for every day use—I have plenty of narrow Valenciennes—I

* A life-long friend of Canning's since Oxford; he later became Foreign Secretary.

should think they ought to cost about 8 or 10 francs. Then I want also a black silk mantelet with a silk border or crêpe as lace would not be mourning—and I should like also something black lace-sort of "*fichu paysanne*"—to wear in *demie deuil* in the evening in the country— & if you are buying black open work stockings I should be glad of a few pair & also some black thread if any are to be had. I tell you all these commissions now that you may not have the trouble of going on purpose to get them but to buy them when you see them. Give hundreds of loves to Ly Lincoln if you see her. Pray always tell me what you hear of her.

But by June 4th Char settled for Paris despite the mourning which would prevent her from participating in any entertainments. 'Lady Stuart has just been with me, sitting up on her hind legs in great distress' wrote Lady Granville. 'The fêtes, the young lords, the Cannings coming, the London season going . . .'[8] No mother with a marriageable daughter could afford to disregard such contingencies.

From Paris the Cannings travelled to Bad Ems in Nassau with all the hazards attendant upon land travel. Canning with no arduous task to occupy him at the House of Lords where he sat on the opposition benches, had time at his disposal; Charlotte hoped to benefit from baths and from the waters which were recommended as a cure for 'certain disturbances peculiar to the other sex', and for sterility. (Neither Char nor her sister were destined to have children.)

Halting on the road at Coblenz Char was unaware, while recounting the final stages of their journey, that the Royal Mistress whom she was later to serve, had mounted the throne of England. William IV had died that morning at Windsor Castle. (Unfortunately no further letter survives until twelve days later.)

Coblentz, June 20th 1837

We were delayed a good while at the Belgian frontier, after that we had very bad posthorses, the post boy got a tumble & ever after kept getting off and mending the harness. In going down a gentle hill all three horses fell down against a house, which prevented the whole concern from overturning—the poor man groaned so that I thought he would die, but when he was pulled out of the mass of horses he was found quite sound & one horse was found in a cellar out of which it was not very easy to fish him. As nothing was the worse for the disaster we soon went on again.

We mean instantly to begin learning German: every time Carlo uses a few words he knows to make the post boys go on, they stop the carriage & come to the door to ask what he means, and when I got out of the carriage at the time of our catastrophe a whole village full of women began talking to me whilst I could only stand still & look like an idiot. They were goodnatured people for one of them, seeing a little cow walk towards me, took me by the hand & led me out of its way, I suppose expecting me to be frightened, & another began to make my gown tidy & pin down my collar in a most benevolent manner.

We are much disappointed with Ehrenbreitstein—there's no beauty at all in the castle itself & Turner's picture of it & all the prints I've seen give one very magnificent ideas—I don't think at all to be compared with Dumbarton.

I put off writing to you until to-day thinking that the letters would be a long while getting to you from Luxembourg or Longwy—tell me how long this is on the road— & tell me what this costs.*

Nothing further is heard of Charlotte's determination to learn German, a shortcoming she deplored, as will be seen, when she later accompanied Queen Victoria to Saxe-Coburg.

Ems lies on the banks of the Lahn, backed by sloping hills. The waters were strongly alkaline and it was customary half way through the cure to change the type of waters—and consequently the spa—in order to advance the improvement of the patient. As has been seen, Spa in Belgium was chosen as their second destination, the mineral waters there being chalybeate. This was once a fashionable watering-place but having been considerably damaged by fire thirty years before Char's visit its charm had diminished, though an observer could write approvingly that there was 'surprisingly little of the vulgar ostentation, fast life, and society of the black-leg, and demi-monde character'[9] which was only too obtrusively manifest at other spas.

* The cost from Coblenz to England via France (always an expensive route) would be about 10p. The letter reached London on June 26th (postmark).

After a short time the place proved weakening and the heat oppressive, and though the walks were beautiful there was little time to indulge in them as it took Char a long while to drink her four large tumblers of water at fifteen minute intervals, and there were only two cool hours in the early morning and late evening when it was possible to move. A jingling pianoforte with such loose notes that it was impossible to play upon was an unwelcome acquisition, and though they found many acquaintances, and 'poor Carlo is quite resigned to his fate', the mode of life did not please them and she thought it a dissipated life to gossip for three hours every morning and evening. In the middle of July when about to leave Ems, she began a letter: 'All the people here ask us every day if the absurd stories about the Queen & Ld Elphinstone* are true & if he is to come back to England to marry her?', and closed it with the admission that she had been 'guilty of the dissipation of going to see a ball here in the gambling rooms, some Poles danced the Mazourka very well'.

The stay at Spa was of short duration for the Cannings were eager to get home to catch the steamer to Inverness which sailed at fortnightly intervals. This allowed very few days in London into which a visit to Lady Stuart must be fitted: 'Will you one of the two days take me to the Lodge to see Granny for I shall not have either carriage or horses.' There would also be little time for shopping but the King's death necessitated a decent mourning dress. 'I wish you would order me a poplin gown to be my best—plain black is the most useful or with a small pattern.'

* A rumour prevalent in 1836 that Lord Elphinstone, Lord of the Bedchamber to William IV, was in love with the then Princess Victoria and that his attachment was returned, had been sufficient to despatch him to Madras where he served as Governor from 1837–42.

3

To Venice by 'Gondola'

The following year, 1838, a long journey on the new yacht *Gondola* took the Cannings as far as Athens; they were abroad eight months, from August to the following April. Charlotte was a good traveller, prepared to enjoy everything that came within her range, while her delight at coming upon friends from home in the midst of sightseeing—a pursuit, one surmises, strictly chosen and regulated by Lord Canning—was an endearingly youthful trait. Over a period of twenty-five years her letters written while abroad lost their touch of naïveté and established a surprising excellence in which her enthusiasm for travel never deviated despite the fatigue of travelling with the Queen, and, in later years, the weariness of camp marches on the high road to Tibet.

That she was never sea-sick was a matter for self-congratulation, and she was equally pleased with Sarah Norris, her lady's maid, who after succumbing at the outset, later enjoyed the same immunity. Her father accompanied them part of the way which must have added to Charlotte's pleasure for he was a seasoned traveller, delighting in adventure of any kind and, to those who understood his eccentricities, a diverting companion.

Brest, [*Thursday*] *Aug 30th 1838*

Dearest Mama, We have had a very prosperous voyage from Lymington having left it on Tuesday at daybreak. I ran up on deck the moment I woke to catch a last glimpse of Highcliffe, but was too late for we had passed Poole & only a scrap of the Isle of Wight remained to be seen.

The first day was perfectly beautiful—late at night there came a good deal of wind so that we rolled about & Sarah [Norris] was sick &

I am ashamed to say that after waiting a good while for breakfast both Carlo & I became a little squeamish but *not sick*—however it did not last; on the whole it has been quite delightful. The captain proves excellent & our cabins are very comfortable; we have still been breakfasting on the herbs and brown loaf; the peaches & apricots & ginger bread are not near finished & Lou's bouquet is still in great beauty & swings very ingeniously in an immense soda water glass in my cabin. The Pianoforte was in perfect tune when I first tried but since yesterday two or three bass notes have changed a good deal, however it does beautifully to play upon.

We have just heard that *La Gondole* under the Capitaine Canning is out of quarantine, for all night we have had a yellow flag so now we are allowed to go on shore and get water which is the principal object in our coming here.

Once on shore—and Char found 'the old picturesque town the most thoroughly French I ever saw'—they made haste to get the water casks refilled and provisions attended to.

We walked about for two hours buying stores of wine & comestibles which we did not profit by for the shopman never found our boat & we came off without them; we have never ceased regretting *saumon frais* & green peas. Next day outside Ushant we were completely becalmed; I amused myself fishing up extraordinary Polypus like crystal beads in slime & little jelly fish, with a glass & a bit of string; the water was so clear that in the sun one could see millions of atoms like the Ancient Mariner's 'thousand thousand slimy things'. Then there came two sharks which gave us great amusement, they would not let themselves be caught but one could see them snifting the beef hung out for them.

Sarah has never been sick since the second day in the Channel and sits quite happily at her work as if she was on land.

At Gibraltar Char had her first sight of Moors and Spaniards, 'like [J.F.] Lewis's drawings, & women in mantillas & carrying long green fans. I think Lou would have been quite enchanted—it was such a bewildering sight that I almost forget the details of the costumes but every group was exactly like a picture of Lewis's'. Few of her sketches of this period remain; perhaps she was too occupied with her letters and her nautical life, and always modest of her own gifts she felt her sister's pencil would do greater justice to the new sights and customs which met her eye.

She was pleased with everything: they called on the Governor of Gibraltar and his wife, riding through the galleries in darkness (Char on a donkey) and dismounting to 'peep with more comfort through the holes for the guns'.

In the first week of October the *Gondola* sailed up the Adriatic and anchored at Venice at the 'entrance to the Grand Canal close to the Dogana & with the best possible views of the Piazza & the Ducal Palace & of the Gd Canal'. As Venice was celebrating the visit of the epileptic Emperor Ferdinand I of Austria the Cannings felt 'the advantage of carrying our house on our backs here more than anywhere, for other people are spending their fortunes in paying for the most miserable lodgings'. Lord Stuart de Rothesay returned almost immediately to England, intending in Milan to call upon the Marquess of Hertford (Viscount Yarmouth of his Paris days, and Thackeray's model for the 'Marquis of Steyne'), but not before he had indulged in an extravagance on a trans-atlantic scale, for surely the '*lord americain*' of Char's next letter was none other than Lord Stuart himself.

Directed by Canning and guided by the Venetian authority Mr Rawdon Brown, sightseeing was thoroughly attended to but one catches a hint of relief at escapes to other distractions; finding friends among the visitors heightened Charlotte's enjoyment. She noted down their names: Princess Mélanie Metternich, third wife of the Chancellor, whose overbearing manner was well-known in the capitals of Europe; Sir Frederick Lamb (later Lord Beauvale), a younger brother of Lord Melbourne and at this time Ambassador at Vienna; but the most valued of all was the companionship of Lady Lincoln. Also in Venice was Baron Philipp von Neumann whose activities often coincided with the Cannings own; he had known them and the Stuart de Rothesays in London where he had been Secretary and later Counsellor at the Austrian Embassy. Twice he dined with Sir Frederick Lamb and found there the Lincolns and the Cannings;

at the Court ball where Sir Frederick presented Charlotte, he noted that there were 1500 guests present.

Venice, Oct 14th 1838

My dearest Mama. I hope you will have heard of Papa's arrival in England by the time this reaches you for the only stoppage he talked of was to see Ld Hertford. We have been seeing sights and shows from morning till night, & now that we have got through the Emperor's we begin to think we should have done wiser to miss a good many of them. The 1st procession of gondolas, & the same gondolas at the Regatta, & the illumination of the piazza & piazzetta of St Marks last night, were worth coming any distance to see. By the bye, to our very great delight and surprise, we found the Lincolns were here; she is more improved by her travels than by [Dr] Jephson or any sort of doctoring, & is quite able to amuse herself like other people; now that we have very nearly done the round of sights ourselves we are showing them all the best.

The morning's amusements have not been half so pleasant for we were foolish enough to go in a steam boat with about 200 people to Chioggia to see a sea fight and a boat race of Chioggia women and the Murazzi—and the Emperor was to lay the 1st stone of a pier. The moment we were outside the lagunes in the middle of the sea fight very nearly every creature became sea sick—without giving the least warning to their neighbours or taking any sort of precaution. Never was anything so disgusting. Ly Lincoln fainted away & did not recover till we were again in smooth water. The moment we got to Chioggia our first object was to get a boat to take us back by the lagunes for it was utterly impossible to encounter the same again. The boat was found and stocked with Chioggia provision & we sailed delightfully back to Venice in about 4 hours—a very merry little party with the Duc de Richelieu & the Lincolns who had both recovered from the steam boat effects. The race must have been very pretty but we hardly saw anything of it.

We went on Wednesday to a court ball; Sir Frederick Lamb had Lady Lincoln, Mrs Craven* & me presented to the Empress who spoke to us civilly. She is goodlooking & has very ladylike manners. The Sardinian Ambassadress presented us & treated us all three very much *de haut en bas*—I don't know why. Another day we went to a launch at the Arsenal for the Emperor, there was but little to see except the

* Novelist, and wife of a diplomatic attaché.

launch. Papa's friend Mr Brown has shewn us a great deal: the Ducal palace, pozzi, piombi, models, cameos, and all. The Armenian Convent, St Giovanni e Paolo, was one good day's work, another with him was the Museo Correr, Palazzo Vendramin where there are some fine velvet hangings, the church of the Miracoli very small but much the most picturesque I have seen, the Manfrini pictures: the Scalsi church and the Ghetto—another long day you will think. In the Ghetto (the Jew's *Quartier*) I bought a good yellow damask coverlid which Mr Brown bargained till he got me it for 2 napoleons, & a sort of net veil as in the Venetian masked pictures. In one shop a man told us he had sold 4 *portières* to "*Un Lord Americain*"—I think you may guess the name of that Lord.

Sir Frederic Lamb has been most extremely kind to us, we dined there twice with Papa; on Friday we went again there to meet the Lincolns & to-day again, besides he has sent us tickets for every show without our asking for them & we have twice had places in his Opera box; another day we took a box for the 1st representation of *Lucrèce Borgia*, a dreadful story for an opera but with four or five very pretty *morçeaux* in it. The Prima donna Melle Ungher is an excellent *actrice*—her style of singing is good but her voice is not much better than Persiani's. Mariani the tenor many people prefer to Rubini; I don't like him as well but I allow that his voice is better and fresher. He never by any chance sings a note in *voce di testa*—he is poisoned at the end of *Lucrèce* & becomes so Blue & Green that he almost made me sick, so next time we came away before the end.

We expect to be in Corfu in about a fortnight or 3 weeks. Many loves to Lou, & Believe me Dearest Mama Yr affly

Char

I must tell you that we have given up the idea of going to Padua and Verona. We gave it up when the Lincolns came that we might have a little more of their company.

To her Grandmother Hardwicke she wrote further details.

Venice, Oct 19th 1838

Dearest Grandmama. At last we have got rid of the Emperor, in consequence of his departure Venice is as quiet as ever, but I hope a little richer. He went yesterday & to-day we are all to pay 5 francs for our gondolas instead of 20.

The Lincolns are our usual companions. She & I have come to great disgrace among the connaisseurs here for insisting on going *two days running* to the Old Clothes Shops in the Jews quarter in preference to a number of churchfuls of Tintorets and Gianbellinis. I know very well that you & Mama would have followed our faction—so I may confess that we bought 4 beautiful old gowns, not *very* dirty & the little dirt there is, is noble for they assured us that all of them belonged once to Doge's wives!! As to the company we have met here it has been exactly like London, about 30 English that we know very well & no others. It has been quite like a lottery to find who we should meet on the Piazza next. Papa was considered a great prize when he turned up. Of course he found numbers of old diplomatic friends—we profitted very much by them, for the great people have been most amiable to us ever since. Metternich extremely so; we dined with him & besides he was very civil in taking us to see the old collection of Archives. His wife is very handsome but most disagreeably brusque & noisy. There is a story of his saying on hearing of some rude speech of hers, '*Vous savez que j'ai la femme du monde la plus mal élevée*'.

I think I must tell you a little about our sea life. Sarah Norris has never been sick since the 2nd day off the coast of England, is never frightened. Of course I am never sick or frightened either. The worst change in us is that we are grown rather greedy & think & talk more of our dinners than we used to do, indeed in the 23 days we never touched dry land the ordering of dinner became so interesting that we used to examine all the stores every morning, and hold a council of state with Papa for the head, & the steward as prime minister.

Goodbye my dearest Grandmama. Pray believe me Yrs very affecately C Canning

Greece appeared terribly bare and parched to Charlotte who likened the one running stream she noticed to 'the black ditch at Tyttenhanger', but the Castalian fountain at Delphi surrounded by washerwomen was another matter. Here the water was plentiful; they picnicked beside it, eating watercress 'which grew in the Pythoness's bath. I was a little bit frightened by a woman who would have acted her part well who came very close to me, screaming something in my ears & with both hands pointing to my face, almost touching it. I dreaded an embrace & called for help to our interpreter who found she was in the greatest astonishment at my face being white & my hands dark green, she not understanding the use of the gloves'. At Athens there was much to see and admire and liken to something familiar. 'The ground lies really like Edinburgh with the Castle Hill for the Acropolis, and Arthur's Seat for Hymettus', she wrote, adding (and here one can surely detect an observation of Canning's), 'this would not be very correct as to the relative bearings but gives an excellent idea of them.'

The travellers reached Malta in mid-December and were obliged to undergo ten days discomfort (including Christmas) in a quarantine lazaret where unexpectedly they found Lord Pollington 'looking very well but rather strangely dressed in a Persian cap', and were able to visit him in the *parlatorio* at a distance of about eight feet. As a classicist he had been Kinglake's companion in Greece, had figured as 'Methley' (the name of the Yorkshire family house) in the early chapters of *Eothen*, and had also travelled widely in Russia, Persia, India and the Caucasus. Coming from Alexandria his 'imprisonment' was for twenty-one days but before he was liberated the Cannings had sailed for Naples. From Genoa they continued to Nice, 'where,' wrote Lord Canning, 'we staid three days & quite enough too. English swarmed, but not of the first order—excepting the Ashburtons. Yesterday morning we left Nice & ran over to Antibes, a very snug little port, and from that went by land to Cannes to look at Brougham's doings. His house is prettily situated about half a mile to the west of the town—but it is small & rather cockneyish. A few of the upstairs rooms are nearly done, amongst others his bed & dressing-room—the first paper'd with bright crimson—& the second in sky blue enliven'd by a trellis-work pattern in silver. The port is going on most vigorously & when the Mole is finished will be infinitely better than Antibes—or any other near it. At Antibes we had only just one foot of water to spare as we lay inside the pier—& at Cannes there was a vessel of nearly 800 tons within the new works. He deserves great credit for this, for I believe it is thanks to him'. In the winter of 1834 Lord Brougham had been forced, through an outbreak of cholera at Nice (then the Italian frontier), to spend a night at Cannes. Finding the country beautiful and the climate beneficial for the health of his tubercular daughter, he chose a spot on the route de Fréjus and built what Lord Malmesbury called 'a Cockney whitewashed house, close to the high road, which passes between it and the sea, with an apology for a garden round it'.[1] To Lady Holland, the great Whig hostess, it had seemed a 'strange, ugly building';[2] yet the Château Eléonore Louise survives, having undergone conversion. Brougham was buried in the cemetery and a commemorative statue erected, which from those who abused him called forth the sobriquet of 'Baron de Cannes'. At an earlier date Napoleon had spent the first night there on his return from Elba but had left no mark, so it can be rightly claimed, that having by his example made it popular among his countrymen, Brougham had been the founder of Cannes.

Malaga, which impressed Char as 'being truly foreign' and where the Vice-Consul spoke no word of English, was followed by an expedition to Granada in the wake of Prince George of Cambridge who had appropriated almost all the available horses. Besides the delights of the Alhambra and the Generalife, a number of low white-washed buildings were observed with over-hanging brown tiled roofs 'like old English cottages'. The Duke of Wellington's place, Soto de Roma, struck Char as being in a 'very dirty condition' and the *administrador* 'wearing a pointed hat and jacket with numbers of silver tags was the very image of Lord Abercorn'. Mid-April found the Cannings in Lisbon, having failed in Tangier to obtain orange and pomegranate trees for Highcliffe. A day or two later they learned of the death of Lord Caledon, and Char, grieving for her aunt, was thankful to be able to look forward to being soon at home.

Yet in July of the following year they had again left England in the *Gondola* with Lord Lovaine, eldest son of the Earl of Beverley (later Duke of Northumberland), accompanying them in the *Turquoise*, and together they had put in at Corunna, Gibraltar (where the heat was intense and Char 'found it the greatest comfort' to have already done her sight-seeing there while Lord Lovaine had it all to do), and Genoa; by the end of September they had reached Palermo. Here Charlotte was intrigued, as many have been, by the 'famous dried people in the Capuchin convent,—the monks in niches in low galleries—and ladies and gentlemen who choose to pay, packed up and laid on shelves. All the men have dresses like us there, but the women have all kinds of coloured gowns & smart gloves and shoes and stockings. Of course it is a disgusting & horrible sight but so curious that I would not have missed it for anything. Many corpses have not died more than 8 or 9 months & some are 200 years old—one box held a General who died last week but he will not be shown for several months. One looks at them with very little feeling for it is quite impossible to bring one's mind to consider them human, they are so like worm eaten blocks of wood, or the cork of which models are made'.

Two incidents occurred after leaving Constantinople which were of interest. At the Consul's house in Syros they met Tarsitsa Kamenou, Trelawney's second wife; and from Cefalonia Canning reported a curious happening. 'A vessel was driven into the harbour at Argostoli from stress of weather, & whilst there, hoisted Greek colours—a Frenchman, who was passenger on board, came ashore & gave information to the authorities that she had slaves concealed below the decks. The vessel's papers mentioned the number of the crew, & no more—& when a search was made they found 20 blacks confined below. She was detained as having false papers—but the *Tyne* which is stationed at Corfu, could not touch her on the score of the slaves as we have no treaty with Greece. It has been ascertained that she had shipped them at Tripoli, & was going to dispose of them in Candia & the fact of this traffic being frequently carried on under the Greek flag has long been known in Athens.'

Charlotte had greater leisure to ponder over news which several months away from England had brought her. The one to touch her most closely was the death of Lord Somers, for her Uncle Eastnor would now assume the earldom and relinquish his seat in the House of Commons. Would her cousin Car Cocks resign her service as Maid of Honour to the Queen in order to assist in the settling-in at Eastnor Castle? Family concerns were always absorbing; so too were the marriages of friends, and that of Lord Shelburne (later 4th Marquis of Lansdowne) she found 'very odd', principally because he had earlier been refused by the bride's sister.

February found the Cannings arriving in Rome in the midst of Carnival. 'We came into the Piazza del Popolo and were pelted with sugarplums [made of chalk] and bouquets.' But bad news awaited Charlotte; her grandmother Stuart had died leaving many debts which would have to be discharged by the sale of belongings; her house in Whitehall Yard, left to her son, might have to be given up, while Thatched Lodge at Richmond returned to the Crown on Lady Stuart's death.

Besides sightseeing to attend to there were a few English friends they were glad to see, among them Lady Lyttelton with two daughters, of whom one, Lavinia, would later marry a brother of Mrs Gladstone, a friend of Charlotte's youth. Within a short space of time Lady Lyttelton and Charlotte had positions at Court, the elder, already a widow, in the capacity of Governess to the Royal Children, while for thirteen years Charlotte was to hold a place close to the Queen, both at Court, and in the affections of her Sovereign.

An early visit must have been paid to the studio in the Corso of the sculptor Lawrence Macdonald, for there in April of the same year, Mary Richardson (Ruskin's cousin), a most unexpected chronicler, came upon 'marble busts, or casts, of an immense number of celebrated people, among them were . . . Lord and Lady Canning'.[3]

As excursions followed upon antiquities, Char found it hard work to detail all she had seen.

Rome, March 16th 1841

I think now you will really believe that we shall be back in England in May as Easter week has not power to keep us, in fact it is no great sacrifice for I only cared for the fireworks, the trumpets in St Peter's, & the Pope's blessing the people, & I think they would hardly be an antidote to the bore of the ceremonies. We have almost finished the first round of sights which has been hard enough work but I have enjoyed it very much indeed when I was not tired to death. Every thing are the worse for winter for they look so very ill kept & almost rubbishy, which with plenty of leaves and long grass would not be the case.

Lamenting that for want of time she had only one ride about the acquaducts in the Campagna, she had yet been twice to Vespers at St Peter's. Of Cardinal Fesch's great picture collection at the Palazzo Falconieri she had not much to say; he had been Napoleon's uncle and had amassed a fortune and many treasures, and now two years after his death, these were soon to be sold. 'There are but few I very much admire for the pride of his collection, his Flemish & Dutch pictures, are so out of place in Rome. His Rembrandts though are beautiful.'

But time pressed and there was still much to see; breathless and not a little exhausted Char was 'Just now going to the Cupola of St Peter's and the Vatican gardens', and with a triumphant: 'I am sure you never saw half of what we have' closed her letter—only to start a new one a few days later.

Rome, March 31st 1841

Yesterday night we did the Vatican by torchlight which I think must be rather a new fashion for I never heard you talk of it—both for the locale and the statues it ought to be seen, for beautiful as they are by daylight they certainly gain seen in this way. The torches make but one strong light for they are tied up in a bunch and fastened under a shade. It is usually made a junket of but we sent for our permission late & had not to ask people and saw it all the more comfortably.

The same day we went to some of the studios. Gibson* had just modelled a hunter holding a dog [*Hunter and his dog*]—quite a magnificent thing, about the best modern piece of sculpture done yet. We have seen very few people here; the Princess Doria has receptions & we had a very dull 1/4 of an hour at one last Monday. The Londonderrys are come from Naples—poor people, in low spirits as well they may be

* Twenty years earlier this English sculptor (1790–1866) had befriended Severn during the last months of Keats' life in Rome.

at the loss of Wynyard*—it has been ruined till 2 years ago which makes the loss of the whole value still more provoking.

Two days, by the Siena road, brought the Cannings to Florence where, owing to Holy Week, they were prevented from visiting the galleries but were obliged to stay on, not wishing to travel on Good Friday or Easter day. As soon as they could they pushed on to Genoa, taking four days to reach there. But Charlotte's thoughts were already turning towards home and domestic details could not be overlooked. 'By the Bye, I must not forget my business about the servants for we shall be back in the middle of May and shall want our footman restored to us by you & the underbutler by Grandmama Hardwicke.'

Avoiding the 'stupid Piacenza road' they reached Brescia from Milan, and at Verona, finding they were able to see all they wanted in one evening were so tempted the next day by a steamer on Lake Garda, that they continued their journey by water to the top of the lake. Char had such a 'horror of getting to Paris in rags and a few days there of the hardest work in shopping, commissions and visits', that they decided to go by Innsbruck and Munich to Frankfort instead, and thence by the Rhine to Rotterdam, but in writing these plans to her mother her confusion was such that she admitted that she could not even count up the days.

* Wynyard, the Londonderry seat in Co. Durham, had recently been rebuilt and furnished, and though still uncompleted had already cost about £130,000. After the damage by fire on Feb. 19th another £40,000 was spent on the rebuilding which started immediately.[4]

4

Lord Waterford's Courtship

The year 1841 brought many changes. Lord Melbourne's government fell and with Sir Robert Peel in office, Canning, echoing his father's appointment fifty years earlier, was nominated Under-Secretary for Foreign Affairs. His chief, Lord Aberdeen, appointed Lord Stuart de Rothesay Ambassador at St Petersburg in succession to the Marquess of Clanricarde who had held the post for two years. Lady Holland reported that 'Never was man more pleased than he is at quitting Russia. He describes the Court & society as detestable, pomp & show with such a mixture of meanness that altogether is unsuitable to persons who have enjoyed polish & ease of a refined society'.[1] Lord Stuart had known St Petersburg as a young Secretary of Embassy at the beginning of the century and was now returning as Ambassador at the age of sixty-two, unsound of health, but anxious for some profitable occupation, for his mother's debts had not improved his circumstances.

The Whig government had resigned on August 28th but Lord Melbourne did not immediately sever his connection with the Queen. 'It cannot greatly signify who is Ambassador at Vienna, or even Petersburg', he wrote to her from Woburn in early September, '. . . Stuart de Rothesay and Strangford are not good men, either of them, but it will be difficult for Lord Aberdeen to neglect their claims altogether.'[2] With his appointment confirmed, Lord Stuart was eager to be off and allowed no time for a formal leave-taking from the Queen who read with astonishment of his departure in the newspaper. Her displeasure was at once communicated to Sir Robert Peel.

25th October 1841

The Queen saw in the papers that Lord Stuart de Rothesay is already gone. The Queen can hardly believe this, as no Ambassador or Minister *ever* left England without previously asking for an Audience and receiving one, as the Queen wishes always to see them before they repair to their posts.[3]

When Lord Stuart de Rothesay left so precipitately on October 23rd it had been decided that his wife and Louisa would not join him until the following summer in order to avoid the severe Russian winter which closed the navigation of the Baltic and was already setting in. The most usual route from England between May and November was to cross to Rotterdam, continue to Hamburg and on to Lübeck where the traveller would pick up the packet on a Tuesday (or at Travemünde on alternate weeks), sail along the Baltic, and after four days put in at Kronstadt in the Gulf of Finland, entering St Petersburg by the Neva. This was the course adopted by Lord Stuart, as also by the United States Envoy who travelled by the same vessel. The new Ambassador reported his arrival in the Russian capital on the evening of November 7th in a despatch to the Foreign Office and the following day the Embassy plate was handed over to him; the cold had suddenly increased to 10 degrees Réaumur and navigation was closed. A few days later he was received in audience by Emperor Nicholas I who manifested 'more kindness both in manner and words than it would become me to mention.'[4]

On the day of Lord Stuart's departure Baron Bunsen and his wife paid a call at 4 Carlton House Terrace. Bunsen was a scholar, earnest and devout, forever seeking the Lord with Prussian thoroughness—in the previous decade in Rome when attached to the Legation to the Vatican, and now in London where he had been appointed Prussian Minister. '*Oct. 23 1841.* We went together to Lady Stuart de Rothesay . . . I saw the incomparable designs of Miss Stuart . . . Raphael-like compositions, such as were never yet made in England. The impression I received was such, that the following day, in spite of business (whose name is Legion) I spent an hour there for another sight of them.'[5] He was impressed by Louisa's drawings and appearance ('her Grecian outline and eye of soul displays a style of beauty still more refined'[6]) and equally by Char ('the face of Lady Canning always grows on me'[7]). He was also impressed, which was of still greater value to Lady Stuart de Rothesay, by the Carlton Terrace house which she was glad to let in order to move to Whitehall Yard with Louisa.

Bunsen was pleased with his new residence. '*9th Jan 1842.* Two days ago the sky was clear, and I saw the prospect across the Park to Westminster Abbey . . . the quiet is delightful—we scarcely hear the wheels of the carriages as there is no thoroughfare', and on a later occasion: 'We have had our prospect again for the last week—the Park and the Abbey becoming visible after three months' fog.'[8]

But matter of greater consequence than the temporary disposal of Carlton House Terrace was occupying the Ambassador's family, and it was something more than the Russian climate that had delayed his wife and daughter in England. Louisa had fallen in love. She was by now twenty-one; to von Neumann she was 'one of the most beautiful girls in England'[9] and there were few who quarrelled with this opinion. Her mother had watched her refuse a number of eligible suitors, but to her astonishment the one with seemingly the least to recommend him to her daughter's affections was the one to capture her heart.

At the age of fifteen the 3rd Marquess of Waterford had succeeded to his father's titles and to the estates in Ireland and Northumberland; he was now thirty and was renowned for his fearlessness on the hunting-field, his recklessness, and his handsome bearing, but there was nothing in his practical joking nor in his interests concentrated entirely on the stable and race-course, to complement Louisa's artistic talent and gentle manner, nor the piety on which her life was founded. They had met in the late summer of 1839 at 'Lord Eglinton's Grand Tournament, given at his castle in Ayrshire . . . the principal knights who performed in the lists were Prince Louis Napoleon, then in exile . . . and Lord Waterford',[10] who was long remembered for his dazzlingly handsome appearance. From the first he had pressed his suit, but slowly and with diffidence. Louisa was left to make her own decision though from the start the proposal had not wholly commended itself to her mother, while Lord Stuart, more able to appreciate the brusqueness of manner, and not against encouraging the match, and Grandmama Hardwicke, the champion of all betrothals, were heartily in its favour. Waterford's sister, married to Viscount Ingestre, later 18th Earl of Shrewsbury ('not a good example for Waterford to follow'), had been named with the Duchess of Montrose as chief protagonist in the incident in which Queen Victoria had been hissed at Ascot in 1839 as she drove up the course, shortly after the painful story of Lady Flora Hastings' death had precipitated a further outbreak of hostility towards the Palace. Although Melbourne was emphatic that Her Majesty had not believed the story, the fact, in spite of the indignant denial of the ladies, was true though directed more at the 'general contents of the procession' than at the Queen herself, and Greville jotted down in his *Memoirs* that by some 'not decorous or feminine noises they testified their dislike or contempt', and that this was 'openly, evenly ostentatiously done'.[11]

Charlotte endeavoured throughout to preserve an open mind and was able to write composedly to her father on the subject of table glass which he hoped to have copied in St Petersburg, although a few years earlier during her travels in Russia Lady Londonderry noted in her journal that this glass was in no way superior to the English.[12]

Grosv Sqre, Dec 7th 1841

Dearest Papa. We were so happy to hear of you safe at your journey's end—it has proved that you had no time to lose in getting there.

I have not forgotten your commission about the glass & have been to look at some patterns, but it seems to me the style of the English glass is so different that I think it will hardly answer to send patterns except for some very slight alterations, but that if you want any of the very light & thin glasses a few of them might be got here & the heavier sorts there; but I am to take Mama some glasses to look at & I promise not to forget it. Ld Granville [on leaving Paris] sold his glass &

Viscountess Canning, *c.* 1838, from an engraving after J. Hayter

Viscountess Canning, 1849, by F. Winterhalter

china for something enormous so that purchase would not have answered. His plants went for nothing; Ld Cowley [the new Ambassador and younger brother of the Duke of Wellington] had the refusal of them at 500£ & the orange trees went at the sale at 5frs a piece. I suppose the sum to be a figure of speech but that was the news brought from Paris; as it is, there is now not a stick in the Embassy greenhouse.

There have been no end of deaths this last month. Ly Normanton & Ly Durham, besides Ld Lothian, Ld Harewood & Ld Elgin.

But besides these deaths there were other topics engrossing London society. Chief among them was the constant postponement by the bridegroom's family of the marriage between Lady Sarah Villiers, eldest daughter of the 5th Earl of Jersey, and Prince Nicholas Esterhazy, whose father had long been Austrian Ambassador in London. Her mother who 'walks about like a grenadier, fat, beautiful, delighted with herself' was much blamed for having pushed her daughter into the marriage, and to Lady Palmerston there never seemed to have been 'a greater piece of folly. She turned poor little Sarah's head with flattery—she is a good child but rather stupid, and at present dreadfully unhappy'.[13] Prince Esterhazy had resorted to every kind of hindrance for he disliked the source of Lady Jersey's large fortune—Child's great banking house in Fleet Street—which with its undertone of commerce was thoroughly undesirable to this powerful and wealthy patrician. A natural obstacle was the mourning occasioned by the death in December of Lord Westmorland, the bride's grandfather, and now while at Ratisbon at the beginning of 1842, he procrastinated still further by pleading gout.

Of closer interest for being of the family was the engagement of Char's cousin, Lord Pollington, who had chosen Lady Rachel Walpole as his wife, daughter of the 3rd Earl of Orford of the second creation, an alliance which did not find favour with the Mexboroughs for she had a host of admirers and was known to be flighty and unconventional. Shortly before her marriage she had made a stir by being the first to dance the polka at a ball, and on her introducing it at Norwich 'produced almost as much sensation . . . as when Ld Townshend first introduced Turnips'. Lady Holland considered her 'very wild and gay; but most people believe it is merely from excess of animal spirits, & that her "Boys" as she calls her troops of suitors, are merely playfellows. But as [Pollington] is perfectly satisfied, the dragons of Virtue must be silent'.[14] The Orfords were known to be dissipated and to have gambled away a fortune; the bride's brother, Lord Walpole, separated from his wife (granddaughter of Lady Holland) shortly after their marriage, and his entanglement with Lady Lincoln was one of many; her sister Lady Dolly (Nevill) was notorious for her eccentricities. In short the family was considered *déclassé*.

Charlotte and Louisa kept their father abreast of family events.

Tyttenhanger, Jan 3rd 1842

Dearest Papa. How very good of you to write a letter expressly to me when you must have so many other things to do. We have been here about ten days and Mama means to stay on till Whitehall is ready. The workmen there have been very slow about it and it still smells of paint. Grandmama is perfectly well and happy at this moment having Pollington's marriage to Ly Rachel Walpole to talk over. He kept on denying it long after the other side had publickly announced it. Pollington is now playing the *attentif* in Norfolk and the announcement over, seems quite satisfied.* Ld Westmorland is dead & the Esterhazy marriage put off another month or more, however had he lived, Prince Esterhazy was putting them all in a great fright by remaining at Vienna and asking Nicholas to come over to him. I am very sorry for poor Sarah.
I suppose your winter is fairly set in. I am glad to hear you have a *clean* house as they say the bugs & fleas there are tremendous. Goodbye dearest Papa, Your affec daughter
L Stuart

Charlotte added her quota of news:

Tyttenhanger, Jan 3rd 1842

GdMama is very happy to have Pollington's marriage on her hands.

* In spite of indication to the contrary the marriage was a happy one; Lady Pollington died in 1854.

At last [he] allows his to be talked about & letters of congratulation fly about *de part et d'autre*. The Orford family talk of Pollington's excellent qualities & how his wife is to deserve such great happiness—while the answers from his side look rather hypocritical though they do not attempt to reach Lady Orford's raptures.

Esterhazy is not yet come & now he will probably use the excuse of Ld Westmorland's death for some time to come. Ly Jersey looks very low & told us she did not know when the marriage would be. Lou & I have sent our small presents which had long been on our consciences. The trousseau was shewn a month ago & I believe it cost £2000, it was very handsome & plentiful, 72 of each article. I have no more room or time to go on.

An outstanding piece of news, and one to make Lord Stuart proud, was that of Charlotte being the only woman invited to luncheon by the Bunsens to meet King Frederick William IV of Prussia during the 'riot of parties, day and night',[15] occasioned by his visit to London to stand sponsor to the baby Prince of Wales. The other guests included 'clergy, Quakers, scientists, and politicians . . . a queer medley', as Mrs Gladstone remarked,[16] but it had been the King's wish to have the opportunity of meeting a cross section of society who might not otherwise have had access to him, and Bunsen felt the object of the luncheon had been achieved; among many others he was able to present 'Carlyle the historian, Dr Arnold from Rugby, Archdeacon Hare'.[17] Charlotte wrote her own account.

Grosv Sqre, Feb 1st 1842

Dearest Papa, I was at Bunsen's wonderful breakfast for his King on Saturday. I was very much astonished when I arrived through a string of hack-cabs reaching to Waterloo Place, to find myself, besides Madame Bunsen, the only woman among eighty savants. They were a curious collection—Quakers, missionaries, American, German, and English; savants, artists, musicians, clergy—high and low church. The King held a levée first, and then there was a luncheon downstairs, on one immense table, filling both rooms and passing through the door, and it was really handsomely done. Your dessert service and ornaments were borrowed, and looked very smart. I was put on one side of the King. His bear-leader is half distracted with all he has to do, what with reading up *laqais de place* answers at all the sights and drives about the streets.

The Brunnows [Russian envoy in London] say you are very happy in St Petersburg and that everybody is enchanted with you, & that you are not a day older, and all kinds of pretty things. They have a dinner for the Jerseys and Nicholas Esterhazy & Sarah Villiers. She is as happy as possible, & they are all overwhelmed with the bustle of the trousseau.

Over sixty years later the bride's magnificent trousseau was still remembered, 'above all the ornamental lace and flower tops to the long gloves, of which there were dozens and dozens, as it were a provision for a lifetime'.[18]

Writing to her husband a few days later, Lady Stuart was able to add a postscript that the 'King of Prussia is gone, pleased with high and low, and having done handsomely in the snuff-box giving line'. And 'At last,' wrote Charlotte, 'the Esterhazy marriage is over. It was settled in such a hurry at last that the invitation only got to Mama & Lou just in time to bring them from Tyttenhanger an hour too late for the breakfast. I was at it & everybody in London too except Mme de Flahaut,* an unwise omission, & I cannot think why Lady Jersey did not ask her. The bride looked really beautiful, much better than she ever did before & the Grandmother Esterhazy sent her a quantity of magnificent pearls with which she was loaded.' Queen Victoria later remarked that she did not wonder at Prince Esterhazy being displeased with the match, the grandmother of the young Princess 'having been a daughter of Child the banker'.[19] Within a few weeks this seemingly humble lineage was of great resource to the bridegroom, for being on the point of arrest for debts, he was obliged to pay up hurriedly to avoid a scandal.

* Margaret Mercer Elphinstone, Baroness Keith and Nairne in her own right, had married in 1817 the Comte de Flahault, reputedly an illegitimate son of Talleyrand, and earlier the lover of Queen Hortense. From 1860–62 he was French Ambassador in London. It was she, the 'Fop's Despair', who as an unmarried heiress at the time of his disgrace, had teazingly remarked to Lord Byron in the house of his highly influential supporter Lady Jersey: 'You had better have married me, I would have managed you better.' Her half-sister had married the Jersey's second son.

Lord Waterford's Courtship

Although an onlooker at the Opening of Parliament in February 1842 might have been struck by the graceful figure of Louisa Stuart dressed in turquoise velvet, he would have been ignorant of the overtures to marriage she was receiving and of the diffidence they engendered in a nature so wholly unassuming. Lady Stuart was at pains to mention it to no one but Grandmama Hardwicke and the Aunts. She was comforted by the knowledge that Lord Stuart trusted entirely to her own judgment, yet she admitted that his absence complicated everything. Through modesty Lou had had difficulty in writing to her father and could only bring herself to mention obliquely the man with whom a closer acquaintance was about to be made; the confusion in her use of noun and pronoun was entirely consistent with an upbringing in which no young girl in a similar position would have brashly used a pronoun of the masculine gender.

Jan 17th 1842

Dearest Papa, I can never thank you enough for the kind and affectionate letter which you last wrote to me and which I received two or three days ago. I am very grateful to you for putting me at my ease upon a subject which I did not like to begin upon, & I hope you did not think it very strange and formal of me not to have mentioned it in my last letter to you; if you did, pray forgive me, and believe me it was entirely from false shyness and not exactly knowing how to begin with so little to begin upon—

I assure you I never had any prejudices against that person, on the contrary I often thought they were very unfairly abused—so I am perfectly satisfied to make their acquaintance with a free and unbiased mind. I shall be very glad when the first making acquaintance is over, for that is what I dread as I shall be sure to do or say something absurd or awkward. The idea that it pleases you tho' is every thing to me.

So believe me your affect daughter

Louisa Stuart

Meanwhile at St Petersburg Lord Stuart was unwell. Very probably he had undergone a stroke though he seems to have made sufficiently light of it to his family for Char to hope it was no more 'than what you call a warning for it would be very disagreeable if every winter's cold in that horrid climate turns into such an illness'. Later much blame was laid on the Russian stove which was known to omit a poisonous gas and suffocate people unless carefully attended to, though if properly managed *Murray's Handbook* could recommend it enthusiastically as 'the most complete device that was ever imagined', for 'in spite of the great external cold there is a perpetual summer indoors', and no additional blankets were considered necessary.[20]

By early March, though matters were still going slowly Louisa, with complete freedom of choice, seemed to be making up her mind and Char wrote to St Petersburg that there was no 'fear of her marrying him without caring for him. She may be quite happy with his odd but amiable disposition, & if she bears his rough manners now she is sure not to mind them afterwards. Gdmama has worried herself almost to death with thinking about Lou, she is Ld W's most active & violent partisan & is longing to have him brought to Tyttenhanger'. She closed her letter hoping that he was none the worse for 'cold air & what is much more unwholesome, hot rooms with stoves—plenty of exercise must be needful to balance the two. Ever yr afftly C Canning'.

Lady Stuart de Rothesay was distracted at not having her husband with her, for society was beginning to talk. The presence of Lord Waterford at a *soirée dansante* (a *breaking in*, as she called it) which she, the Ingestres and Lou attended, also the still faithful Mr Tomline, was so unusual that the *Morning Post* commented upon it. Within a few days he had left for Dublin to ride in a steeplechase. His boisterousness and rough manners were Lady Stuart de Rothesay's special grievance and her sensibilities must have been shocked by the letter which Lord Ingestre, having seen by the papers 'that Waterford had had an accident which perhaps might alarm *those interested in him*', enclosed with his own.

Bilton Hotel, Dublin, March 24th 1842

My dear Ingestre.

I daresay you will see that I had a cropper yesterday, however I got caught by cramp *tous directions*, and am all right again. I was so unlucky yesterday, I was winning the first race in a canter with Blueskin, when in the last field a brute of a horse ran against me, & knock'd me over.

In the second race I rode a stone above the weight, won the first heat in a canter, and would have done the same in the second, but the fellows would not start before half past seven, when it was so dark that my mare put her foot in a hole in the last field, & tumbled over me. I found on passing through Dublin these races were to take place next day, so I sent for Columbine & Blueskin from the Curragh—we had very good sport.

I shall be in London about Wednesday next.

Yr affec Waterford

Give my love to Sarah [Ingestre] and Co.

As letter followed letter to St Petersburg, Lady Stuart de Rothesay was able to open her mind to her husband, and though she had many scruples there was no doubt where Tyttenhanger sympathies lay. 'Tyttenhanger remains very anxious for his success', 'At Tyttenhanger, they are optimists', 'Tyttenhanger continues to patronize', was the refrain. '*You* would be quite to the Tyttenhanger fancy' she added, while 'I am thought over-cautious', but if Louisa 'once comes to the point of acceptance, I am determined to hear nothing *against*'. By mid-April the happy news that Lord Waterford had been accepted was conveyed to Lord Stuart de Rothesay by his wife, who had also written to Queen Victoria.

When I wrote just now to tell the Queen I said 'I hardly dared hope that, consistently with your duties in Her Majesty's service, you could leave your post even for a short leave, tho' it would be great gratification to us that you should be able to join your family on such an occasion'—

Mama is delighted at getting at last to the *dénouement*. Pollington and his bride were at the Queen's ball where she looked very pretty, and danced with great delight. It was her first ball: and in another way, it was Lou's *last* and made me feel that my occupation was gone.

The next day she wrote again to say the Queen was all compliance and had immediately communicated with Lord Aberdeen, hoping that if it were possible Lord Stuart was to have leave to come home for the wedding. Charlotte wrote on the same day as her mother.

April 19th 1842

Dearest Papa. I think you will be quite happy when you get this batch of letters & hear that Lou's marriage is quite settled. She looks as happy as possible & Ld Waterford has become much more gentle & amiable, & he is so devoted to Lou that he will do anything to please her & she is certainly not *éxigeante*. It is a very good thing that he voluntarily has set about suiting himself more to her tastes. All his family are in the greatest possible state of joy, as well they may be. I believe we shall go to Tyttenhanger, & Mama & Lou take Ld W to introduce him there. Gd Mama is really dying to see him & was quite ill with anxiety when it was still pending.

I hope you will be able to make it possible to come over even if it is but for a few days, & that as much for your sake as for ours, for nothing could be more wholesome for you than the passage after a winter passed in such unwholesome stove warmed atmosphere. Goodbye dearest Papa.

Ever yr affec Char Canning

Lord Waterford's letter followed a few days later.

London, April 25th 1842

Dear Lord Stuart. I thank you for completing my happiness by giving your consent to my marriage with your daughter, and hope that you will find it practicable and convenient to be present at my wedding; if not that you will inform us whether it is agreeable to your wishes that the ceremony should take place on the 1st of June, by which time all matters can be arranged.

Believe me to be Yrs very truly

Waterford

Of the visit to Tyttenhanger Grandmama Hardwicke wrote a rapturous account to Lord Stuart, though judging from the postscript ('Pollington's little wife is a gay, wild, pretty creature & I suspect very clever—they were *not* of our party') she considered one erratic visitor at a time was enough.

Lady Stuart added her description.

April 26th 1842

It went vastly well. The young pair of Pollingtons, who went away that morning, having been in great fashion, were quite forgotten in the interest of the new acquaintance, and there were also Charlotte and Canning.

We should all have liked prolonging our Tyttenhanger country life a day or two, but I thought after the Queen's civility and kindness, it would not do to shirk her invitation to a concert last night. The concert turned out a ball for want of music as the singers were all sick, and as Lou did not want to dance, it allowed of a very early return. The Queen came forward and gave her an embrace. I don't think she recognised Lord Waterford, but he stood an introduction to the Vice-Queen* who, of course, told him that Louisa was much too good for him. However, she meant to be gracious, and he was only amused, and thought the business done at a cheap rate as we came away soon after ten o'clock.

On the day of the above letter Lord Aberdeen sent Lord Stuart the following despatch:

Foreign Office, April 26th 1842[21]

If the event of Your Excellency being desirous of returning to England for a limited time in the course of the spring, I have to acquaint you that you are at liberty to do so, and that you can leave St Petersburg for that purpose as soon after the receipt of this despatch as may suit your convenience.

To which Lord Stuart replied:

St Petersburg, May 14th 1842[22]

I purpose availing myself immediately of the permission which your Lordship has granted me to return to England. I have already taken leave of several members of the Imperial Family and shall embark by the first steamer for Lübeck.

After the hesitations and long-drawn out suspense of many months the final arrangements were concluded with speed. Lord Stuart sailed on May 17th and dined in company with the Cannings at the Russian Embassy in London on June 2nd. There is no account of the effect his appearance made on his family, though from impressions noted down at this time there emerges the semblance of a sick man. In writing of his return from Russia

* Probably Countess De Grey, wife of Ireland's Viceroy.

an acquaintance remarked that '*Lord Stuart en est revenu apoplectique, et même, dit-on, un peu atteint dans son intelligence: on pense qu'il ne retournera pas a Saint-Petersbourg*',[23] while Nesselrode (Russian Secretary for Foreign Affairs) terser and just as discouraging, described him as a '*cadavre ambulant*'.[24]

Louisa was married on June 8th by special licence at the Chapel Royal, Whitehall (the Banqueting Hall), the first wedding to take place there for almost fifteen years. Converted into a chapel by George I Divine Service was held twice on Sundays, but it had never been consecrated and was considered one of the dreariest places of worship in London. The honeymoon at Curraghmore gave Louisa her first introduction to her Irish home where she would live in perfect happiness until 1859, when her husband was killed out hunting.

5

An Honourable Distinction

At Buckingham Palace Queen Victoria, aged twenty-three and married two years, made an entry in her Journal on June 1st. 'Lady Dalhousie has resigned & I wrote offering Lady Canning the post, which she has accepted.'[1]

Two days earlier Charlotte had received a command from the Queen to which she immediately replied.*

Buckingham Palace
May 28th 1842

My dear Lady Canning,

The reason for wh I now address you is to acquaint you that I am desirous of offering to you, the Office of Lady of the Bedchamber, which has just become vacant by the resignation of Lady Dalhousie.

As I have had the pleasure of knowing you ever since *we were* Children, I should be very happy if this would suit you.

Pray believe me always
Your's very sincerely Victoria R.

Tyttenhanger, May 29 1842[2]

Madam

Your Majesty's gracious Letter calls for my warmest and most heartfelt thanks.

Under any circumstances it would have been a source of pride and gratification to me to be selected for the honourable distinction of serving Your Majesty's Royal Person, and I trust that in expressing to Your Majesty the sincere Pleasure with which I undertake this grateful Office, I may be permitted to add that the kind terms in which Your

* The rough draft in Lord Canning's hand survives amongst Lady Canning's papers.

Majesty has been graciously pleased to confer it can never be forgotten by me.

I have the honor to be
With the greatest respect
Madam
Your Majesty's
most devoted
Humble servant
C. Canning.

The Queen had chosen with discernment. Following upon a period when the vexed question of the Queen's Ladies was still in the mind of the public, she had done well to make an appointment in line with the government.

In her seven years of marriage, despite the somewhat austere character of her husband, Lady Canning had lost none of the tolerance which was so engaging an aspect of her nature, neither had her enjoyment of life and people been suppressed. She was two years older than Queen Victoria and her sense of duty had developed early. At home in most spheres of society, life at Court did not intimidate her though her innate modesty preserved her from complacency, as did a disposition to observe life with an amused eye. Above all, her character was unimpeachable. Her own misgivings arose from the paucity of her wardrobe and her ingenuity was often put to the test, for the Cannings had no great wealth and had a London establishment and a carriage to maintain. There is no account of her first waiting; the only indication that it probably took place in July is from Lady Lyttelton, the Royal Governess, when referring to a 'very pleasant talk with Lady Canning in the afternoon; she is exceedingly agreeable and admirable in every way, I think—so simple and unselfish.'[3] She also wrote admiringly of Charlotte wearing a wreath of real dahlias (of a small size one ventures to hope), for among her other accomplishments this was one which appealed to the Queen, and Lady Canning was often required to make the Queen's wreaths—of heather, when in the Highlands.

Two events, not unlike in circumstance, occurred soon after

Louisa's marriage. The Duc d'Orléans, eldest of Louis Philippe's five sons, and heir to the French throne—the 'flower of the flock'—whose marriage only five years earlier had been the occasion for Lady Stuart de Rothesay lingering in Paris, had fallen from a moving carriage and had died almost instantaneously leaving two sons, the Comte de Paris and the Duc de Chartres. France was thrown into grief at the suddenness of the tragedy, and on Queen Victoria's visit to France the following year the stricken widow was the object of her interest. At present the Queen could only echo the general feeling voiced in an English journal on the inscrutability of Providence: 'Alas! who can reckon upon tomorrow?'

The second accident which at first was reported to be equally grave, befell Louisa herself within a week of her arrival at Curraghmore. Her husband was driving her in a phaeton and on descending a steep mountain road the horses took fright, Lou was thrown from the carriage, and falling backwards suffered severe concussion. Her husband carried her home insensible in his arms. The first to arrive was Aunt Caledon followed closely by Lady Stuart. Bulletins were issued in the newspapers until her improvement made them unnecessary, but there had been an interval when her life was despaired of and once again the penetrating truism which von Neumann noted in his diary, that 'Beauty, wealth, rank, all were here united, but all are equal in the face of the blows of Providence' must have found an answering chord in the thoughts of many.[4] Her long hair had had to be cut to relieve pressure on the brain and reduce the fever; Lord Waterford himself discharged this duty and ordered that at his death the tresses should be laid beside him in his coffin.

In consequence of this unlooked-for circumstance the Stuart de Rothesays did not reach St Petersburg until October. Two letters survive from Lady Stuart to her mother, one affording a glimpse of their reception at the Alexander Palace, Tsarkoe Selo, by Nicholas I and the Empress Alexandra Feodorovna. Of their daughters, the three Grand Duchesses, the eldest, Marie, aged twenty-three had been three years married to Duke Maximilian of Leuchtenberg; Olga, the future Queen of Württemberg, and Alexandra, were as yet unmarried. The Tsarevitch had recently married the daughter of the Grand Duke of Hesse but it was not a marriage much liked in the family, for as Lady Holland had heard, 'her education & manners have been more carefully attended to. She is grave, relishes books & correspondence; whereas all the other Princesses beginning with the Empress are very great hoydens full of practical jokes and giggling'.[5] However one member of the Imperial family, the Grand Duchess Helene, wife of the Tsar's brother Grand Duke Michael, was of a serious turn of mind with a preference for intellectual pursuits and the New Michailoff Palace (now the Russian Museum) was notable as a centre of scholarship and learning.

No doubt this letter to Lady Hardwicke from her daughter went the round of Tyttenhanger.

Petersburg, 12 os [old style]
24 ns [new style] [*Oct 24th 1842*]

Dearest Mama. I had the delight of a letter from you, though rather of old date, yesterday morning, before starting for Czarskoe Zelo & it gave me spirits for enterprise to have the last tidings from home. The Courier is going back directly so I must abridge my history of "the Court of the Czar", which I have been writing to Lou as she was made my principal topic of Imperial graciousness. Lord Ingestre had gone to Peterhoff if you remember just after her accident, so they knew all sorts of details about it.

I thought all I saw very splendid though I saw only the small Palace, the sort of Trianon to the larger *corps de logis* as big as the Tuileries. I believe they always have a sort of reunion on Sundays, & for us it was made still grander; there was a little French Play & a ball afterwards, & the hurried change of toilette is rather hard on a new comer, for we had not the guide of the turbans or hat that we had been introduced to in the morning to help me to the face below it. When the dinner company assembled at three o'clock I was taken into the next room, & the Imperial Family made a very dignified, & yet very interesting appearance, a *Bonhommie* about the Emperor prevents any *aire*, & they all took at once an *acquainted* manner, which always *takes one in*, for I believe it goes no further.

Amongst the *alentours* of the court I had been told I should see a vulgar talking English woman, married to a Russian general, & I am sure you or Cath [Countess of Caledon] will remember the person it turned out to be, one of a family who used to walk the beach at Mudiford [near Highcliffe], to have a talk with whoever she could get hold of; & this elderly young lady somehow picked up a Russian husband & seemed very familiar with all the Imperial Family, & of course chose to be an old & intimate friend of mine. She was of use to me however as I could ask her the names of forgotten acquaintances of whom I find many, grateful for *my souvenir*, which is *forgotten*. The young Grand Duchesses would be beautiful girls in any family, & dressed in a perfection that must be the result of much labour, but all the Court puff them as *anges de bonté* & they certainly all seem amiable & affectionate, & very civil doing the honours more than any Princesses I ever met with. I am to go to-morrow to the Grand Duchess Helen—sister in law—who is a very different sort of person from the rest, less frivolous, but not so popular.

Lord Stuart had a good rest between the morning & evening duties and so did not feel very fagged & the Empress was always desiring him to sit down. I suppose to give the Men something to do they were ordered to be *en frac* for the Evening—having been in Uniform in the Morning. For the Ladies both Toilettes seemed equally fine, but the Morning the most solid. I was afraid I was going to have a cold but it has only come to a sort of ear ache rheumatism that I have some times.

I think the Berryhood [Misses Berry] will be with you soon & so I write to none of the two, though I hope to hear from each in turn. I got back in time for the Courier, I shall miss him however if I add another line & so adieu Dearest Mama & affectly yrs E S de R

Following upon the departure of her parents Charlotte was in London. The running of Highcliffe Castle and the estate had been left in her hands, and the letting of the house in Whitehall Yard fell to her also and appears to have given rise to the same difficulties as are encountered today, and whether to sell or let was a continuous harassment.

In her next letter Charlotte was able to elaborate upon the paragraph contained in the *Illustrated London News* of August 22nd which Lady Stuart had read before her departure from England:

H.R.H. The Duke of Cambridge, accompanied by Baron Brunnow the Russian Ambassador, arrived at Stockton upon Tees at 1 o'clock by a special train from Darlington en route to Wynyard, on a visit to the Marquis and Marchioness of Londonderry.

The Duke was kindly and of generous proportions; like many deaf people he was an incessant talker, speaking always at the top of his voice, and irrepressible in his jokes. The Queen had been unnecessarily offended by his behaviour in connection with Prince Albert's precedence at Court, so that he and the Duchess were not popular with their niece. Further it was rumoured that Lady Augusta Somerset, the Duke of Beaufort's daughter and Lady of the Bedchamber to the Duchess of Cambridge, was with child by Prince George of Cambridge which the Queen, with an ear for gossip, was willing to believe though there appears to have been no truth in it. Charlotte's opinion given in her letter of Nov. 5th was surely the correct one.

Grosv Sqre, Oct 10th 1842

The account of the Wynyard visit is wonderful. A whole week was spent *promener*-ing the company all over the country, breakfasts at Stockton—dinners at Durham—three balls at Wynyard at night—then races, & at last the whole party were carried to Sunderland & billetted there and at Seaham, and brought back again next day. Brunnow all but died of it & nobody but the D of Cambridge was happy.

I have not heard a word about Ly Lincoln & the P of H. I think Douglas's marriage must be coming to pass now it is so publickly talked of—they say Ld Shelburne was refused by her.

Gossip relating to Lady Lincoln seems to have reached St Petersburg. Candidates for the 'P of H' were not abundant, though the name of Charles, Prince of Hesse (1809–77) suggests itself. He was married to Elizabeth, Princess of Prussia, and their son was the future husband of Princess Alice, second daughter of Queen Victoria. (The sixty-six-year-old Palatine of Hungary does not seem a likely competitor.) However, the suspected engagement between Lord Douglas, once Louisa's suitor, and the Princess of Baden, 'one of the most distinguished beauties of the continent',

Chateau d'Eu, the arrival of Queen Victoria, 1843, water-colour by Charlotte Canning

Viscount Canning, 1852, by George Richmond R.A.

was greatly intriguing society at this time. Besides his measure of good looks and his skill as a dancer, Lord Douglas was notorious for a fractious temper. 'What have you heard about the rumour of Lord Douglas's marriage to the Princess Marie of Baden?', Lady Palmerston wrote off hastily to Princess Lieven whose husband had been Russian Ambassador in London. Swiftly came the retort: 'I do not greatly approve of this new fashion of marrying outside one's class. But there are many good customs forgotten nowadays'.[6] Conjecture was general as to whether the lady would take her husband's title or retain the dignity of a princess.

6

A Commission from the Queen

Portumna Castle, 'a wild place on the shore of the wide part of the Shannon called Loch Derg', in Co. Galway, had been gutted by fire when the Cannings stayed there at the end of October with its owner, the Marquess of Clanricarde, and his family. The cheapness of posting from Dublin (where Gresham's Hotel was found to be as 'bad & dirty as possible') had permitted them the luxury of four horses and the distance of a hundred miles had been covered triumphantly in ten and a half hours. They all lived in the stable which had been comfortably fitted up and the Cannings found their holiday a capital innovation, but the Waterfords were expecting them at Curraghmore, and Charlotte was longing to get her first sight of her sister's Irish home and to prolonging the visit for some weeks before her next waiting at Court claimed her on December 5th.

Curraghmore, Nov 5th 1842

Dearest Mama. At last I write to you from Curraghmore after waiting so very long to come here. Lou looks & is as well as she ever was, she is in perfectly good spirits and entirely happy. Waterford is as kind & goodhumoured as possible. I have an incident to tell you worthy of a French novel. On Thursday when we arrived here C found a letter for him from the Frankfort or Munich secretary—I forget which—formally telling him that Douglas's marriage to the Princess of Baden was by the same post formally announced to the Queen by the Prince of Leiningen!! Wasn't it a curious piece of news to greet us in the first moment of our first arrival in this house? This morning's post has brought for C a letter with D & C for the seal.* I shall have to send off

* The fact that Canning, as Assistant Secretary of State, had been officially advised of the engagement of the Marquess of Douglas and Clydesdale (once

this to you before I hear the contents for C & Waterford are gone out to hunt. Before I came away from London I heard that the Grand Duke of Baden would not consent to the marriage; I suppose he has relented. I cannot help pitying Douglas for we shall all be so inclined to laugh at him & Her Serene Highness Ly D & he must find it an uncomfortable sort of *ménage*; besides all of which he used to object to, what must be the case now in marrying a Roman Catholic—if she is like her cousin Mrs Ernest of Coburgh it may do well—for I never saw a simpler, more countrified or amiable little person.*

À propos to court news. You must have read that a deal of scandal has been talked about Ly A Somerset. I have always believed that the extent of the truth was that she had flirted violently & openly with P George & the Cambridges prudently gave her a *congé* for a time. The Beauforts never admitted for a moment that she was dismissed by the Dss of Cambridge, & Ly A was at Badminton with a house full of people which shewed that one part of the story going about could not be true. Now she has gone back to the Cambridges which is a sufficient contradiction to all but the flirting story, which is true.

I see in the paper that the Queen goes for a few days to Walmer before Brighton, again driven away by fevers in the town. How often fevers must be as near as Pimlico or Windsor & then nobody minds them, but every journey gets put off by the doctors.

I must tell you how much I have seen here. The beauty of the place is above my expectations even now that I see it with hardly a leaf left. The house is decidedly ugly but it is a good thing to be so totaly void of a bad sort of taste & the offices are of a very good style. Lou's projects are excellent. She has made the drawing rooms very pretty & comfortable with chintz covers on all the sofas & chairs and all sorts of china and ornaments spread about. Lou has a number of commissions to give me for she has used her summer trousseau bonnets till now & they are become dirty rags. She has a very good crop of hair about 1½ inches long, as thick as possible & inclined to curl, & she looks very well with it. She has entirely left off caps & in the morning wears your brown silk net with the Isidore† front & the chenille net in the

---

Louisa's suitor) while in Louisa's own house, could not but add piquancy to the communication.

* Princess Alexandrine of Baden had married Duke Ernest II of Saxe-Coburg in May 1842.

† Mr Isidore, hairdresser of 14 Bentinck Street, Manchester Square.

evening, both of which make her head so exactly of the same shape it used to be that one cannot believe that her hair is gone. Give Papa my love. Yrs aff Char

Once home in London after crossing to Bristol in strong wind and with four hundred pigs on board, Charlotte's attention was claimed by Court affairs for she found a letter from Lady Lyttelton calling her to Walmer Castle where most of the Household accompanying the Queen had gone down with fearful colds. The house which the Duke of Wellington as Warden of the Cinque Ports had placed at the Queen's disposal was unprotected from the violent wind which continued to blow at a 'brisk gale' throughout the stay; the long passage was warmed by a stove which was admitted to be a peculiar construction, and the rooms used by the Court faced east, those of the Royal Children in a northerly direction. No small wonder that the Queen suffered from face-ache.

But St Petersburg was never far from Charlotte's thoughts, in particular her father's health. (At the end of November Princess Lieven was asking Lady Palmerston: 'What news of the Stuarts in St Petersburg. Is he still alive?')[1] She was particularly provoked by the imputation that her sister-in-law, Lady Clanricarde, had been the author of the recently published *The Ambassador's Wife*, by the prolific novelist Mrs C. G. F. Gore, whose work Thackeray delighted in parodying. The book, partly in epistolary form, owed its notoriety, not to its nicety of construction, but to its highly-coloured version of pampered society life in St Petersburg and the ambitions of an imaginary low-born Russian Ambassadress at a foreign court; it would have ill-become a past Ambassadress and sister of a present Under-Secretary of State to have been associated with so fictitious a representation.

Windsor Castle, Dec 5th 1842

Dearest Mama.

I went on Wednesday last to Walmer and found the Queen with a bad cold and pain in her face, so much so that the 2 first days she did not dine at table. The cold had run thro' the house & everyone had had a share of it. Car [Cocks] & Ld Hardwicke I found both in waiting besides Fanny Devereux, Ld C. Wellesley [Chief Equerry] & Sir E. Bowater who has got the Lodge. He seems very fond of it & has brushed it up very much; he has added a passage or two & what he calls 'a little something at the top of the stairs' which I perfectly understood & believe must be a gt improvement, & a chimney to the thatched house.* Car & Miss D were lodging near with the Ansons† & I was the only person besides Ly Lyttelton of the suite, in the Castle. It is very small & is literally a fort & upon the beach.

We came here on Saturday, it was amusing to be of the party on such a journey; the day was fine & crowds of people lined the road. The Queen is as kind as possible and I find I shall see much more of her now there is no Baroness to carry messages.‡ She asked after you and told me to make you tell me all about the Gd Dss Helene's daughters for she suspected them to be very ugly; I said I had already heard from you that such was the case.§ Then she talked of the finery and said it would be hard upon you to dress & undress so often & I assured her you had taken a very good set of fine things with you.

Poor Car has had to go back to Eastnor to-day for it seemed that she was a good deal wanted there for Hatty has been ill again. What a wonderful and abominable idea I hear they have got hold of at Petersburg, that Ly Clanricarde wrote 'The Ambassador's wife', she is very indignant about it but has sent for it never having read it—it is notorious to have been written by Mrs Gore who has never denied it. Douglas is coming to settle the preliminaries of his marriage almost immediately. I hear that here it is thought rather a *mésalliance* for the Princess. Charles Murray [Master of the Household] says she is to be called Ly Douglas.

I hope Papa is more prudent than he used to be & that you have pursuaded him to put on a little flannel. Good-bye dearest Mama, give my love to Papa. Ever yr aff Char

At about the same time Lady Stuart was writing to her own mother of her difficulties in finding a suitable Embassy, for there

* Sir Edward Bowater, Equerry to Prince Albert, was now installed at Thatched Lodge, Richmond.

† George Anson had been Private Secretary to Lord Melbourne from 1836 until he filled the same office, as well as Treasurer, to Prince Albert in 1840. In 1847 he was appointed Keeper of the Privy Purse.

‡ Baroness Lehzen had left at the end of September.

§ The three young Grand Duchesses were not renowned for their looks.

was no established house for the Ambassador. Before settling into the neighbouring house, the Stuart de Rothesays had gone to the magnificent palace fronting on the English Quay, owned by the Demidoffs whose fortune had sprung chiefly from mines in the Urals. Count Paul Demidoff, the elder of two brothers, had married a Finn and their son inherited not only his father's estates and riches, but also those of his uncle Count Anatole Demidoff who now in the second and last year of an incompatible marriage with Princess Mathilde, daughter of Napoleon's youngest brother Jerome, had had no children. Prince Oldenburg, also mentioned by Lady Stuart, was a connection of the Tsar; his palace on the Neva beyond the Hermitage stands beside the house which eventually became the British Embassy.

To the Dowager Countess of Hardwicke from Lady Stuart de Rothesay

Petersburg, 15 os
27 ns [*Nov 27th 1842*]

Dearest Mama. You shall have the first of my pen & ink, after the transfer into the House we have taken for a *twelvemonth*, I like my first friend best though we shall be able to lodge our *Monde* better here, but the high finish of the lavish expenditure of the Demidoff, makes this simple House look rather Bourgeois & had the Lady of the Mansion next door arrived before we had *signed* for *this*, I think I should have continued to have made the junction which baffled the architects, & have kept the salons I borrowed, which are lost to every body. Her large House is very fit for an *Ambassade*, but not very commodious, & she is spoiling it by contrivances she is very proud of in the ball room, & if we are destined to move again, I had a fancy for that house & reproached Mme Demidoff for not consulting *me*, which she quite seemed to think it would have been her duty to do. She is a remarkably pleasant & handsome woman, who weeps over a strange almost mad husband, & rejects all her suitors, to devote herself to her only child, the heir of all the wealth of the old Demidoff you remember. The younger brother Anatole who is also here this winter married the daughter of the Duc de Montfort, a Bonaparte King & she has royal connexions of her own. She is very handsome, but sighs after Florence where she was brought up, and therefore is not popular here, besides it was thought rather impertinent on the most simple ball dress to have more diamonds than the Empress at the Palace *Fête*! However I did not learn that the Empress thought so, & the other Mme Demidoff who was quite as splendid is her particular favourite.

I thought I should have done a little patronage there with the Princess of Oldenbergh, who thinks of nothing but her nursery, for Miss Withers, but it was a real *scrubbing damsel* she wanted, at least for the *tub* & *towell* work to assist a head nurse; she was a Nassau & is not held quite of Imperial rank, at least the Emperor took me to *Polonaise* before her, but her Husband who is a cousin by his mother, has charge of a great many Institutions & in an unpretending way they are very useful people, but keep aloof from balls when they can & one might have been sure she would invent the contrivance of a *pocket* in her *ball* dress! & she was very proud of all the things she had stored away in it.

A connexion of ideas leads me to the Selkirks, & the magnificent fur which Lou is enjoying, & has I hope properly thanked for; I should like some messages from me, as I had no opportunity of goodbyes.

The year closed with Charlotte still in waiting. The Queen spent Christmas at Windsor and enjoyed the big Christmas tree in her private sittingroom, while a second one was set up in the Oak Room for the Household when each member received a present. On New Year's Eve the Queen and Prince dined in their private apartments and the Maid of Honour, the Hon Georgiana Liddell, youngest of a family of sixteen, found the evening remarkably long and dull.[2]

On the day of the following letter Queen Victoria made an entry in her Journal: 'After luncheon walked out with Lady Canning who is a remarkably nice person, so quiet, unaffected & gentle & so ready to do anything.'[3]

Windsor Castle, Dec 20th 1842

Dearest Mama, That I may not forget it I will at once give you a message from the Queen, but she told me to beg you not to mention it to any of the Russian court. It is a commission she wants you to do for her—to get a number of lithographed or engraved portraits of the imperial family, *not* of the Emperor himself for she has several and of the Empress—but of the Grand Duchesses young and old—married &

single—the wife of the Czarovitch and all—to put into a collection of lithograph portraits. The reason the Queen wishes you not to say a word about the commission is that whenever she has wanted any portraits of them they have always sent her *presents* of oil pictures—and this she wishes to avoid. I should think there can be no difficulty in getting these things and sending them to the Foreign Office & then through me to the Queen.

This week nearly all my fellow servants change which I am sorry for—for I had got so used to the present set. Fanny Devereux and Miss Murray I got on very well with & liked very much—Miss Lister & little Georgy Liddell take their places. The Queen is very kind & pleasant and I do not at all dislike being here. Canning paid me a visit of four days and I suppose will be asked again at Christmas. Pray tell me what year it was we were at Ramsgate? for the Queen says she perfectly remembers us there, that you were lame & Lou & I were brought to see her with a little boy—which was Alexander. I think she was only 2 or 3 yrs old, & I should like very much to know when it was.*

There is no news at all just now, all the wars being ended and everything going well. Major Malcolm† who brought the treaty home from China was here for a day & gave us a great deal of curious information about it. The bravery of the Tartars was quite extraordinary & many anecdotes were as wonderful as Roman and Grecian traits of Heroism. The suicides of the Tartars were too horrible and it was with great difficulty they could be prevented from killing themselves, their wives, & children, deliberately. Even some Chinese did the same but they were more easily reassured. He told us of the house they went into in which 22 people had hanged themselves. The Chinese generally did not interfere in the least in the struggle but used to run in crowds to see what was going on as if to a review, whilst our troops fought with the Tartars. They crowded to our hospitals as soon as any town was taken, & almost all the sick & wounded treated by our surgeons became very friendly. Pray give many loves from me to Papa & Believe me Yr aff Char C

* The Queen stayed at Albion House, Ramsgate in 1824, the first of many visits; she would have been five years old. Alexander, the only child of Aunt Caledon, was born in 1812.

† Secretary of the British Legation, Nanking; the ratification of the treaty marked the end of hostilities with China over the import of opium.

Windsor Castle, Jan 2 1843

Dearest Mama, I go back to town to-morrow & am glad not to be of the Claremont* party next week. I suspect it will be very cold for the first frost of this winter is just setting in. I have liked this quiet waiting very much but of course I am very happy to go home again. The Queen has been exceedingly good to me & I have seen a good deal of her. Very few people have been here—I think the Duke of Wellington was the only visitor & a very few people have dined. We had a great deal of feasting at Christmas in the way of very enormous meats & pies & German trees with sugar plums & presents given to every body. I have had my bracelet with the Queen's picture, really a nice thing to have. She gave me also a Paisley cloak & an Annual for New Year's day.

Little Georgy Liddell has been in waiting these last 10 days, I like her of all things & better than her sisters. She is cleverer & more solid I think & has all their good temper. Miss Lister is the other "Maid". She is very babyish but perfectly harmless & not disagreeable. I wish we met Ly Lyttelton oftener.

Back in London Charlotte felt she had been away a long time. In her absence Canning ordered *The Ambassadress* from Cawthorn's, of Cockspur Street, to be sent to Lady Stuart de Rothesay, and Charlotte in writing to her mother referred once again to the 'vile Petersburg report' that attributed the authorship to Lady Clanricarde and nailed the lie to the 'spiteful little Chreptovich,† I hope you have not much to do with her'. (In 1856 her husband, Count Chreptovich, was made Russian Ambassador in London, and was known to have no liking for the English.) A book more to Lord Stuart's taste, and one which Charlotte found the most interesting thing she had ever read, was Eyre's book of the 'Affgan war' (*Military Operations at Cabul, January 1842*) just then published, which went into a second edition the same year. She also forwarded, this time to her mother, the *Jardin des modes* which she guessed had come from Lady Cowley in Paris. 'I suspect,' she

* In Surrey, where Princess Charlotte of Wales had died in childbirth; though still the property of King Leopold, Victoria and the Court frequently stayed there.

† Daughter of Count Nesselrode.

added, 'that it is not at all what you want and I hope you will tell her if you write about it to have it directed to Canning & not to me in Downing St, for I shall be in a scrape. I am sure Prints would suit you much better & give you a great deal more to see each time than that foolish little doll.'

Matrimony and deaths were always news of consequence, and in the middle of January Charlotte had an astounding piece of information to impart: 'Do you know that *Lady Falmouth* is going to marry Ld Auckland!!!' By the next letter the Miss Edens had denied it, and indeed their brother died a bachelor. He had recently returned from a six year assignment as Governor-General to India where his sisters through affection and loyalty, and at great sacrifice to themselves, had accompanied him. Emily Eden was later known for her two novels and more particularly for her *Letters from India*. Charlotte collected all the news she could find with which to divert her parents and gave an account of an evening at the ventilator at the House of Commons, 'not like the old ventilator for it is a long narrow slit opposite ones eyes from which one is able to see & hear everything, and all the ladies shut up in the box had equally good places'. She chose the evening debate on the recovery by Lord Ellenborough (a former Governor-General of India) of Hindu temple gates from the Afghans and later found to be imitations; this she pronounced amusing and violent. Lord Stanley pleased her the most for he was eloquent and *entrâinant* while Sir Robert Peel spoke more in the style of a very good actor; Macaulay was by far the most amusing. She recounted a story of Lady Ripon to make her father laugh: 'Her idolized son had a dreadful cold in his head—she of course was distressed & what do you think her anxiety made her imagine to cure him with—a blister on his nose! This horrible invention somehow inflamed his nerves & threw him into the most violent convulsions. He remained insensible for a time & as nearly as possible died of it. A doctor was got from London & with great difficulty he was cured. He has since had the chicken pox & the story I have told you has been kept very snug.'

An unfailing source of conjecture was the rank which the

'Douglas Princess' was to assume. Lady Lincoln was in a scrape and it seemed doubtful if she and her husband would ever be reunited. The young Turkish Ambassador had dined with the Cannings and had seemed tolerably civilized, and the poor Miss Berrys looking miserably ill kept up their dinners and parties in Curzon Street. One of the new types of Paisley gowns was being sent to Russia with the caution that should it be too gaudy for Petersburg taste it would make a cloak. Simultaneously she rebuked her mother for being neglectful of her family in England. 'I must tell you from Gdmama, Aunt Caledon & myself, that we are rather discontented with yr letters for we want to know exactly what you do all day long & Papa too—when you get up, dine, & go to bed; when it's light & when its dark; what you eat & drink & clothe yrself in; who you see & everything else & how cold it is & how much snow.' Furthermore the commission for prints of the Russian Royal Family had not met with complete success. 'I have just been at the unrolling of your prints at Colnaghis. I am sorry to say the Queen has already got four of them; pray send me the bill & I will get you reimbursed.' And a few days later: 'The prints I gave last week, a great many were duplicates and are returned on my hands. By the next courier you are to have a Print of the little Pss sent you by the Queen.'

7

Queen Victoria's Russian Turquoises

By the time of the next courier's departure Charlotte had been in waiting a fortnight or more. The Queen had now set her heart on acquiring Russian turquoises and wished the commission to be undertaken by Lady Stuart de Rothesay. Charlotte, mindful of her mother's lively enthusiasms, recommended a proper caution. 'I was given another commission for you to do and that is to know the price of some turquoises of rather a *light* colour, single stones not for *paré* and of different sizes, you shld send the size and the price—mind you do not *buy*, only let me know what the cost wld be. You must send *drawings* & prices of the size of the turquoises & remember they must be *light* coloured.' Queen Victoria added her own instructions:

Tuesday morning [*Feb 28th 1843*]

Dear Lady Canning,

I send you here a Print of our little Girl wh I wish you wd kindly send to Lady Stuart in my name.

When you write to her, I wish you to beg her to send drawings of the *sizes* of the *turquoises* with their prices: I wish them to be of the light kind & not *dark* as they often have them.

Ever
Yours affl V R

Charlotte was leaving nothing to chance:

Grosv Sqr, Feb 28th 1843

Dearest Mama. To-day's messenger will take you a print of the Princess Royal which the Queen desired me to send you from her. I will give her your thanks when you get it for it is too small an occasion to send them straight to her, & she has told me to bring her yr answer abt the turquoises myself. In case you have not got the letter I may as well say over again that she wants drawings of turquoises of the light colour of various sizes, with the price given of each. She does not want you to get the turquoises themselves.

My waiting ended last night with a very amusing French Play '*Une Dame de L'Empire*'* acted by Mme Albert very cleverly indeed, dressed in a Josephine like lamé gown. The Dss of Norfolk succeeds me, for Lady Dunmore is nursing her Mother in Law who has had a paralytic stroke. There are a number of people very ill, Ld Ripon has an inflamation of the lungs and Ld Fitzgerald has been spitting blood & looks like a ghost, & the Stanleys are in gt anxiety about their eldest son who is nearly grown up and has an internal inflamation which has put him in gt danger. Hatty Cocks is again improving but hers is an anxious case. Aunt Mex has got the Pollingtons in Dover St for the moment; she [Lady Pollington] is tolerably good but she does not do well with them & I am afraid is not very amiable. She ran riot abroad & there are no end of stories of her odd pranks.

At Tyttenhanger Charlotte heard the same complaints. Lady Pollington was 'as much in want of being kept in order as ever, and the pleasant things about her diminish. Pollington is dreadfully afraid of her and Aunt Mex too—so no one will do her the slightest good'. From Highcliffe to which Lady Clanricarde accompanied her (considering it more handsome than Wrest Park, Bedfordshire, the 'complete Louis XV chateau' designed in 1834)[1] Charlotte was obliged to hurry back to London to be present at the consecration of the new chapel at Buckingham Palace, which was followed by a luncheon for the Household and their wives. There she heard the shocking news which she hastened to impart to her mother, of the sudden death of Lady Louisa de Horsey† of scarlet fever; she was much to blame for having concealed it when it attacked her husband, and though she took bella donna as a preventative she became ill herself and

* At the St James's Theatre in a season of French plays; the Prince and the Duchess of Kent accompanied the Queen. Thérèse Albert played the title part.

† Her daughter Adeline Louisa Horsey de Horsey later married Lord Cardigan.

refusing to listen to the warnings of Dr Curie her homeopathic physician, or of her surgeon Mr Tupper, she continued to go out and have people to the house. When she became ill she was dead in twenty-four hours. 'It attacked the brain and was never thrown out—the Saturday before her death', Charlotte added without taking breath, 'she was at Ly Palmerston's.'

In March Charlotte learned with consternation that her father had erysipelas, and from now on his health was a matter of the gravest concern; a note of anxiety is sounded in every letter to her mother to whom the information that the Duke of Sussex was also in a bad way with erysipelas upon an abcess in the neck must have seemed of questionable comfort. Added to this was the horrifying tale of Fanny Devereux, while in waiting at Claremont, having to hasten to Honfleur where her mother Lady Hereford was in danger of having her foot cut off owing to an acute infection; her sufferings were so terrible that amputation could not increase them. Recovery from paralysis followed by collapse and death of Canning's great-aunt Lady William Bentinck brought him £2000, a legacy as welcome as it was unexpected. Occupying Char's thoughts during all these months was the health of her cousin Hatty, Aunt Somers' second daughter. It is hard to recognize from her symptoms and treatment what was the cause or nature of her malady. Of marriages there was a plentiful new supply. One just settled was between Lavinia, the youngest and prettiest of Lord Lyttelton's sisters, and his wife's brother (also Mrs Gladstone's) the Reverend Henry Glynne, rector of Hawarden 'a clergyman with a very rich living of £3,000 a year. They are all very much pleased about it for it is quite a family party, but she is pretty and so good that tho' he is a friend of ours and very excellent, I cannot help wishing she had married someone in a greater position'.

Lady Stuart had already been told of the Douglas marriage at the Ducal Palace at Mannheim and how the Duke of Hamilton had appeared on arrival and introduction, his head bound up in diaculum [plaster] after a recent tumble, dressed in his Lord Lieutenant's uniform with improvements of his own and many ridiculous and curious details.* The Cannings were invited to one of the three great dinners of ninety people at each, given that summer by the Duchess of Hamilton to introduce all London to Lady Douglas who, already expecting an heir and preferring to take every precaution, remained in Paris. Consequently Charlotte's account of their meeting was slightly delayed, but when it took place she could write honestly to her mother that her manner was perfect and that all the family doated upon her. A week later they met again at dinner. 'She looks ill and her *state* is making her very uncomfortable. She is very quick and pleasant and is adored by the Hamilton family. The first thing I remarked about her is that she reminds me very much of Lou; she wears her hair arranged in the same way & tho' her features are different there is certainly a likeness. I cannot help admiring her tho' there are ugly things about her. Douglas looks radiant & young again; he calls her Marie or Ly Douglas. The D of Hamilton sometimes the one, sometimes "Princess" or "Votre Altesse". She has been presented to the Queen & had "Votre Altesse" said to her all the time by Albert—so the question of her rank remains in abeyance.' To the bride's mother there was no such uncertainty. On Charlotte unintentionally displeasing her by enquiring how was the Marquise de Douglas, she was rewarded by the reply: '*Qui? Qui? Qui?*'. Lady Holland recounting the episode to her son continued the story: 'Lady Canning saw her error and then said "La Princesse Marie", to which a most gracious answer was given. The D of Hamilton calls his daughter-in-law the Marchioness Princess. Our little Queen is less gracious, not having spared Prince Albert to take her in to dinner.'[3] The epic is taken up again later when the Grand Duchess of Baden, a Roman Catholic, wished to be godmother to her grandchild, but the Bishop of London objecting, Lady Douglas was so vexed that she refused to attend her baby's christening.[4]

Besides social gossip there was also the failure of a tenant for Whitehall. There had been a nibble from Sir David Baird Bt.,

* He was famous for his courteous but somewhat affected mannerisms, and for wearing small combs in his hair, by no means concealed.[2]

whose uncle had acquired military fame as Commander-in-Chief at the capture of the Cape of Good Hope and had lost an arm at Corunna, but the offer was of so pitiable a nature that Canning thought it was not 'worth bargaining with such a man, for after finding that two months (the term which he had at first proposed) would not suffice him, he offers 150 guineas for three months! not *per month* as, at first blush, I construed it—but for the whole term. I believe Sir D B's offer is just half what used to be paid in old times—viz 25 gs a week. We had better trust to the chapter of accidents than accept the worst terms so early in the season'. A tenant with a wife was found for the month of June, their three daughters demanding a room each was thought a little excessive; however with nine servants in attendance they managed to pack in comfortably.

In Russia Lady Stuart de Rothesay was exploring summer villas on the Neva; to Charlotte they sounded very aguish. Fortunately the navigation was opening for she had a present of poplins from Lou to forward—the prettiest she had ever seen, with bunches of lilac all over, but she lamented that 'no Pines can go to you for the Queen's birthday, Lou has none ripe and Aunt Mex has not yet been offering any'.

Results of Her Majesty's commission for turquoises seemed slow in materializing and it was just now that the Queen was feeling the want of jewels, her Uncle Ernest of Hanover being in a fair way to recovering the diamonds of Queen Charlotte which he claimed as his own. In early April when thanking for the print of the Princess Royal on her mother's behalf, Charlotte had reported to the Queen that the stones were as expensive as in England, but she urged her mother to send sketches of sizes, for after the Queen's confinement (Princess Alice, April 25th) she would feel obliged to show something. Examples and prices were forthcoming and there was gratifying news to send in return.

Dearest Mama. Here is the answer about the turquoises—I sent on Saturday to ask when the Queen would see me, I felt sure I shd not be appointed till Monday but was very much distressed to find I had been sent for on Sunday when I was at Tyttenhanger, so impatient was she to know what you had done. Yesterday I went & took your turquoises; she was very much pleased with them & kept them all. Of course she would like better ones but she likes the light colour. I return you as a pattern the stone worth 20 roubles which you sent with the mock one. The Q wishes you to get her 20 more like it of the *same size* or a little larger, but not smaller, & of exactly that colour & to send it back with them. I return you the paper of drawings; the Queen has marked a cross opposite to the descriptions of all those she wishes to have. She will always be glad to hear of any fine stones, particularly such a one as the mock one would have been in real.

I forgot to carry your paper with me but had to send it by Caroline [Cocks] to-day. I felt quite ashamed to think how long I had delayed asking to bring your answers, for the last week I put it off until the deep mourning [for the Duke of Sussex] was over that my own black clothes might do. She has been exceedingly pleased with the commission & is very much obliged to you for the trouble you have taken.

I have got you a very gay tarlatane at Potts [lace warehouse of Pall Mall], price 2.12.6. I think you may like it at a breakfast & I think it not too smart for you there. I send also

30 yards of 3d lace
6 yards of 1d lace
6 yards of 1d–2d lace

a scarf as a present, an ugly but convenient & cheap brown striped muslin & a pretty white one, both as presents. Yr aff Char

The list of stones is missing from the correspondence but Charlotte added one of her own; forty-two turquoises were to be bought for the sum of three thousand five hundred roubles. In the middle of June a further letter on the same subject arrived from Lady Stuart which needed discussing, but Charlotte was not in waiting and had no immediate opportunity, though a reinforcement being needed to the usual staff for the occasion of a Command Performance of *As You Like It* (Macready playing Jaques, and concluding with a farce) she had accompanied the Queen to Drury Lane, but the next morning was in no mood for writing to her mother. 'My wits have left me to-day for I have not got over standing at the State Play last night for four hours & a half behind the Queen's chair.'

Her waiting which was to have begun on the first day of August was postponed, the Queen preferring to have her on the sailing expedition at the end of the month and Char thought she would enjoy it a good deal better than a month at Windsor, though she was in a sad puzzle to think how she would 'fit up clothing that will suit a Court & sea combined'. Before July ended there were a great number of balls and concerts; and the competitive exhibition of cartoons at Westminster Hall to determine who should paint the frescoes in the new Houses of Parliament was well worth a visit. To Charlotte it seemed a far more creditable exhibition than any held at the National Gallery; of the eleven prize-winners, mostly newcomers (G. F. Watts among them), Parris and Joseph Severn were the only names known to her. The two frescoes to impress her most were C. W. Cope's *First Trial by Jury*, and *Caesar's First Invasion of Britain* by Edward Armitage. Then from St Petersburg came the news Charlotte had been so much fearing since the first intimation in the late winter of her father's ill health. Lord Stuart had had a second stroke.

Dearest Mama, Canning has just had your letter, it brings us sad news, but I have so long been prepared to hear it that I am almost glad to know that is all & that I hear no worse. How hard it is for you to be nursing poor dear Papa with none of us to help and comfort you. Every letter I have seen of your writing for ages I have looked for what is in this— & I am grateful to think that Papa has not in any degree lost his consciousness or faculties. I suppose as soon as Papa can move he will come home & no doubt that will be best for him— & the easiest way of having no more to do with Petersburg. What has now happened shows one that the same, unknown to Papa, must have been the case before as I think we all felt was very probable, but we could hardly even mention it to each other. It will be a great comfort to have you both here again & I trust by God's mercy Papa will stand the journey—really even in this sad trial we have much to be thankful for. I believe Aunt Caledon may be in town to-day & I shall go to her— Lou comes back to-morrow from Tyttenhanger.

God bless you & Papa, & Goodbye dearest Mama yr aff Char C. I hope that nothing will prevent Papa from returning here if he is able to do so, for I dread that when he is better he may think himself well enough to stay, for that I almost hope the journey may not be put off very long, for it would be impossible for you to attempt to bear another winter of such anxiety. Goodbye again Dearest Mama.

In the first two weeks of August the *Illustrated London News* reporting Lord Stuart's illness and probable departure, hazarded two candidates for his place, the first being the Duke of Beaufort; the second week an anonymous 'Noble Marquess' was mooted, 'but had declined'. The difficulty lay in getting Lord Stuart to relinquish his assignment. Charlotte's letters began to assume a new authoritativeness; no doubt Canning as Under-Secretary of State foresaw an awkwardness arising in a father-in-law who though not prepared to come home, was yet unable to carry on his obligations abroad. Besides, her duties at Court were at hand and this might be one of her last opportunities to advise her mother to make haste before the Russian winter set in. On August 15th she wrote:

Canning will tell you all he can find out about a steamer—*he* cannot, without being authorized by you, ask for one, so what we hope & trust is that by return of post you or Papa *will* authorize him to ask: this might perfectly well be asked for in a letter by the coming post to save time, for it is driving it off very late in the year & in a month more wd be too late. Your letter of last week puzzled me very much for you talk of 'its being fair to expect a steamer to be sent from home, when the *advice to return* must come from home'. That almost looks to me as if you expected Papa to be recalled—now there does not appear any chance of that— & that is certainly a mortification he ought not to be exposed to. What I hope & trust to hear of as yr decision will be that he asks for a steamer & returns on 'leave'—that I equally hope he will not think of going back to Petersburg is also true—but of course he shd not be tormented to resign at once—but it will be time enough to do so when he gets home. I cannot tell you how I dread hearing that you have decided to stay; not thinking about right or wrong as far as the Embassy or people's opinion is concerned—but merely what is to us the most important which is Papa's safety.

One more letter from London told her mother that her cousin

Car Cocks would be in waiting at the same time as herself which would be of the greatest comfort, and that their headquarters were to be Brighton. She had been to Deptford to see the new Royal steam-yacht, the *Victoria and Albert*, and found that much space had been given to Dr Reid's plan for ventilation and that the sides of the cabins being straight it was not in the least like a ship. Lord Liverpool [Lord Steward] and Lord Aberdeen were to accompany the Queen. London was now deserted, and among her relations left were only her Aunt Mex (determined to outstay the Pollingtons) with her daughter, Lady Sarah Savile, who in turn 'looked bored'.

From Windsor Char wrote in some excitement, the more so as a crossing to France to stay with King Louis Philippe was anticipated.

We embark to-morrow leaving this place at 7. We go on board at Southampton & sail about the Isle of Wight landing at Ryde. We then go to Weymouth & Plymouth & then to the Château d'Eu for 3 days. I expect it to be very amusing. We return to Brighton & there is a rumour of afterwards spending a day at Ostend.

I had enjoyed the idea of doing all this with Car so very much, & yesterday when we both met here arriving our different ways we talked it over with such pleasure & she was so glad to go, if to-day's account of Hatty was good. However this morning very early an express came to fetch her back to Eastnor. Car told me many symptoms yesterday wh seemed to me extremely bad but I could not much judge. It seems that on Monday last poor Hatty was conscious of a gt change in herself; she said she felt sure she was going to get well & she has continued to say it ever since, but at the same time she grew frightfully thin & weak & her feet swelled & her limbs stiffened— but she said she was sure the sore place in her stomach had healed & that she could eat. It is a dreadful grief for them all for Hatty's is really an angelic character, she is so truly religious & so cheerful and grateful for every enjoyment left her— & she is so good that life or death are alike happiness to her. She keeps up their spirits & is an example of content & patience & religion to them all.

Before closing her letter and preparing herself for an early start

Charlotte reverted once more to her father's health and her anxiety for her mother. 'I cannot bear to feel that I am so utterly useless to you & cannot go & take care of you both & that makes me amongst other reasons so anxious that you shd if possible return.'

8

On Board the Royal Yacht

Queen Victoria was in high spirits. The previous day she had celebrated Prince Albert's twenty-fourth birthday with fireworks on Virginia Water and today the 'acquatic excursion'[1] on the new yacht promised an exciting measure of felicity, while on her side Charlotte Canning with her capacity for enjoyment was as eager as her Mistress. Fine weather had been prophesied, the late summer morning promised well, and Charlotte had laid in a stock of paper for a daily journal in lieu of letters.

Windsor Monday, Aug 28 1843 At ½ past four I was awakened by S[arah] N[orris] just about to begin her journey, & to finish my packing. Got dressed (with many contrivances for carrying away brush & comb &c) by Ly Dunmore's maid. After meeting the Suite in the corridor, and spending ½ an hour in trying to disentangle contradictory orders about getting one's letters, the Queen came, & with her all the Babies, who were kissed & we immediately set off. Georgy Liddell & myself with the Queen & Prince. The Prince talked of all the farms and properties he ought to buy to improve his shooting, & the Queen was in the greatest spirits, making projects & conjectures about her voyage. At Farnborough we got into the railroad carriage, which was fitted up for the occasion, & had a great crown at the top. Crowds lined the road at every station and we caught a glimpse as we passed at full speed of rows of faces not so easily distinguished as the roadside poppies, & heard cheers drowned by the railroad noises. The Queen & Prince set to work to read the contents of 3 red boxes, a large packet of Stratford's [de Redcliffe] of whose voluminous writings H.M. complained, saying he has always so much to say it is sometimes quite alarming. Ld Howard [de Walden, Minister to Portugal] filled a box, & of him she said nearly the same, & laughed very much at both these being cousins of mine.

About 1 hour & ½ took us to Sthampton. An invention by which a lamp was thrust into the top of the carriage instead of an embroidered crown as if by magic when we got into the tunnels was amusing, however for the last & longest part it appeared to have got out of order, for we were left in the dark. It was the Queen's first sight of tunnels & she did not mind them a bit—not like Ld Ely who was found in tears at the end. A great crowd had assembled at the terminus. A carriage & 6 was ready & into it we scrambled receiving and carrying a load of cloaks, red boxes, & bouquets & baskets of flowers from the ladies of Southampton. At this time a sea fog & drizzle had set in but the crowd did not mind, & lined the road which was round by lanes & fields by a great circuit, which finally brought us to the top of the High St. We drove to the end of the pier and there embarked in a barge, the steamer being aground a few yards off. The luggage was pouring in at the moment by another gangway, and the confusion great.

The Duke of Wellington [Lord Lieutenant], Ld Haddington [First Lord of the Admiralty], & a crowd of great people lined the pier-head. In time the tide floated us off, & we steamed away in a fog which concealed both shores, Albert believing the New Forest side to be the Isle of Wight, & quite satisfied with the Hitchin river for the Southampton Water. Passing Cowes we anchored at Ryde. Sir Charles Rowley's [Flag Officer, Portsmouth] barge then took the Queen on board in a little cockling sea. Of course a number of officers were clustered on the steps, & the midshipman at the bottom, when trying to fend off the boat as she bumped against the side, got upset & thoroughly ducked. He reappeared in time & struggled. Shrieks came, I believe, from the Queen, who gave me a violent pinch. The poor youth was pulled out all shivering & dripping & none the worse. Landing at Ryde was well managed, the crowd were kept back by the coast guard, whom Albert calls "guarda costas" & a shabby carriage of Ld Liverpool's was ready to carry the party to Ly Cath Harcourt's place, St Clare, looking over the Ryde corner of the island with sea on three sides. The Wharncliffes [President of the Council], De La Warrs [Lord Chamberlain], & Cavendishes, in bright silks & muslins were all waiting to receive H.M. who looked, as well as her Suite, rather dowdy & wet—for she had been perpetually running on deck in the rain.

Getting back to the boat was no easy matter: the Queen was of course well protected, but the crowd followed so closely as nearly to lift us off our feet, and the Preventive men defending the Queen with their ramrods gave us many a poke. A damp cloudy night, yachts showing blue lights & throwing up rockets & grand fireworks at the yachtclub; the Queen amused herself looking at these until so sleepy as to go to bed.

Tuesday, Aug 29 All on deck & breakfasted by 8. The Queen got into her barge, the first time of using the new white one built of mahogany for the yacht. We rowed in & out between the yachts, hailing them & learning their names. All their yards manned & dressed in their colours—30 or 40 at anchor of all sizes, the owners in conspicuous places, Ld Wilton particularly so. Ld Yarborough's gesture of delight [Commodore, Royal Yacht Squadron] when he heard the Queen meant to board him was worth seeing.

We landed at East Cowes, & went to Norris Castle.* Everything about it the Queen remembered, & kept constantly comparing it with the Pavilion, to the disadvantage of the last, & regretting she had not bought it when it was to be sold. Albert asked why she did not, to which she answered very simply she had not then money enough. P[rince] A[lbert] says there ought to be 5 miles of property to every Royal villa which ought certainly to put the Isle of Wight out of the question. The Proprietor is now the editor of Bell's *Weekly Messenger.* A maid was found to let us in, & the Queen insisted on going upstairs into all the bedrooms until she was stopped at one room by hearing a gentleman was in it in bed, & by a half dressed man peeping out of another & meeting her face to face. Wharncliffes, De La Warrs & much company lined the way as we returned, & we were under weigh at 10. A heavy swell set in as we rounded the southern part of the Island. The Queen had made me sit by her for a time on one of the sofas fitted up on the poop, and a few minutes after telling she was sure she would not be sick, & was determined not, she moved to the centre of the vessel to avoid the motion. In this new position the smell of oil was detestable & very soon she fairly gave in, & went below and became very uncomfortable. P A looked much more wretched, Lds Aberdeen & Liverpool too; & Sir J. Clark† wandered about

* The house occasionally taken by the Duchess of Kent for Princess Victoria; they had first stayed there in 1831.

† Physician to the Queen. In Rome he had cared for Keats in his last illness and had stood beside the grave at his burial.

doing what he could for them in no better condition. Georgy Liddell too took to her cabin, & Ld Adolphus [Fitz-Clarence, Commander of the Royal Yacht] & I proceeded proudly to luncheon after sending to consult the rest with an offer of some.

The haze hid the Hampshire coast & I could see nothing of Highcliffe as we passed the Needles on the outside; the Queen soon after sent for me. I found her lying down perfectly happy & well again, for her sickness is like a child's, & lasts but a minute at a time. Her cabins are delightfully cool & sweet—not so our part: the doors of the galley have never yet been shut; the smell of bilge & oil is powerful, the scuttle over the officers berth is always open & the smell & heat altogether enough to knock one down. The berths are otherwise perfectly comfortable, & full large enough. The place where we dine is always sweet. The poor officers are wretchedly off, & lie on the deck or at our doors. I believe there are a dozen of them. The fog concealed the coast & we anchored for the night in Portland roads. The Prince & all the Gentlemen landed to walk about Portland; the Queen kept me with her & amused herself watching the strange boat-loads of people who gathered about us from all parts. At last the Mayor of Weymouth arrived with his mace bearers and was produced to make his bow dressed in his chains with a tight black evening suit, particularly ridiculous. I sat up writing & reading in my own berth until ½ past 11 for I thought the gentlemen expected possession of the dining room & we never ventured to reappear there.

Wednesday, Aug 30 Under weigh at 7½ to go to Dartmouth. The Queen was early on deck looking quite well again. Coasted along Dorsetshire & Devonshire, past Lyme Regis, Axmouth, Sidmouth, Exmouth, Torbay & Torquay. The Queen told me Sidmouth was the Place where her Father died & asked me to make a little sketch of it. She made me afterwards do the rocks at the entrance of Torquay.* The Queen was very anxious to arrive early at Plymouth that the Prince should see it to advantage, & by ½ past 5 we reached the breakwater. The variety of outline & the in and outs of the harbour reminded me of Malta. Soon came Authorities, admirals & generals, Ld Haddington & many others. One Admiral the moment he was presented put his hat before his eyes & said 'The sun's in my eyes, I can't see' which has been thought a capital joke ever since. Plans were made for the next

* Two sketches made this day are at Windsor Castle Library.

day's work & a very heavy dew at last drove us below—it was very dull and silent—in that respect rather fortunate, for the Queen has since told me she saw us through the skylight while walking on deck & heard what we said, which was only Ld Liverpool pressing everyone to eat macaroni. Our dinners grow very bad for wherever we go the shops are shut, and nothing can be had. We have milk from the cow on board, and a sheep was given to the Queen at Portland, but she has taken an affection for it & it is not to be killed as long as she is on board. I have let Sir James Clark try to make my cold well; I wish he could mend our skins for we grow browner every day. Ld Aberdeen's complexion alone stands the sun.

Thursday, Aug 31 Received orders to be ready to go on shore with H.M. at ½ past 8. Here that is easy for we always breakfast at eight & the noise over head wakes one very early. It was at that hour a very thick fog with a dew on the deck enough to wash it. The Queen's barge was ready & no one seemed to think the fog an objection, feeling sure it foreboded great heat, so we went ashore at Mt Edgcumbe close to our anchorage. Carriages were ready, the sun had come out & blue sky appeared over head. We wound up the hill by a zigzag road thro' fine woods with magnificent Spanish Chestnut & oak, imagining the views we could not see. At last the Queen gave orders to turn about & go to the gardens. We went back to the bottom of the hill & got out at a little door leading to a narrow walk between 2 walls of evergreens. It ended suddenly in the most perfect Italian garden I have ever seen in England; an orangery at one end, a pond with a marble fountain, a simple pattern in grass, & edging the grass magnificent orange trees in perfect health and in full blossom in cases; statues in the middle of each compartment of the parterre & aloes in vases.

By the time we had walked through the shrubberies of ilex & all sorts of beautiful evergreens the fog had cleared; the heat was intense by this time, & we returned on board for the Prince was to see the dock yards with the Lords of the Admiralty. The Queen made Georgy Liddell & me sit and draw in the Pavilion. Letters came; one from poor Car gives as bad an account as possible of poor dear Hatty. She is quite calm & knows exactly what her state now is—her appetite is returned & I cannot help thinking it is just possible that may save her for decided atrophy is sometimes cured. Her loss will be very great.

I had hardly time to write to anyone, for the Queen wanted me very soon, for all the Mayors & Corporations of Devonport & Plymouth were coming. They arrived in numbers & passed by as at a Levée, giving their addresses to Ld Aberdeen. The hardest part of the day's work was still to come. We landed at the Dock yard & found the Queen's carriages to take us a drive at foot's pace all over Devonport, Stonehouse & Plymouth. The Queen & Prince, G Liddell & I were in one carriage, the Gentlemen followed in another. The mob in the dock yard seemed quiet till we got into the town, & there it would have been possible to walk upon their heads; flags waving & a noise absolutely deafening. The hills were steep & the drag was often put on and off; the worst was any place less crowded where the people could rush down like a torrent carrying all before them. Quiet women we saw lifted up in this way & taken great distances before they could get out of it, with their clothes in rags. The crowds were in the highest good humour & most loyal; they looked well dressed, & prosperous in general. The heat all this time was quite unbearable & we grew very tired & were rejoiced to get back into the dock yard. At the stairs we embarked in the little steamer *Ariel* to go on board the *Caledonia.* She is a 1st rate man of war & ready for sea. We went over every part of her & the Queen looked pleased. The Prince knows nothing at all about a ship—he ought to study the subject a little before he goes upon this kind of expedition. The height between decks in our steamer is very apparent on comparing it with that of the *Caledonia,* & the size of the deck is much nearer that than I could have guessed. My respect for this vessel increases.

The boat mob was greater than ever coming on board in the evening. Ld Liverpool I think the most provoking of men, & if I was Ld Adolphus I could not help swearing at him. He interferes with everything, hollers out all sorts of directions in the barge; stands up to wave his hat to people to get out of the way, & makes the most undignified noise, when there are people whose duty it is to do all this quietly & properly. I think him odious & very disrespectful to the Queen. Ld Aberdeen I suspect is as bored with him as I am.

We all dined at the Queen's table, Ld Adolphus too. A great bonfire was blazing on the Plymouth hill & the Queen ran up before dinner was over to see it. At 9 fireworks began, & the ships in the Sound were all illuminated; we staid all the evening on deck. We were glad enough to get to bed the moment the Queen went below & my ears were still ringing with the noise of Royal salutes from about

4 batteries & 8 ships, which we had undergone about 15 times during the day. The Queen minds saluting when she is very near & gives orders that no firing shall ever take place when she is on board. This happened to her once long ago & she said 'we had to submit to it then, for we were not the greatest people'.

I should like to see many of my friends accept the post of Lady-in-Waiting—to get in and out of carriages & boats with rarely, if ever, any one to hand you—out of the barge, never; for the Queen goes 1st, then the Prince, & me next, so every one but me is too far off to lend a hand—so it is necessary to be active. Then for those who mind a shot, perpetual firing; then for those who are frightened in a carriage, mobs, scrambling, kicking horses, receiving the utmost provocation.

Friday, Sept 1 Again a beautiful day. I was so tired & excited I could not sleep & shall stay as much as I can below to-day. There was very nearly a very good scene this morning which Ld Aberdeen enjoyed intensely. He & Ld Liverpool are next door neighbours. Ld A heard a great noise: 'Hand me a pair of pincers thro' the port'. 'Yes my Lord'. This was very often repeated, he thinking Ld Adolphus required this, & not paying much attention. At last, after more noise & the pincers being lowered to him by a string, Ld Liverpool who had bolted himself into his cabin succeeded in getting out after having almost made up his mind to be drawn out thro' his port from the outside. We all regret this was not done. At 9 we were under weigh. I am busy packing for Eu; we cross over to Cherbourg to-night & hope to arrive at Eu to-morrow in daylight.

Reached Falmouth at 1; the Barge was lowered for H.M. to row round the bay. We were anchored at some distance from the town—a number of men of war's boats were ready to clear the way and the Barge got thro' well enough. We passed a pier where Ld Liverpool told us he once fell off backwards & was very near drowned. The barge had distanced the boats meanwhile, and on reaching the end of the bay we doubled round the bight to return, passing under the town. Our pursuers saw this & cut across by a shorter cut & in a moment we were in the midst of the fray—cutters, luggers, barges, lighters, jolly boats, a steamer, gigs, all loaded with people, two Corporations with Mayor & beadles, an immense proportion of women with very young babies. All these people cheering at the top of their voices & standing up & most of the steerers in the sailing boats entirely forgetting their business when they got near the barge; sounds of crunching & smashing of boats in all directions. The Queen grew rather frightened, Ld Aberdeen tumbled off his seat in pushing off a boat in the act of running up against it; a man of war's boat ran straight into a gig & left it in a baddish condition. The first opportunity to get out we set off full speed & they chased us, but the Queen was safe on board again.

The Corporations arrived on time. One Mayor was a terrified Quaker, deadly pale, his lips moved for a long time before any sound was heard, & with this terror he had the courage to keep on his hat & clearly to avoid calling the Queen 'Your Majesty', by always mentioning her in the 3rd person. The heat was very great all day. I found a shady cool place on deck before the Paddle, close to the cow shed in a dirty undignified part of the vessel. In time the Queen came there to sit with me and G Liddell. I afterwards heard from Ld Adolphus that he had perceived a commotion among the men who had just finished their supper. He asked what was the matter; the answer: 'Please my Lord, the grog tub's jammed'. 'What?' 'The grog tub's jammed'—'What do you mean?'—'Please my Lord, Her Majesty's right afore it'. The Queen saw something was wanted & volunteered to move so it was got out & she sent for some to taste.

Passed the Eddystone before sunset. Sat on deck till bedtime, the sea like a lake & not a breath of air. The Prince de Joinville expected very early.

9

Majesty Abroad

Disembarking in France added a new dimension to an already delightful voyage. The French Royal family were spending the summer at the Château d'Eu and the novelty of sharing five days with the French Court was one which appealed to Charlotte; besides, this was the Queen's first journey abroad. The King and Queen Amélie were of an advanced age; of their six surviving children—the Duc d'Orléans having been killed the previous summer—there remained Nemours, Aumale, Montpensier and the Prince de Joinville who in May had married Francesca de Braganza, daughter of Pedro I of Brazil. Of the daughters, Queen Louise of the Belgians was the consort of Victoria's Uncle Leopold, and Princess Clementine had made an indifferent match in April with Prince Augustus of Saxe-Coburg, Albert's first cousin. Besides the French Household and Ministers, Comte de St Aulaire, French Ambassador in London, and his wife and the Cowleys with their daughter the Hon Georgiana Wellesley, were the only other guests.

Saturday, Sept 2 At 5 received a message that the Queen was getting up & the Prince de Joinville was on board. Found the Prince on deck with him. The P de Joinville & his officers as smart as their best uniforms could make them; our decks, covered with water & our officers in their shabbiest undress & nobody up of the Suite but me. The Queen came soon & sent me down to get them all roused. P de Joinville looks very sickly and has a bad high shouldered figure, but is very tall & has handsome features & a great quantity of beard. The day was as fine as the last 4 & not a breath of wind. I believe we are to land at Tréport, if it is not exactly high water they have to use a bathing machine.

The great part of this afternoon the Queen has sat on the bridge near the Paddle. G Liddell and I stood on each side holding our petticoats, & the 2 Princes on the Paddle box. The *Circassian* saw us all making this strange group & probably we were well laughed at. Off Tréport a white barge & a Machine were seen approaching & soon the P de Joinville told us he believed his Father & brothers were coming to meet the Queen. The steamer was stopped & Louis Philippe stood up in his boat & in a moment was along side our stairs. The Queen stood at the top, the King came up actively enough. They met with an embrace on both cheeks & the King kissed the Queen's hand; his sons followed & Mons. Guizot [Minister for Foreign Affairs] & some more of the ministers & Ld Cowley, all the party in full uniform. The Queen was asked to land in the King's barge which she did with P A & as many as the boat could hold of the party who came with him. We waited for the Queen's barge which was soon lowered & we very nearly caught up the others but were not quite in time to see the landing. As we followed between the jetties on each side of the river the wind from each gun fired every few yards from us—facing us—actually stopped one's breath for a moment. On the top of the Quay a large open tent was built, in it were all the Princesses with the Queen of the French and all the ladies now at the Château d'Eu.

After a few minutes the people cried out for a time '*Vive le Roi*', & '*Vive la Reine d'Angleterre*', then came troops, & then the most wonderful carriages, a mixture between one of Louis XIV's time and a marketing cart from Hampton Court. The body was like an enormous coach with a good deal of gilding & coats of arms & containing 2 or 3 rows of seats. The top was flat & supported with little pillars with draperies & curtains of flowery chintz. This was drawn by 8 Wouwerman-like fat jumping horses, very much caparisoned; the coachman & servants had coats of *ancien régime* covered with curious old fashioned lace. All the Royal family got into this (except 3 Princes who rode) & we scrambled into another with 6 horses, less like Louis XIV & more like Hampton Court. We were carried at full gallop thro' clouds of dust till at an arch the royal carriage attempted to turn in, the horses refused and the carriage looked very much as if it wd overturn. After a time the attempt was given up and we went on to some distance and entered the place at a more convenient gate. An odd winding road zigzagging through terraces edged with high trees brought us past the front of the Château to a square court between it and the church; a number of troops were assembled playing 'God Save the King' which they had been practising for a week. The Queen and the royal family all went upstairs and showed themselves to the multitude from a balcony for a minute & we were all taken down again & to our rooms. The Queen of the French in the civilist way told us how sorry she was that G Liddell & I could not be better lodged & that our rooms were high up; we were agreeably surprised by finding them very good. I have a bed room & sitting room & she is next door to me. Every one is as civil as possible to us. I have found several people I know, Mme de Chabot [wife of the Lord Chamberlain] and Mme Villain XIV [Lady-in-Waiting to Queen Louise].

The dinner was put off till late to give the Queen time to dress which we were glad of for it was no easy matter to get any clothes. We established ourselves in a room next the Queen's; in time the Q of the Belgians came, & then all the French Royal Family, to fetch the Queen & take her to dinner. I fell to M Guizot's share & had the P de Joinville on the other side. About 50 people sat down to dinner in a long gallery on the ground floor hung with portraits, as is the whole palace. Since the Grande Mademoiselle* baptised a collection begun by the Guises & the House of Lorraine there have been portraits added by last generations, & L Philippe has completed it with a number of copies; it is very well arranged. The dinner was very handsomely done. Why does Louis P have a pile of bread & rusks of all sorts at his side? Our Queen did not know what to do with her great French loaf. The table was not tidy & every body's bread & crumbs & dirt stay all thro' the dessert. In the evening what Miss Burney calls the Royals went into a room by themselves—and the Duchess of Orléans came, she does not dine with the rest & is still in very deep mourning. We were sent for to sit with them in time; I was behind & between the Q of the Belgians & Pss Clementine. The pretty little Princess de Joinville amuses us very much; she gets dreadfully bored & now and then jumps up as if quite unable to stand it. She goes & whispers to somebody or to help herself to a glass of water & then back to her place; she looks very young & has a graceful figure—in her own country she was shut up as in a convent. The evening was soon over & the Queen went to her room. Louis Philippe looks much older than I remember him, he is evidently in great spirits.

* Duchesse de Montpensier, niece of Louis XIII, also of Queen Henrietta Maria of England.

Sunday Morning, Sept 3 Got up early & had a small breakfast in my room. G Liddell & I & our two maids read the service to-gether. We had a visit from old Mme Angoulême [daughter of Louis XVI]. As breakfast time drew near we went to wait in the Queen's drawing room. She is lodged very comfortably on the ground floor with windows opening into a formal garden, the curtains and furniture are of Beauvais tapestry—bunches of flowers on a pale pink ground—very pretty indeed. Soon Louis Philippe came, with all his family, to fetch the Queen to breakfast. All walked arm in arm upstairs, as if to dinner, to long tables in 3 or 4 rooms. I sat between the Duc de Montpensier & Ld Aberdeen. Breakfast began with soup, & hot meat of all kinds & wine; then came eggs; then sweet things & then tea, coffee & chocolate, & bread & butter. All the meals of the day in one. At last I have heard a little of the Queen's impressions of all she has seen. She is as amused as a child could be, and very much pleased with her reception. Louis Philippe tells her over & over again how enchanted he is with this visit. We had a visit upstairs from the Marquise du Roure, who came to offer us all kinds of help. She is one of the Queen's Ladies, but at this moment is lent to the Princesse de Joinville—as much to teach and train her into civilised ways, as for the common use of a *dame d'honneur*. They all say the difference between her manners now and when she arrived is not to be believed. I think much more training will spoil her, for her manner now is very pretty—almost like a child, & full of grace & so perfectly natural. She is very well dressed & has a beautiful figure and cannot be induced to wear stays; they one day put her on a pair but it made her so wretched they gave up the point.

Before the drive we were taken all over the Château to see the pictures. The King showed & explained them all to the Queen. To make the collection complete there is an addition of an immense quantity of bad copies; they are intermingled with good originals, so that even their merits have to be searched for with difficulty. Melle de Montpensier is there at all ages, beginning from her *maillot*; many portraits of the Orléans family; all the Guises; & in the King's own sitting room many of the Kings of France. Mme Adelaïde [the King's sister] has the pleasantest room; it has been less renewed than the rest, and is ornamented with the Grande Mademoiselle's *chiffre*, & the portraits of her friends as she placed them. The [French] Queen's room is very gay & pretty, but very much modernized, & gilt & painted in compartments; at the head of the very large bed without curtains are the portraits of all her children & grandchildren— & in her dressing room Louis Philippe showed us the picture of the Chapel at Palermo where they were married.

The vans, or char-à-bancs then came to the door & we bundled into them. They were all alike on this occasion & drawn by six grey horses each. We were taken along a road winding & serpentining very curiously thro' a little bit of Parc Anglais: it led us at last into the high road thro' the arch the horse refused to pass thro' when we arrived. From thence we were taken for some miles along a very narrow field road, in deep dust, & over stones, & ruts & holes, till we expected to be overturned every moment, & did not at all approve of the Queen's running such risks. P A & the Ducs d'Aumale & Montpensier rode comfortably. We had on our front bench Ld Aberdeen & Ld Liverpool with Guizot bodkin; Georgy Liddell & Miss Wellesley with Sébastiani [Marshal, and lately French Ambassador in London] bodkin on the next; then Ly Cowley & I, & Ld Cowley & the Baron Maco (or some name like it) [Mackau] Minister of Marine & Colonies.

At dinner I had the Duc de Montpensier & Sébastiani to sit by. The first of these is a very odd youth; far more civil, & courtly than his brothers & evidently by way of being very literary; he talked of Shakespeare & his fondness for reading Beaumont & Fletcher, & owned afterwards he had once known English very well but had almost forgotten it now. He has been my neighbour several times now & asks curious questions about England, always reminding me what a small country it is—whether any gentlemen live in Wales? Whether there were mountains in England? He told me what numbers of English came to take *bains de mer* in France— & '*Il n'y a pas de bains de mer en Angleterre*?' That evening was dullish, we dawdled on a long time in the downstairs gallery, & then went up. The Queens & Princesses sat round a table & Louis Philippe walked abt. We had albums & sat behind them in a double row for they filled their table.

Monday, Sept 4 The project for to-day is an expedition to the Forêt d'Eu. Waiting for breakfast P A brought us the English newspapers, & read out some of the accounts of our voyage. A letter in the *Times* headed 'Her Majesty at sea', from 'A Gentleman on board', makes him very indignant for he is said to have suffered a good deal, & the Queen not.

The Queen sent for me early; a band of 50 men was playing under the Queen's window & almost deafened her. The same form was observed as at all the other meals—the whole family in a body came to fetch the Queen. I was delighted to see Mme de St Aulaire who is just arrived; she came post haste from Burgundy, travelling 2 days & nights without stopping. The Ladies of the Court are all rather tiresome or I am stupid, & do not get on beyond civil phrases with them. It is an immense party, we were 68 at dinner yesterday, Harriet [Clanricarde] wd not be pleased with their dress; the Psse de Joinville is much the best, the others are rather dowdy. All the Ladies were taken by surprise & had no *grandes toilettes*, for they wear anything on other occasions here; all the young ones wear wreathes of natural flowers, and diamonds & very fine gowns. I was very much distressed to see our Queen appear in scarlet china crape the 1st night, when it was so very hot. The little Comte de Paris was brought into the gallery after breakfast to-day by his mother [Duchesse d'Orléans]—he is a very nice merry child; he is particularly fond of his grandfather, & ran from a distance to jump into his arms the moment he saw him.

This day's drive was to the Forêt d'Eu in the same vans as before & all the company were told the number of their van & were left, as before, to climb up to it. It is rather tiresome to be always put with the same people, but I suppose it is to honor us. Ld Liverpool's incessant talking in disagreeable French bores one to death. The springs of the vans are rough & the seat high & without backs—so that a long drive in them tires one very dreadfully. For 2½ hours we drove about, after a good while longer we came to a long open tent with a great luncheon spread out. The King made the Duchess of Orléans sit by him; I observed she looked very pale & they afterwards told me it was the first time she had ever sat at table with the family since the death of her husband. They all walked round the *carrefour* afterwards; the people called '*Vive le Roi*' & '*Vive la Reine d'Angleterre*', the poor Duchess followed them with her little boy all in black. Many voices called '*Vive la Duchesse d'Orléans*', & she came back to the tent looking quite overcome; she had never yet appeared in public. She is very much beloved by all the family & is very clever & strongminded—they all say she is so *abattue* & changed since, that one cannot imagine how pleasant & agreeable she used to be.

After this occurred a curious scene relating to a small tent guarded by soldiers, at a little distance in the brush wood—but it cannot well be described. We jogged back again by a shorter road, had no time to rest for some letters had to be written, & it is always difficult to be in time for these 7 o'clock dinners.

In the evening the '*Musique du Roi*' performed symphonies of Beethoven, Gluck &c. I believe 100 people have been brought from Paris on this occasion for these concerts. There was to have been an Opéra Comique and the theatre was actually built & the actors had all arrived from Paris; the pieces to be acted had not been chosen & the only two the actors brought were objectionable—one was so improper, & the other ridiculed the English—so we wait for something suitable to be sent from Paris. The little Princesse de Joinville says '*Moi, j'aime beaucoup la musique, mais je ne sais pas pourquoi, mais elle m'e donne l'envie de dormir*'. I suppose the 6 leagues drive was another reason for the same—for I could scarcely keep my eyes open, but la *Symphonie en 'La'* by Beethoven was perfectly beautiful & played as if by one instrument.

Tuesday, Sept 5 As usual began the day with a private breakfast at ½ past 7. Sat by the Duc d'Aumale at breakfast. He was my neighbour also at the Forest luncheon the day before & it was only on that occasion I have heard him allude much to his campaigns; a horse got entangled in the ropes & gave the tent a shake, this eventually brought forward the topic of living in tents.* I do not think him at all bad looking but his manners are very *ton de garnison*, & he obviously approves of looking very weatherbeaten & soldierlike. He is civil enough & not disagreeable in conversation. The hour or two in the gallery after breakfast is rather tiresome, it lasts longer & longer every day. The Queen of the French is always anxious to make people sit down & to put them at their ease; I am quite surprised to see how little form there is in comparison to what we are accustomed to. The Queen sent for me & talked a long time abt everybody here. She is very much pleased with them all & says she feels as if she was one of the family. At ½ past 3 we all met to be shown the church; in the Park, as they call it, the carriages stopped & we all bundled out to gather & eat peaches. They have all been very civil asking after Papa & Mama & sending messages. Mme Adelaïde said he was one of the oldest friends she had & the Queen & Louis Philippe told me the same sort of thing.

* Now aged twenty-one, he had served in Algeria for three years. In 1886 he made over to the Institut de France his estate of Chantilly with its library and collection of paintings.

Dinner we were told wd be as usual at 7. About ½ past 6 G Liddell & I began ringing for our maids & continued to do so until 3 minutes before 7 & calling to all the servants who passed along the passage. At last S Norris arrived pale as death with a long story of how they had gone to the forest & how the horse had knocked up & they had lost their way. Strange to say I was in time & my clothes shook themselves into order; the King was happily a little late. I have never been too late yet—but for everybody it has been a disagreeable race against time. The dinner was long and the room hot as usual & I had the same neighbours, M Guizot & the D de Montpensier. In the evening there was another instrumental concert & some solo playing on violencello, & pianoforte, and on the French Horn by a man who has made great discoveries in the power of that instrument—he is able to sound chords, 2 or 3 notes at once—somehow it was not pretty & the sounds had the power of making everybody laugh. The Duc de Montpensier had the giggles & it caught from one person to another till all were in tears & the poor performer's sounds became stranger & stranger. I kept grave very long indeed but my lips shook & some very deep notes vanquished me at last. I was very sorry for the poor man, but his back was partly turned & I hope he did not find out, & between each spasm every good natured person called out "*c'est étonnant*!, *merveilleux*!", & Mme Adelaïde went to compliment him & found him well satisfied.

Wednesday, *Sept 6* Another beautiful day. The Queen sent for me before breakfast to know whether I had drawn anything & to bespeak a sketch of the house from the avenue—the spot from which we first saw it as we arrived. The Queen had a paintbrush in her hand when I came in, & she owned she was trying to hide herself behind the curtain & to sketch the French soldiers who were serenading under the windows. It had been intended that the yacht should be shown to the King & Queen, & the sea was calm enough but it was found the tide did not suit, and to embark in bathing machines from the beach was happily thought undignified, & the project given up. The Queen had been buying a number of very pretty things made at Dieppe of ivory. I was sorry to miss seeing the man's stock, for the things sold to the Queen (little vases and statues) were uncommon & not dear.

At breakfast an amiable dispute between Louis Philippe and his sons on the subjects of distances to certain spots in the Forêt d'Eu ended in a project for a very long expedition—as they could not agree on the time necessary for performing it (the accounts vary from seven hours to four) we were invited to assemble at two, and the luncheon was ordered to be sent on. As soon as we could get away G Liddell & I rushed with drawing materials to the avenue, & got thro' the ordered sketches. Then came the char-à-bancs; we were packed differently & more agreeably; I was put with Mme de St Aulaire & Ld Cowley behind—and to my great astonishment I saw M Guizot by an active stride push Ld Aberdeen into the bodkin's place where he was very efficient acting as a damper on Ld Liverpool. Lady Cowley, who hates the char-à-bancs said she had a headache & begged to be excused. I rejoiced at it for she is a particularly disagreeable neighbour on these expeditions, for she never ceases grumbling & abusing everything in the most ill bred way, & it is so difficult not to appear an accomplice when one is grumbled to. I asked Ld Aberdeen whether our conversations could be heard on the other benches. He says not, but I think he is getting a little deaf. G Liddell & Miss Wellesley were put with some of the French Court ladies & I think the variety suited them too. Mme de Chabot is very pleasant & good natured. She has a delightful fat French maid who makes us dahlia wreathes every night & taught Sarah Norris her art. She comes in the morning to ask the colour of one's gown and sends a written order to the gardener for suitable flowers—the flowers are not very good or plentiful but they do not spare them—and after dinner brings us '*les bouquets du dîner*' every day, & four large bunches for the porcelain vases in my bed room & sitting room.

The drive was along the same road as the 2nd day for some distance, but we turned at last into an older part of the wood. The *bût* was the *ferme* Ste Catherine—a common farm house in an orchard, with a little garden overlooking a wide valley. The table was laid in a grove close by—at least 50 people sat down. I believe Louis Philippe has a great fondness for these expeditions; the apparatus is complete; camp stools for everybody, one or two tents, & a great table—the whole packs up, & it is curious in how short a time it is put together. The King plans all these things himself & no details are too small for him. I believe this was a melancholy expedition for the poor Queen of the French & the Duchess of Orléans; for they had been there often with the D of Orléans, and I saw the two sisters were very sad & they were all silent but the King; & he probably feels these recollections less or he wd choose other spots for these fêtes. Mme de St Aulaire was very agreeable all the way home; she told me that Mrs Fry was very much respected and thought of in France—that she had given advice on the management of the prisons which had been followed with success.*

I had again the greatest difficulty to be ready in time for the Queen's waiting room. The Reine Amélie gave me a most beautiful bracelet as a souvenir of the visit; G Liddell had one too. I was very glad to have this little souvenir to keep of this good amiable woman for one cannot help caring for her & respecting her very much, & she is so kind & sincere— & it is so easy to see that her civility comes from a good heart. I think Mme Adelaïde's manner very delightful but I am told she has not so decidedly the merit of sincerity! M Guizot as usual took me into dinner, & my other neighbour on this occasion was the Pce Auguste of Coburg. He is without exception the dullest man I ever met—I think Ld Crewe† might appear to gt advantage compared with him. I now remember I sat next to him the 3rd day, but he left so little impression on my mind that I put someone else into the journal. I pity Princess Clementine very much, nobody takes any notice of him—but I suppose he is found inoffensive.

Old Mme du Roure is rather tiresome about showing her respect to the Queen, which I always see means that she wants the Queen to take great notice of her. Last night she told me all the Ladies of the Household wished to show their respect to the Queen & to thank her for having been so good to them. It is true that she has taken great pains to be civil, & they were all satisfied, I thought. Mme du Roure ended her speech by saying that when '*de service*' they had so little opportunity of making their *hommages* individually, could they ask to present themselves in her room before her all in a body? I knew this was just the sort of thing the Queen hated. I told her at night & she said she wd talk to me about it in the morning. In the morning it had gone out of her head— & when I begged for an answer she said she had so little time she cd not let them come, & told me to say something

* Elizabeth Gurney (1780–1845), known in particular for prison reform, was by birth a Quaker and had married into another well-known Quaker family. In 1839 she had travelled extensively throughout France where her report on prisons helped to alleviate existing conditions.

† Monckton Milnes was quoted as having once said of his future brother-in-law Lord Crewe that he would 'stick his face in a holly-bush sooner than meet a party of his neighbours'.[1]

very civil indeed to them, & to shew how much she considered their attention. This I saw would not do at all, & I said it wd not be an easy speech to make, but wd she speak to them all in some corner of the gallery? She answered 'Oh that will do beautifully—remind me of it before I go back to my room after breakfast.' I then said, what had been weighing on my mind, that if these people had been received in the Queen's room, wd it not have been necessary to receive Ly Cowley & Mme de St Aulaire also? She said certainly it wd, & that she would speak particularly to all in the gallery. I found the tiresome old Mme du Roure, & told her that if all the Ladies wd assemble the Queen would come to them. It was well received, & they drew up in a phalanx, & it passed off beautifully, & she was thought very civil, & Mme de St Aulaire was talked to for a long time.

The Queen has really pleased them all I think, and many of them have made me speeches abt her which sound true. Another difficulty I had which happened the 2nd day: Mme du Roure said the Ladies felt they had not properly shown their respect to Albert. The Queen of the French the moment after landing pointed them out to the Queen, but to him they had never been presented; this amused me when I remember that I was never presented to him. I told the Queen, who instantly said to him 'The Ladies are in a great fuss because they have not been presented to you'. It seemed rather late to do it then, & he also promised faithfully to go & speak to them all— & by so doing I was saved having to give any answer. I received orders to be ready for breakfast at ½ past 6.

Thursday, Sept 7 At ½ past 6 all the Royal family assembled in the Queen's sitting room in bonnets & shawls, & the men in full uniform, so it was clear we were to be taken back to Tréport in the same form we were brought! The breakfast was on this occasion in the gallery where we always dined; it turned one rather sick to be offered soup & large strong sausages at that early hour. By waiting patiently I got a breakfast of tea, bread & butter & egg; Georgy Liddell was less fortunate & was left shivering over a peach & iced water. Had to act maid for the Queen, & put on her things, for the Dressers were sent off earlier: then I ran as hard as I cld to the top of the house for my bonnet & shawl, & arrived at the door as the troops were calling out '*Vive la Reine d'Angleterre*', and they were all scrambling into the same great *calèche* they arrived in the 1st day.

At Tréport the tide was high and the French barges waiting. The Queen went in the King's, with as many of the Royal family as could be packed in—the rest followed in a gig. We were put in another barge with a cargo of aides de camp. I never saw such cowardly people: before it was half full 3 or 4 screamed out it wd hold no more, that it was not safe—with as much caution another boat was loaded & old Mme du Roure was the only lady brought, the others were not allowed to come for fear of danger. The sea was perfectly smooth, with only enough ripples to make it blue & cheerful. The Prince de Joinville was to see the Queen home again, & to stay two days at Brighton. The poor little Psse de Joinville wanted sadly to come too, and the Queen tried hard to persuade them to let her. There was some difficulty about finding a Lady to go with her, & it was not allowed— & she cried when she had to go back. When they stepped into the barge our crew gave three cheers, and then saluting began on all sides. We weighed anchor, & they disappeared in the smoke.

Before 3 we were in sight of Brighton, at 9 we weighed anchor. I suppose so short a passage was hardly ever known. The sun was burning, & the sea very blue & covered with boats. We passed close to the *Warspite* with all her sails set & studding-sails—her shrouds manned, & they gave 3 cheers. The *Grecian* was near us, & far off in the haze we could just distinguish the 3 line of battle ships, the *Caledonia*, the *St Vincent*, & the *Camperdown*—all saluting at once. It was low water when we reached Brighton; the beach was thronged with people & even the shallow water was full of boys & bathing women wading about. With all these spectators we had every reason to wish to land tidily, but at the foot of the stairs a little stage with red cloth was placed, about four feet higher than the boat, so that by no possibility could we get upon it. Several inventions were tried, by any of which the Queen would surely have tumbled into the water, & for full 5 minutes we sat looking at this in despair, surrounded by a throng of boats: it was very difficult not to laugh or cry. At last it was suggested it was best to cut away the fastening & overturn it, & get to the old steps which go down to the water's edge, & below it— & thus was our landing effected. The P de Joinville must be well amused. The Queen was well received as she walked along the pier by the crowds below.

The Pavilion, Brighton. In this strange palace it is difficult not to fancy oneself on the stage in ballet. I do not like the style, but it is impossible not to admire the perfect finish of the decorations, & how well every thing is made to suit. At the same time it has the objection of being very dull—the garden is about as good as a London square & there is no other view— & the still greater objection of being so close & hot that one can hardly breathe in this boiling weather. The Queen is quite unhappy to leave the yacht, & to have to live in a house again; she says it feels like a prison, & she longs to be at sea.

10

A Visit to King Leopold

The Queen had not long to wait. On the evening of their return from France while Charlotte struggled to keep awake over a game of mouche, decisions for a further expedition were being taken. A few days later the *Victoria and Albert* sailed to Ostend: the visit to King Leopold was expected to last a week. Charlotte had barely time to scribble a letter from the Pavilion (where she found it the oddest sensation to be 'actually living amongst all these dragons & nodding mandarins') to tell her mother of the presents of Sèvres china and two pieces of Gobelin tapestry representing the *Hunt of Meleager*, begun for Malmaison thirty years earlier, with which the French Royal family had 'loaded the Queen'. When the Hon Eleanor Stanley came in to waiting at Windsor in October she described how one of the pieces was put up in their breakfast room and caught the eye at first glance, the design being 'so very French, nothing but arms and legs'. But this was only a temporary measure, for together with the second tapestry, '*Atalanta weeping over the dead body of Meleager*, or some such thing', they were to be set into the panelling of the Oak Room 'which is to be pulled to pieces for that, and, as the two sides are not near long enough to admit the tapestry, it is to be turned back about 2 feet to make it fit . . . and the Prince after that flatters himself he is a man of taste, and talks of encouraging the arts!'[1] Charlotte's letter ended with the news of Hatty Cocks' improvement, and the usual quota of deaths.

Tuesday, Sept 12 1843 Went on board the Royal yacht with the Queen at ½ past 8. As soon as we got under weigh the clouds cleared off and it blew hard from the North Eastward. Staid the whole day on deck; the

Queen was very proud of being well tho' it blew so hard, but the water was so smooth near the shore that she had little provocation for sea-sickness. Passed close to Hythe, Sandgate, & Folkestone, all very picturesque towns with wooded hilly country beyond. Opposite Walmer we found 3 line of battle ships. The Duke of Wellington came on board; it made one nervous to see him on the ladder with the boat dancing about, he seems well but is very tottering. The Queen meant to keep him to dine with them, but they happily decided not to do so in this rolling sea. Getting him back to his boat in the dark wd have been very unsafe. As it was it made one very nervous to see him danced about at the bottom of the ladder held by 2 Captains who watched a safe moment to get him in & in so doing were all three soused up to their waists by a sea. He staid only till the Queen's letters were ready to be sent ashore & until he knew at what hour the Queen sailed to be ready with his salute.

The morrows plans were talked over. First it was pronounced impracticable to take the yacht into Ostend, & to get into a boat there with the wind on shore was out of the question. Ld Aberdeen advised the only safe plan which was to decide at once to go to Antwerp, & then by railroad to Ostend. This was objected to for many reasons; such as the distance, & how odd it wd seem to go past all the places they would have to return to afterwards, & to pass thro' Dutch waters was considered an objection—so this, the only really safe plan, was not listened to. The council of war went on more than an hour—one captain after another was sent for, and at last came Capt Smithett of the *Ariel*, a horrid little steamer. The King & Queen of the Belgians have often crossed over in her, and he is supposed to know the coast exceedingly well. We were told in time that it was all settled, that the Queen & Prince were to go on board this wretched *Ariel* at 7 in the morning, with me & Miss Hamilton [the Hon. Clementina, Maid of Honour], & some servants; & that Ld Liverpool, Ld Aberdeen, & the maids should be transferred to the *Prometheus*. At least it was simplified to that, for it was a much more complicated plan at first. Poor Miss Hamilton was obliged to take to her bed as soon as we anchored, & from that time was miserably sick. We were all very cross, & thinking of nothing but the disagreeable day before us.

Wednesday, Sept 13 The thought of getting into the boat to be shifted into the *Ariel* kept me awake half the night with visions of dropping the

Queen into the water, & being myself dangled at the end of a red string I had seen preparing. At 6 S N came into my berth, having been distinctly desired by me to be ready & to have me dressed by that hour, & baggage & all to be disposed of, as might be ordered. Dressed in desperate hurry—sunrise, cloudless sky, as much wind as ever, & more swell. Guard-boat dancing very uncomfortably; saw in one an officer showing a tub with a hole in it and a seat—the dreaded accommodation chair itself! Heard a welcome voice say it wd not be wanted—S N whispered that a rumour reached her that we were not to be moved—a woman servant of Ld Aberdeen's knocked at the door and confirmed it. Too late to go to bed again—so I ran on deck to know the reason of the change & found all the party wishing each other joy of the change. Ld Aberdeen claims the credit of it; from his little window the dancing of boats distressed him so much that he had seriously sent for Ld Adolphus to see if any thing could be done to prevent putting the Queen into such jeopardy. Ld Adolphus meanwhile discovered the yacht could after all get into Ostend!

We sailed at 7; salutes all round, & a gay blue dancing sea. Poor Miss Hamilton I found in gt misery, in her bed, & in her boots. She had in 3 attempts got thus far in her toilet, then nearly fainted, & had made up her mind to be left to her fate, as it was easier to die than to dress; & so she remained, & worse & worse until Ostend. Found a very heavy sea beyond the shelter of the Goodwin Sands; P A flattered himself he was getting used to the sea 'it does not lift me off my legs so.'* The Queen was stoutly breakfasting in her Pavilion. She made me sit by her for at least three hours in one of the sheltered Paddle-box seats & was in high spirits all the time, except for five minutes under the influence of an over powering smell of roast goose—even then a little O de Cologne set her right, & she laughed heartily at the sight first of P A dreadfully overcome, then Ld Liverpool, & then Ld Aberdeen, all vanishing in haste. She owned that had the passage been in the *Ariel* she wd not have stood it better than they. A midshipman begged me to let him doctor Miss Hamilton with quinine—I asked her consent, & she was enchanted to try any thing from any body, & it stopped her sickness.

Steering into Ostend was nervous work with so long & large a vessel; it wd have been impossible to get into boats. It succeeded

* Queen Victoria's Journal records that 'I resisted entirely, though I did not feel very comfortable, but poor Albert succumbed.'[2]

beautifully & in a moment we were in still water alongside the quay. The King & Queen [Louise] came on board in a moment. I had commended poor Miss Hamilton to the care of Sir James Clark, but in one minute she had come to life, finished the toilet begun in the Downs, & was able to land, & go on with us. We were packed into *calèches* & four & at a foot's pace proceeded thro' an ugly French looking crowd. This is an ugly little town with shabby small houses, and the King has a number of these to live in when he comes for sea air. The Queen [Victoria] is put into his best which is neatly fitted up. We are in the next street; we lodge with a very civil old woman, & we have persuaded her to let our maids sleep in a spare room & not to be sent out of the house. All the gentlemen are billeted in different houses & we feel rather friendless.

Sir Hamilton Seymour [British Minister, Brussels] came to offer us his services. The Queen has decided to send the steamer to embark at Antwerp—this is not expected here, & Sir H Seymour began to talk of the difficulty of passing thro' Dutch waters, & that the King of the Belgians never did so because of some affair abt lowering his flag—but what can that matter to the Queen? Of course she wd not be expected to lower the Standard! We assembled in the Queen's rooms & were taken on to the Hotel de Ville to dine there, as the house could not hold us. I sat between Ld Liverpool and the King; he told me to remember him to you when I wrote, & said many civil things about you. The evening was short; we were very formally placed in a circle & before 10 were carried home.

Thursday, Sept 14 Went to the Queen very early to give her the parcel I received the night before. She was exceedingly pleased with its contents and thought them [turquoises] cheap & well chosen. I waited for her in a room with her collection of gowns hanging round the walls: they are very decidedly badly chosen, & quite unlike what she ought to have. Her dresser never ceased sighing & lifting up her hands and eyes all the time I looked at them, & lamenting how little she cared abt her dress. Some gowns just come from Paris were less fitted for her use than the rest. The Queen & Prince breakfasted alone & we were told to come at ½ past 10 to the *déjeuner à la fourchette* of the Household. This was a very dull long meal & it is a bore to undergo it every day, for we had really breakfasted long before.

We were left all day to our own devices with orders to be ready for dinner at ½ past 6 & to go afterwards to the Play. The dinner was again at the Hotel de Ville, and we assembled before at the Queen's. The King brought in his three children, two nice looking boys with long noses, & the most lovely little girl I ever saw;* she is 3 years old, very dark, with immense dark eyes, red cheeks, & a tiny mouth, quite a darling & very much petted naturally. The Duke of Brabant was a very beautiful child once, but his nose spoils him now, but he would still be handsome if it stopped growing, & the rest of his face grew up to it—he is exceedingly like Mrs C[umming-] Bruce. At dinner Miss Hamilton had the Senator of Ostend for a neighbour—a wonderful man—who in the course of conversation offered to arrange a marriage between her & his son, & asked her address. I believe she civily refused the proposal but told the old man that letters directed to the Court of England reached her.

Sir E Bowater is ill; he has had an attack of cholera, he nearly fainted at dinner the first night & has been in bed ever since. After dinner we went to the Play, *L'Héritière* was given first—then an act of *Guillaume Tell*, very well sung in French. The theatre is very small and plain, all the public boxes on the *balcon* were smartened up, and in the middle our Queen sat between the King & Queen of the Belgians; I was next to Albert & we amused ourselves pointing out the English faces—the young ladies with bare backs in the pit could not be mistaken. The heat was unbearable and it was difficult to keep awake. Between the two pieces the orchestra played 'God Save the King' & everybody got up; there was clapping & a little noise. They went away just after the trio to avoid a song about liberty which the audience generally applauds more than the King likes to hear—at least they are in the habit of so doing at Brussels, and they did not know how it would be here. I was told afterwards it had not been applauded at all; it was very absurd to go away. '*On ne savait pas s'il y aurait du tapage, et on en aurait pas voulu en presence de votre reine.*'

Friday, Sept 15 Miss Hamilton & I are conjecturing whether or not the Queen will go to Waterloo. It is a sin that she should not see it—and perhaps somebody or other might take offence if she went there. It is odd that I have heard no one mention it as a thing to be seen. Ld Aberdeen is thinking over the subject.

* Duc de Brabant, Comte de Flandres, and Princesse Charlotte who married Maximilian, Emperor of Mexico.

This has been such a busy day that I can hardly remember all we have done & seen. We were taken at 12 to the railroad & packed into a carriage nearly as good as those of the Gt Western Railroad—I even think it was wider. We went to Bruges at a good steady pace of about 20 miles an hour, thro' country as flat as water, and cultivated like Battersea fields. At Bruges we were met by a crowd of Authorities who muttered long *discours*, and we were put into carriages and four, following the King's in procession. We had a stuffy luncheon with the Authorities & went next to the Government House & were made very angry by a very simple squinting Governor's wife who was in a state of bewilderment which had dispossessed her of all her faculties, & she applied to her husband for advice & assistance when she had much better have judged for herself of the capabilities of her house. From this moment the sightseeing began in good earnest. We saw first the Church of Notre Dame, the Cathedral was our next sight,* ancient vestments were shown, and I was very anxious the Queen shd see some trimmed with the deep old lace we have so often had turned into flounces. I think she is exceedingly amused with the foreign look of everything, people, Churches, houses, & all—more than by each particular sight. P Albert naturally enough being used to all this pays more attention to what he is shown, & as to the merits of pictures & statues he really can judge well. The most interesting part of our day's work was the next: a visit to the English convent of Augustine nuns. This is a very strict order, no one is allowed to cross the threshold except on the visit of a crowned head. The nuns were all very old and ugly & as simple as babies. There are thirty-nine, several lay sisters, and about 50 *Pensionnaires*; these were little girls in white, with long garlands of flowers in their hands & wreaths round their heads, arranged in a pattern like a ballet figure & backed before us the whole length of the cloister.

From here we went to the Palais de Justice; the programme for today's work gave us 2 more sights, but the Queens were tired for once & we went to the Governor's house to be ready for the railroad. We kept the squinting lady in order by strong compulsion, & by 5 o'clock went back to Ostend by our special train. Lady Seymour, Ld Aberdeen, & Ld Liverpool were my carriage companions during all this expedi-

* 'There are stalls in the Choir, just as at Windsor', the Queen noted approvingly in her Journal, but she was dissatisfied with 'the French they speak', finding it 'something too dreadful.'[3]

tion, & I suppose they will be every day, for I find they are very etiquettical here.

I fitted myself for dinner by lying down on my bed till the last moment before dressing, & was less sleepy than usual for the evening. My dinner neighbours were again the King and Ld Liverpool. Between the dinner & railroad the King & Queen had found time to go & walk on the digne! & after dinner they thought proper to stand a full hour. Royal legs are surely of other stuff than ours. Tomorrow's work will be harder still; we are to go to the railroad at 9. The Queen has been very much amused. Eu was 20 times better fun for me.

Miss Hamilton has had no end of apologies made to her for the odd speeches of her neighbour at dinner yesterday. It is universally allowed he is cracked & she is not to sit by him again; they are mistaken to think she was offended.

Saturday, Sept 16 A very long busy day. The carriage fetched us at ½ past 8 before we had done breakfast & gave us a good half hour of the waiting room. Sir E Bowater reappeared, well again of his cholera. It is difficult to imagine how his name can be troublesome to learn, but here it is considered so & the Comte d'Hane [Master of the Horse] after taking infinite pains calls him Sire Water-bo. We found at the station the Seymours & were placed in the 2nd division of the King's carriage as before. Ld Liverpool thought we were crowded & very kindly put himself into another to our gt relief—for his incessant chatter & jokes at the beginning of such a day's work pass our power of endurance.

We passed Bruges & two smaller stations & had only a minute at each for the Authorities to say something & the wheels to be greased. Ghent is seen for some time before the railroad reaches it as it makes a bend round the town. We went first to the Government house, then to the Cathedral of St Bavon, a very fine church but much spoilt by white wash. On a triumphal arch it was written that the town rejoiced in again welcoming a Queen of England & on one side was written 'Victoria' & the date, & on the other 'Philippa of Hainault 1348'. After the Cathedral we had a long drive to a gate which seemed the end of the town; it led however into the Béguinage. This is a place where 700 Béguines live together, it is a kind of religious order established in 1234 for women. They wear a nun's dress like the picture of the Countess of Richmond, mother to Henry VII, they take no vows but may remain as long or as short a time as they please, living under the Béguine rules.

There is a collection of small old fashioned houses red brick & stone with step gables; a number of these women live together in each, each has her own cupboard with all she requires for eating & cooking, each cooks for herself & they all dine at their cupboards separately; they work together & I cannot hear that they are of the slightest use to anyone. The Queen was more amused at this than anything she has yet seen. By this time we were quite exhausted with heat and fatigue & were glad to get back to rest at the Government House before luncheon. The *déjeuner* was well done; great pains were taken to procure rareties & there was a dish of roasted gold Pheasants with their heads & tail feathers put on again, & quantities of disgustingly fat ortolans.

The great concert we had been told of so long before was settled to be at ½ past 3 o'clock to allow of our return to Ostend by daylight. We passed along a string of *vigilantes* carrying people in full dress to the concert & the effect of going out of the burning sun into a lighted room was odd enough. It is a most beautiful theatre in rococo style & is very fresh & highly finished. The royal box was beautifully fitted up & we were all served with choice bouquets. The concert was chiefly instrumental; a very fine orchestra, a clarinet player & a violin, a singing woman, & a very curious valse which melted by degrees into 'God Save the King' sung by a chorus of men at valse pace. There was to be a great deal more but we did not stay.

On this occasion I have had much more Ladies' Maid work to do for the Queen than ever before. We were sleepy & silent on our journey & soon after sunset got back to Ostend. It was very wearisome to have to dine & dress so soon after that; rest was out of the question. These dinners and evenings are very formal; the Queens stand & talk to each other for ages & walk round the circle. There are chairs ranged round the wall & two sofas, & when they sit on their's the three or four women sit on another far off & the men stand at a gt distance with their backs to the wall.

Sunday, Sept 17 Prayers were read by a Mr Jessop, the Clergyman here —a Clergyman had been sent for from Antwerp but he never came & this poor man was got at a minute's notice. He seemed very much frightened but read very well indeed. The Queen sent for me & desired me to send some little present to the 4 ladies of the town of Ghent deputed to receive her, & to the squinting wife of the Governor of Bruges. To get their names & titles right she desired me to go for help to Ly Seymour & I got help in my letters, for it required care to make them civil enough yet not too humble. This, & packing up the little parcels, kept me & Miss Hamilton the whole afternoon. I never longed more for a little fresh air by the seaside than after this broiling day; it is August weather & we have not seen a drop of rain since Southampton 3 weeks ago & have only had one cloudy day. I am very much distressed that the Queen has not been better dressed on this journey for all the Belgians remark it & the Ghent day it was sad, her bonnets wd do for an old woman of 70 & her pink petticoat was longer than her muslin gown. I told the maid who can do nothing but sigh and groan.

Monday, Sept 18 We were recommended to dress smart after we arrived at Brussels & Miss Hamilton and I had a box packed with many things to be required in the day. This box was to be especially favoured & to travel with the Queen's things & to be within reach the moment we arrived. My 6 bonnets by this time have all gone to decay for the burning sun they have been daily exposed to has made the white ones brown & the coloured ones white, so we laid out a plan on the road how Ly Seymour was to send off in all directions for bonnets & how we were to be smartened up in incredibly short time. The day's programme made it one of great activity; from 9½ to ½ past 1 in the railroad, then the *entrée* into the town, a *déjeuner*, & at 3 a drive to see sights & at ½ past 4 a concert in the Park in the open air! The railroad journey was not so disagreeable for we had learnt to consider it rest & cool & to value the four hours out of the worst of the sun.

I think this [Brussels] one of the prettiest towns I ever saw. Every house so white & clean & gay like the best parts of Paris. The Palace is not fine or large, it looks into the Parc which is only a large square like a baddish bit of the Tuileries, Miss H & I & the gentlemen are all lodged in this Brussels Palace. The Queen & Prince go to Laeken, the country house, where the King & Queen always live. The heat of the sun was like a blister and the drive at foot's pace thro' the town was real suffering. Of course the selection of clothes in the favoured box was not forthcoming & the carriage with things of P A's & of the Queen's with which it travelled was bodily left behind at Ostend.* I

* Charlotte Brontë who witnessed the Queen's drive through Brussels that day, described the 'little stout, vivacious lady, very plainly dressed' to her

did pretty well with another gown & bonnet but poor Miss Hamilton was in gt distress.

The concert in the Park was a tiresome operation. We were in a booth opposite to an orchestra in a pavilion in the middle of the Park; the interval between the trees was crowded with people all staring into the booth & making noise enough to prevent one from hearing more than a faint tinkling. This lasted more than an hour. The King, P A, & all the men in full uniform with their hats off. In fact it was the means of showing themselves, & my only amusement was watching how long the same could stare at the Queen without moving or blinking their eyes, & how great a crowd could mount the same chairs & stick upon them until undermined from below when they disappeared in the mob, tumbling in a heap on each other. These concerts are only given on gt occasions & are a very stupid invention.

The dinner was late for the Queen first received all the *corps diplomatique*, & the stray carriage & boxes only arrived at nearly 8 o'clock, & poor Miss Hamilton had to hurry on her things in two minutes. Miss H & I were so amused when we were waiting with General Goblet, the Min of Foreign Affairs, in the room next that in which the *corps diplomatique* were, to see him deliberately go to the key hole and look thro' it for a long time. He turned to us & said '*C'est drôle un corps diplomatique, ils ne s'arrangent jamais*', & so he went on peeping at them till Ld Aberdeen came. Peeping thro' key holes seems common here. At Ghent a servant peeped into the room where the King & Queen & our Queen were, & went on doing so before about 20 people; our gentlemen wanted to kick him, but this *métier* proved an innocent one as it was to seize the right moment for opening the door when the royal people came to it. I sat at dinner between Ld Liverpool & the French Ambassador, M de Rumigny, a very agreeable good man, still in gt distress at the loss of his wife who died of the measles. She said before hand if she caught it she would die of it the 5th night. Her daughters fell ill of it & she kept her word and died the 5th night.

The Grand Duchess [Anna Feodorovna], sister of the King, is here. She was divorced from the Gd Duke Constantine; neither the Queen nor P A had ever seen her. She lives a very retired life in Switzerland &

---

sister Emily. The absence of the favoured box probably explains the dowdiness of the Queen's dress on that occasion.[4]

I believe has not always been very respectable. She is very like the King & the Dss of Kent and Agnes Berry & has remains of very great beauty; her manners are very agreeable & she is considered extremely clever. We sat round a table very formally & at 10 the Queens went to prepare for their drive to Laeken. Miss H & I were offered a carriage to go & see the illuminations. The Queen looked as pleased as a child at the novelty of a night drive in the open carriage leaving behind all her Court, which has not happened to her since she was Queen.

Tuesday, Sept 19 Lady Seymour came to us early to take us out shopping which may be done in a very independent way in that quiet town. We were in too great a hurry to see much, & I only succeeded in getting some neckcloths & music. The pretty shops of bronzes & ornaments we thought there was no time for. Miss Hamilton & I found our way alone to the Cathedral Ste Gudule, Miss H got heated with this hurried walk & looked as if she wd have a fit so we thought it prudent to go home in a *vigilante*; I doctored her & did her good. I envied Ld Aberdeen & Ld C Wellesley their journey to Waterloo before breakfast; we could not go. At twelve there was a *déjeuner* & we went as fast as possible to the railroad to meet the Queen at the Laeken station. After many false alarms and standing in the dust & burning sun they came much behind their time & the train hurried along at more than its usual pace of less than 20 miles an hour.

Antwerp, Wednesday, Sept 20
The Queen appointed us at ½ past 9 to go with her to the *Musée*. The exposition of Modern Pictures is this year at Antwerp, every third year it is at Brussels or Ghent. Some of the pictures are very good in the Cuyp, Mieris, or Hobbema style—it is quite different from the Modern German school & they all aim at imitating Rubens or the above mentioned painters. It was not easy to see this collection for the place was crowded with the ladies of Antwerp, many of them with short sleeves & evening dresses & I had enough to do to keep up with the Royal party & squeeze thro' the mob whenever they cut me off. The escort & the Gd Duchess's carriage now always keeps me back for a minute or two so that the crowd get into the church before us & swept us about hither & thither till it swept us out again & we met the Queens at the door. By 'us' I mean the usual carriage party consisting of Ly Seymour, Ld Aberdeen & Ld Liverpool. The Q of the Belgians

when we got back sent for me & Miss Hamilton & gave us each a very pretty bracelet. The Queen has showered snuff boxes & rings & pins on all the gentlemen who have had to do anything for her, & 500£ to the servants. The Eu servants got 1000£ in a lump & some presents besides.

The embarkation was at a little before one o'clock & the King & Queen & Gd Duchess came on bd & down the river as far as Leifkensoek, their frontier fort. The parting was very melancholy & the Queen's eyes were red. We made the north & south Foreland lights before ½ past 10, I got the credit of first seeing one of them. The night was lovely & Miss H & I sat on deck till eleven, very late sea hours. I find the news that the Queen was very badly dressed particularly at Ghent has spread everywhere, even the officers heard of it & asked us whether it was not a false accusation—every detail of her dress on that particular occasion was known to them all.* At twelve we anchored off Margate for some hours.

Thursday, Sept 21 A beautiful morning but hazy & presently foggy; the speed of the engine steamer went on increasing to the last, more than 17½ revolutions in the minute, good 12 knots an hour. We were on shore at Woolwich by 11 and at Windsor before 1. The Queen gave her orders that the yacht would not be wanted any more this year with a heavy sigh. We are all very sorry to leave her, & she behaved like an angel. Most of the officers are to get promotion; I shall be anxious to know who will be the disappointed for each separately confided to me or Miss Hamilton that he thought himself sure.

Windsor looks very grand & gloomy & it is the oddest feeling not to be in a hurry & I shall go to the chapel, & get a good walk.

The next day Queen Victoria observed in her Journal: 'Drove out with Lady Canning. We both agree that it is hardly possible to believe, now that we are quietly reestablished here, that so much should have taken place & that we should have seen & done so much between the time we were last here!'[2]

* The *Times* reported that she had worn the same dress as at Bruges, a pink silk with a lavender bonnet.

11

Reports from St Petersburg and Windsor

Although not in waiting Charlotte was back at Windsor at the beginning of October, this time with Canning, to meet the Grand Duke Michael of Russia, whose reception was an exceedingly civil one. The Queen showed him every attention, but Eleanor Stanley lamented her wearing what must have been the same shockingly unbecoming dress she had worn at Château d'Eu, to which Charlotte had referred as looking 'very hot'. The vividness of its colour, in violent disagreement with the Queen's complexion, seems to have been its distinguishing feature. 'The Queen had on *the* cerise crepe de Chine, trimmed round the bottom with three rows of lace. It is a very handsome gown, and sets off her jewels and blue ribbon very well, but it looks very hot, being, in fact, bright scarlet.'[1] The Cannings met the Grand Duke again at Drayton Manor, Staffordshire, the house of Sir Robert Peel, and from there Char wrote to her mother.

Oct 23rd 1843

We came on Friday by the Railroad & he arrived Saturday from Chatsworth. I think he is a good specimen of a Prince in one thing, that he talks incessantly topic after topic, which when one's own topics are scarce one values. The Gd Duke surprised us by giving out that he wished to go to church with us yesterday, so they took us to Tamworth instead of their village church. It put me in mind of Christchurch only that it is in bad repair & cruelly pewed up. The Gd Duke bore the cold & the long service manfully & said afterwards he was pleased with it & recognized many prayers as the same they had in Greek, which of course is true of many. They are all gone on to pay a morning visit at Witley Ct [Worcestershire] to the Queen Dowager and from thence to sleep to-night at Ditchley, Ld Dillon's place. I believe he made acquaintance at Kissinger with the Dillons or it seems a strange place for him to go to.

I am going to ask you to do me a very little commission and that is to send me a brooch to suit the little *parure* of garnets you gave me. I should like a bow, or a shell, or something pretty that does to wear in the morning at country visits & I shd be glad of 4 buttons of the same also. I pay yr housemaids' board wages 10s. a week, so we can bring our accounts straight in that way if you like for this commission.

The Queen's projected visit to Wimpole Hall near Cambridge to stay with the Earl of Hardwicke, Lady Stuart's cousin, was of consuming interest. The Cannings had been invited, so too had Aunt Caledon but was sending her son instead, and Charlotte was looking forward to her first visit in eleven years. Only a week's notice had been given, so a new bed had to be purchased in the greatest haste and two liveried footmen borrowed from Tyttenhanger, as well as plate.

Grosv Sqre, Oct 31st 1843

I was very glad to see Wimpole again. I remember every thing, only the scale in my recollection was far grander than the truth, only the Library and the trees were larger than I remembered. The Queen was very sensibly & comfortably lodged, they gave her up their own rooms which were Grandmama's apartment, & the dressers, & Lady, & Maid of Honour were close by, & the white stone staircase was given up entirely to the Queen & shut in by two folding doors near the dressing room door. She had the Billiard room & South dining room fitted up as drawing rooms, & the old red drawing room as a dining room to breakfast in. The Ball was in the Gallery, & the libraries were used for our breakfast & luncheon to which the Queen came, & lighted up the night of the Ball. The Greenhouse is dreadfully dilapidated and was made to look as well as could be by the walls being covered with ivy & the whole thing lighted up with coloured lamps.

The visit went off beautifully & I think the Queen liked it very much. They had great difficulty in getting people to Wimpole at such short notice; the Peels could not go for the Prince of the Netherlands was to be with them, & the D of Wellington had to receive the Gd Duke, & in the few days they had to submit their lists to the Queen & send invitations not many cd be collected. Aunt Mex I find was not asked & not pleased with it—I wish they had asked her which they cd very well have done for several rooms were not used—the best bedroom with the Chancellor's bed! They thought of putting the Queen in it but for various reasons found it wiser to give a more convenient and private suite. The Ball was very pretty & gay to look at but the dancing did not last long for they were so much occupied in staring at the Queen as long as she was there, & when she went it ceased, as she slept over the gallery. The chapel is very well done up & they have prayers in it each morning. The first the Queen was so early that she went in before the bell rang & hardly any one was ready. I was late amongst the rest.

Pray send me 11 yds of narrow sable trimming if it is not ruinously dear; it is to go round a sort of cloak if you can get it for abt 8 to 10 £.

Eleanor Stanley who was in waiting at the time found the house 'very old-fashioned, but comfortable, except that the windows dont shut close, so we were all very cold, besides being tired to death'. Having 'done the civil by all the country neighbours' she was thankful when the Queen retired at eleven for she had found the ball very stupid and her partner, Lord Caledon, an unattractive little man. She teased him by telling him that the Queen was sure to dance with him, and, 'accordingly she did dance the last quadrille with him; he did not know the figures and was dreadfully alarmed'.[2]

Before leaving London for a visit to Welbeck Abbey in November, Char received a few additional turquoises for the Queen but decided to keep them till her mother sent accounts for £175 already disbursed by Sir Henry Wheatley (Privy Purse) for the first group. Her own more modest request for a garnet brooch had been discharged, and musk with which to scent her furs had also reached her. But to her dismay her father had elected to stay on at St Petersburg till the late spring, principally because he had lost the use of a leg and was in no condition to undertake the journey home. In her turn Lady Stuart needed some purchases made in England; Charlotte wrote from Welbeck: 'You shall have the lace gown, & I shall order an Irish one for you for Honiton is very dear & not a bit pretty, in fact I think it is more dabby & not so suitable. As to the fly gown, it sounds quite frightful to my ears, & I hope I may use discretion about it & not make the purchase if I disapprove exceedingly. You are to have a printed velvet gown, a printed flannel (which though ugly, might be pretty enough for a dressing-gown), 9 pr of stockings, a limerick lace. I have ordered a white silk to go to you for a slip—for I believe such things are dear at Petersburg.' She was able to collect together other items of news: Aunt Mex was still in a state of great annoyance at not having been asked to meet the Queen at Wimpole; she had seen the Duke of Newcastle and two daughters, 'they are living at Clumber on a very reduced scale, he talks openly of being out at elbows and he lives in two rooms, at the least possible expense'; the Berrys were at their house in Curzon Street, 'they ask about you and preach by the hour, but end in promising always to write you volumes'. The marriage of Emily de Flahault, daughter of Comte de Flahault and Baroness Keith, to Lord Shelburne, as his second wife, was causing a stir for having accepted him, after several times refusing him, she had then broken her engagement in the summer and Charlotte felt that 'having refused him before, she ought to have been very sure before she accepted him. It has clearly been her mother's doing'. In November the marriage went forward and the following month Char had heard that 'people were never more delighted with each other—it is a case very much in favour of *mariage de raison*'.

An invitation to Curraghmore followed Welbeck; Canning could only make it a short visit but Charlotte remained into the new year. Her cousin Sarah Savile was to have accompanied them and was sadly disappointed at being delayed by a bad cold but followed later, and was thought enterprising and 'very courageous to undertake such a journey trusting almost to chance chaperones & I think it marvellous that Aunt Mex had the *courage* to allow it'. Char and Lou wished to see her suitably married: 'We are dying to get people to meet her—a son profitably, but they are not so easy to find.' Earlier in the season Sarah had snubbed Lord Cranstoun and was thought right to have done so, 'for he is really a fool, an idiot is more true, or a madman, & he has a silver top to his head. However he made a very remarkable piece of work abt Sarah for a time; Aunt Mex did not encourage it, he was so very mad it could not be wished'. Charlotte was glad of her companionship as 'a kind of protection' on the long journey home, for Canning having forbidden Char the crossing to Bristol with pigs on board at this season, they were obliged to go round by Dublin. One thing still required to be straightened out with her mother:

Pray send me by *return of post* the account of the price of the Turquoises. I have never been able yet to give the few additional turquoises you sent me for want of it. Long ago I gave in writing the sum owing to you which you mentioned to me, since then you told me it was more than was due, & you sent me these additional stones to make it come right. I will give them whenever you send me the bills or tell me accurately what the mistake was—for as it is, I do not like to say vaguely—that I mentioned a wrong sum, & that these came to make it right. I am sorry to bother you about this but I want to finish off the affair in my next waiting & you have often promised the bills without sending them & there is only just time now to get them. If you have not got me the bit of sable I asked for pray do not mind about it, for I do not care for it much & it will be too late in a little while to use it this year.

Lady Stuart had worries of her own. Her husband would not resign his post though now decidedly less well, but on hearing that the Embassy was to be demoted so as to correspond with the Russian Legation in London he agreed to send in his official resignation on those grounds and wrote to Lord Aberdeen accordingly:

My dear Lord, It has been my intention to have deferred sending my resignation until nearer the time of my departure from Petersburg, but having heard that it is the intention of Her Majesty's Government to change the character of their mission, I feel it my duty to place the Post I have the honour to fill, at your Lordship's disposal, without delay.[3]

The possibilities of their going direct to a German spa were explored; Charlotte hoped they might settle in Whitehall Yard which remained unlet though Sir Robert Peel had thought seriously of buying. Highcliffe was an attractive alternative but the lack of superior medical care was a deterrent. The Carlton Terrace house would probably be put on the market and Lady Stuart anticipated £18,000 unfurnished, till cautioned by Charlotte that Lord Kensington's had been sold to Lord Clanricarde for £15,000, though that was considered 'cheap beyond anything'.

Her next letter was from Windsor:

Jan 23rd 1844

The 3 children are quite darlings so very full of fun with such pretty manners; the little one is like a fat cottage child and the Princess Royal is rather thick & stout but grown since I last saw her & much prettier than she was. She has quite a royal memory & knew me & my name after four months absence; her *bons mots* are wonderful. Yesterday Pss Mary of Cambridge went out walking with her and talked French to the Bonne but made 2 mistakes of gender.* The little Princess heard them & said nothing at the time & mentioned them both after they came home—in private. The Prince of Wales now wears a little dress which I believe is like the Russian moujiks—it is the shape of a short shirt open on one side and embroidered like a blouse—he looks very pretty in it.

I succeeded Lady Douro with her first waiting. She has met with gt success here & has been most kindly treated, in short she thinks Court a paradise and agreeably surprised them all by turning out very merry as soon as her shyness wore off. Reel dancing was the great amusement in the evenings & harp playing in the day time. The Queen made her play duetts with her constantly. I have now my piano strewed with music books for playing duetts on 2 pianos & by 4 people at once. They say the effect is beautiful but it requires excellent time. I shall be in a great fright when the time comes. I have given your 4 little turquoises which were a very pleasant little surprise in addition to the set.

* Daughter of H.R.H. the Duke of Cambridge and the future mother of Queen Mary; she was now just ten years old.

There were many people staying at the Castle, all of whom Lady Stuart would know. Amongst them the Jerseys who having come for three days were obliged to stay a week, Lord Jersey [Master of the Horse] having tumbled over an imperial left by a maid in a dark passage; he was in great pain with a strained tendon and exceedingly provoked, for 'having hunted all the year to be disabled by a bandbox he thinks a very hard case'. The Duchesses of Kent and Cambridge as well as the Queen had asked a great deal after the Stuarts.

At the end of the month details had reached Queen Victoria of the engagements of two Grand Duchesses, daughters of the Tzar and the Grand Duke Michael. The Foreign Office received the following despatch from St Petersburg:

January 8th 1844[4]

The Ceremony of the 'Betrothal' according to the forms of the Greek Church, of Her Imperial Highness The Grand Duchess Alexandra Nicolaïevna to His Serene Highness The Prince Frederick of Hesse Cassel took place yesterday in the chapel of the Winter Palace.

Her cousin, the Grand Duchess Elisabeth Mikailovna, was similarly betrothed to the reigning Duke of Nassau, and both were to receive one million silver roubles (nearly £157,000) as their marriage portion, and half a million silver roubles each (£78,000) in presents for their trousseau. In addition the daughter of the Tzar had a private fortune of £68,000.[5] Queen Victoria was intrigued by every particular. 'The Queen has asked very kindly after you & Papa & you did very well to send all the accounts of the *Fiançailles* for she asked every detail & was particularly anxious to know the state of the marriages, but I could not disentangle the confusion I get into between old & new style, & old & new Christmas & New Year's day, & the 2 Grand Duchesses & their 2 marriages apiece. This has been a very quiet waiting but not for any particular cause, for I begin to believe the Queen is not going to increase the family for she danced English country dances one night most actively.* Quadrilles, valses, &

* Prince Alfred was born seven months later.

that sort of thing she has left off caring about, but now takes delight in Sir Roger de Coverley & all the old fashioned dances. She was anxious to know how the Gd Duchess was dressed at the *Fiançailles* so none of yr details were superfluous.'

The Court was suddenly plunged into mourning by the Duke of Coburg's death, father of Prince Albert. 'It has been a great grief to the Prince, & the Queen has been quite cast down by it too. The poor Dss of Kent has felt her brother's death most severely & there never was such a gloom as it cast over them all. The mourning is Private & will last a year, so we shall wear black gloves in waiting for 8 months, but at home we are to keep to the Court mourning of 6 weeks.'

Except for a few days at Highcliffe with the Clanricardes at Easter Char was now in London until her next waiting at the end of May, and throughout the spring her letters are chiefly concerned with her parents' journey home; Lord Stuart had ventured to express the hope that Her Majesty would be graciously pleased to extend to him the indulgence of a government steam vessel to convey him home, a request with which the Queen was willing to comply.[6] Nevertheless there were a few incidents worth communicating though Charlotte admitted to having no news or gossip, and even a couple who dined with them had nothing to tell, '& had reason to complain of us, for I quite forgot to order some meagres & Canning never found out she was fasting [Lent] & gave her such a miserable 2nd helping of fish that I saw her turn in despair to beetroot & pickles'. She was mildly disapproving of the Ripon's son, Viscount Goderich, now sixteen (he who had earlier suffered the application of a blister)—'though far more presentable than one could have expected'—was allowed to have his own way & do exactly as he pleased and 'he goes to the French Play & wherever he likes by himself'. Pollington and his wife, 'that little wild Rachel', had emancipated themselves from the Mexborough's Dover Street house, and had established themselves in Bolton Street which was in a 'higgledy piggledy state, but she seems to like a house of her own of all things'. At the Queen's Drawing-Room the Clanricardes' daughter, Lady Elizabeth

De Burgh (who the following year married Viscount Lascelles) was presented; she was tall, handsome, and admired. There was also the doubtful distinction of Sarah Savile being offered the place of Lady-in-Waiting to the Duchess of Cambridge. The Duke and his family were considered too easy-going by a Court whose moral rectitude was becoming progressively more emphasized. 'Aunt Caledon & GM thought it very delightful & Aunt Mex was rather for it. Now I think it dreadful & have been working hard to prevent it. C[ambridge] House is very bad company & Sarah would be in no way the better for it, on the contrary being mixed up in a society *mal vue* by the respectable would be of the greatest disadvantage towards her. I think as she never could play 2 bars in time she may get off upon want of music and say something abt not liking to leave home being an only daughter, for which reason she formerly refused the place at the Dss of Kent which was not really to be disapproved of—tho' just after Lady Flora people were shy of it.'

Summer saw the Stuart's return to Highcliffe, and both daughters were thankful to be able to share with their mother the anxiety engendered by Lord Stuart's paralysis. In early September Charlotte was at Court and wrote from Windsor Castle that 'everything Royal that can be collected comes for the Christening [Prince Alfred] at 6 o'clock before dinner, & dinner is to be in St George's Hall'. And a few days later: 'There were so many Bishops & Church dignatories that it looked almost like a Roman Catholic ceremony, for it was in the little Chapel by candlelight just before dinner. The P of Wales & Pss Royal were there looking so pretty & good & the baby himself is a very good specimen—all 4 children were let to be for some time in the corridor afterwards and the three who cd run abt were delighted—it was quite their first piece of dissipation. We went after dinner from the Drawing room to the Waterloo Gallery & had terribly noisy music in the two orchestras.' There had been an accident that morning when the man trimming the lamps of one of the five great chandeliers had, to save himself the trouble of moving the ladder, twisted it round and round till it had become unscrewed and had crashed to the ground; but this was forgotten as the great punch bowl holding a hogshead of mulled claret was borne in beside the cake, which in Charlotte's view seemed too 'small & genteel', but was nevertheless conspicuous for the figure of Peace crowned with laurel rising from the centre.

Queen Victoria (*right*) with her cousin, the Duchesse de Nemours, 1852,
by F. Winterhalter

Viscountess Canning, 1855, a preparatory study by E. M. Ward R.A. for *The Installation of the Emperor Napoleon III as a Knight of the Garter*

12

Blair Castle

The christening over, Charlotte hastened to complete her packing for she was accompanying the Queen to Scotland on board the Royal yacht. Lord Glenlyon, later 6th Duke of Atholl, had put his house, Blair Castle, Perthshire, at the Queen's disposal. Four royal carriages with sixteen carriage and saddle horses besides a number of pointer dogs were shipped to Dundee on the steamer *London*, and the Court having worn full mourning for the Grand Duchess Alexandra (so recently married) were now free of half-mourning for the Duke of Coburg also. The ladies discarding their black ribbons, fans and tippets prepared themselves for the sea journey.

On the day of departure Charlotte woke to an unpromising morning of drizzle following upon a heavy thunderstorm.

Monday, Sept 9 1844 The Queen and Prince took the little Princess & punctually at 7 set off from Windsor to arrive at 9 at Woolwich which was accomplished as precisely. Caroline [Cocks] & I were asked to allow the Swiss governess [Aimée Charrier] & nursery maid for this short journey to the railroad, to be in our carriage & we had no easy task in trying to calm & assuage the poor woman who had quite lost her head in the terror she has of the *voyage d'Europe*. Ld. Aberdeen & Ld. Liverpool were already on board & Sir J. Clark & the party were complete. The little Princess was disappointed to find the ship so like a house & that there were rooms to live in & expected many more wonders.

After the Nore we met a swell & this increased till a good many of the passengers fell sick. The Queen stood it very well for a long time but at last had to lie down on a sofa on deck. Albert remained alone in the corner of one of the comfortable little towers & Caroline & I took care of the little Princess for the poor Charrier was downstairs in a state of immobility, & even the nursery maid had to give in now & then—towards evening weather grew worse. The Queen went down very sick & wanted her dressers but not one of the four was to be had

& Car & I helped by the Stewardess waited upon her: sometimes one dresser came & officiated for a minute or two—but that was the extent they were able to do. The Queen was as goodnatured as possible & grateful beyond anything for any little service we could do. At last she was got to bed & from that time her sickness was at an end. The little Princess did not deserve much pity for she always forgot her sickness when she was amused, & listened to stories the whole afternoon in high spirits unless she was asked how she was, when she always laid down & said 'I'm very ill'. The machinery below is ventilated by Dr Reid's invention & is airy & sweet— & the use [need] of the apparatus was made very evident—for three people were there, all actively sick. The nursery maid got very unhappy at taking poor Princessy there & I went down to look at it, and then asked the Queen if she would like her to be put in a berth occupied by two dressers on the upper deck. The Queen referred me to Albert who said in a groan yes if it were necessary, & wd only talk of being allowed a little rest in Yarmouth roads. As I heard he was determined that if possible the nursery shld be established below I did not like to bear the blame of changing the arrangements & there was no more sea or reason for sickness than would be sure to occur in any voyage, so I asked the Queen to let Sir James Clark decide. He immediately set the Dr Reid's works going— & it was in a very short time quite cool & fresh. The prejudice against the apparatus is still very strong & every noise & smell is attributed to it & it does not always do its duty. For instance with great care & pains the pump was made by mistake to turn the smell of the engine into the men's sitting room.

I had no passenger companions at dinner & sat down to a large table with Ld Adolphus. The Queen could not count upon her dressers enough for me to be away above a few minutes & Caroline was not quite ready for food after all she had seen.

Tuesday, Sept 10 was much finer & by degrees all the sick people began to revive. The Queen got up quite well again & the little Princess was running about saying 'I don't know what to do I am so merry'. We passed Flamborough Head & Scarborough, & Whitby, a little beyond is a beautiful valley with the woods of Mulgrave on the north side. The castle can scarcely be distinguished but we could see the flag flying on the top of the tower. The *Black Eagle* was the only steamer in company with us, she was appointed by the Admiralty as escort & to go ahead of us during the night & the yacht to keep to half speed. All Monday she was far behind & we waited for her to come up after dark; in the morning however she kept up very well when the Yacht went her 11½ & 12 knots, & in the course of the day passed her. By a signal Ld Hardwicke showed that the pressure was higher than that in the Yacht engines—the *Black Eagle* 8lb & the Yacht 6½. The latter might have the more pressure without running any risk, but as it was no object to arrive at Dundee an hour or two earlier as there was no possibility of getting there before dark, the moderate rate was preferred. The improvements have not made much difference; the boilers take up room and the additional space is given to the men, & the engineers have now a berth while formerly they had none. The heat of the engine is very much diminished & the kitchen has been newly done up. The smells are as bad as ever & there are more blacks and small cinders than before & the stern worse than ever. The *Black Eagle* has made all sorts of exhibitions, at last crossing before our bows so near that the Yacht had to stop & Ld Adolphus is in a great rage with Ld Hardwicke for such shewing off which is not quite respectful.

We passed Alnwick & Howick & Bamborough at sunset & went outside the Farne islands, & then at half speed to arrive about 1 off Dundee and at 4 dropped the anchor in the Tay.

Wednesday, Sept 11 The Queen wishing to avoid the crowd as much as possible & to arrive by luncheon time at Blair talked of going ashore at 8 o'clock. She was begged to wait till ½ past 8 for the tide to rise enough to bring the barge to the level of the steps. Ld Hardwicke came on board early & didn't bear his triumph meekly, but owned that he had been very much surprised that he could beat the Yacht. He privately wanted to know whether the pranks of the day before, zig zagging abt & literally going round the Yacht, had given offence.

The Princess was delighted to go in the barge & for the first time really believed she was on the water. On board the Yacht we forgot she is so little that she cannot see over the bulwarks. A little splash of water in her face made her ask 'Who is it spits?'. The landing was beautifully managed, the crowd did not press & the Queen walked along the quay to her carriage on a carpetted path & the people could see her perfectly. We filled four carriages; the Queen & Prince were in the new travelling chariot—the Princess in a coach after them; then the equerries, Sir J Clark & Mr Anson; Caroline & I, Ld Liverpool

& Ld Aberdeen in the last. The decorations of some of the houses of dahlias & heather were beautifully done & dahlia inscriptions were very successful. The fourth carriage of course had the worst horses, one stood up on his hind legs & with great difficulty could be made to go on, but the worst were furnished us at Moulinearn the stage between Dunkeld & Blair. At the steep part of Killiecrankie they jibbed & we slipped back a great way but somehow they were dragged on & as there was a parapet we did not much mind. But at another ascent & that not so very steep but at the top of the pass, & with no parapet, they jibbed again & we as nearly as possible went over. Ld Aberdeen opened the door & in a very short time we bundled out & nothing happened, but dragging *down* hill again we stuck & this time we got out for good. The Stage coach loaded with our servants came along at the same time & we got into it & arrived at Blair by a back way, too late to see the Queen's arrival which I was very sorry to miss.

We got out at the Dunkeld inn [Duke's Arms] & the little Princess was to have some luncheon for it was already nearly 2 o'clock & she was very hungry; of course weak wholesome broth was not what they would bring her without much asking for it, & she had to sit waiting patiently looking at 2 basins of strong giblet soup & Athole Brose* & shortbread and other unwholesome good things. The crowd in the street cheered when the little thing came to the window & it went on bowing its head to them as pleased as possible taking all demonstrations to itself.

When we got to the gate of Blair two Highlanders who guarded the approach sent us on to find our way to the house by a back road. We submitted very humbly for the coach was a very discreditable affair, the hind panel by some accident was knocked out & we did not wish to bring it into the cortège which a whole mob of people had assembled to see. Ld Glenlyon wrote before the Queen arrived to ask that the Athol men should have the honour of guarding her. She consented & is now without any troops. The bodyguard consists of a large number of men about 150 or 200 who are all volunteers. They do their exercises beautifully & are in full Highland dress and armed with Lochaber axes, claymores & dirks & pistols.† There are 5 tents for them in the front of the castle and 24 men & 2 officers are on guard for each three

* A mixture of honey, whisky, and two teaspoonfuls of water.

† The Atholl Highlanders, bodyguard of the Dukes of Atholl, wore the Murray tartan.

days. These sentries are so picturesque & well suited to the country—the group standing about the little camp is always quite beautiful.

Lady Glenlyon was on the steps waiting to receive the Queen & she shewed her all the rooms prepared. We arrived late & wandered about without having a guess as to where we should be lodged or what we were to do. Ly Glenlyon at last appeared on the staircase & showed us our rooms. It is the oddest house that ever was—the ground floor has offices & servants rooms only. On the *premier* is a very good dining room and anteroom—my bedroom* & S Norris's; another dining room used by the gentlemen & Car & me for breakfast & luncheon, & a very good drawing room for me & Car & a little room near it for her. All this sounds very comfortable & so it is generally, but these rooms are very difficult to get at for some open into each other, & other useful communications are shut up & sometimes one has to go downstairs & up again in immense complication. On the 2nd floor the Queen is lodged at the top of the house. There is a very fine drawing room which was still a lumber room a fortnight ago & had not been used for 25 years. The visit must have put the Glenlyons to very great expense; they have put in carpets & furniture & have done all sorts of things about the place. A bridge was built in a fortnight & an approach made & all sorts of things. They have lodged themselves & the officers of their body guard in the factor's house & I suppose will remain there all the time.

Thursday, Sept 12 We mean to keep early hours & to breakfast at 9. This morning's breakfast was a bad substitute for a Scotch one & Ld Liverpool had a great deal of tormenting to submit to when butter & cream came to an end & nothing but the palace baker's rolls & dry toast were to be had. Even the dinner oat cake from London!

The day was beautiful. All the hills round quite clear & a hot sun. The castle has such thick walls that it never warms thro' & they have fires in all the rooms all the year round. The Queen had her usual early walk with the Prince & to go some distance had her wheeling chair. She is not strong enough yet to see much,† for all the walks here are long & most of them very steep. The Prince decided to stay with her all day & to shoot grouse the next day & to stalk on Saturday. So quiet has all the ground been kept that not a shot has been fired this

* Probably the room now known as The Blue Bedroom.

† Prince Alfred had been born only five weeks previously.

year either at grouse or deer & not a grouse was to be had for the Queen's luncheon & Ld Glenlyon went out to get a few for dinner. He has recovered his sight very much but his shooting must be fearfully dangerous to those who go with him.

After writing letters I took Car to visit Ly Glenlyon. We met him [Ld Glenlyon] at the door & he introduced us to two of the officers of the guard, both Drummonds. They live for their 3 guard days in the tents & sleep on blankets on a bit of oil cloth, I am afraid 3 weeks of this romantic loyalty will make the whole force very Rheumatic. At present the men volunteer for the guard, the whole company together, & 20 are taken of each in turn. Ly Glenlyon was on her way to the garden & she took us with her; it is a very good specimen of the North mixture of fruit & flowers. We went on to the Tilt; along the back of it there is a very pretty walk which leads to some little waterfall. We met Albert who left his horses to see this on his way home; it wanted 10 minutes so he had to run which poor lame old Bowater could not attempt & hobbled home ½ an hour after. The Queen after luncheon came & looked at our rooms & sat with us a good while & made a vain attempt to make the Princess repeat the '*Cigale & fourmie*'—which she pretended to forget. They had great difficulty to pack into the rooms prepared for them & changed them all, turning sitting rooms into bed rooms & moving everything. Albert for a moment even thought of changing floors with us & came & looked at all our rooms. I believe they are very uncomfortable for none of the rooms communicate with each other except one or two which are useless by having no other entrance. Poor Mlle Charrier's room is thro' the Princess's which you get at thro' the drawing room; her dinner cannot be carried to her by this road & she with many apologies has begged to dine at our luncheon.

The Glenlyons dined & we got upstairs in the gt drawing room, the Queen on a little chair & Albert walking abt promiscuous & nothing like a Windsor evening. They looked at some pictures of Prince Charlie & Ly Glenlyon told us of a quantity of Jacobite relics she is to shew the Queen. Albert is quite delighted to be here & I think the Queen likes it too, but I think she is hardly strong enough to enjoy it thoroughly. Albert has brought a collection he is making of enamel of the Kings & Queens of Scotland & is seeking information about them & to find out whether they are genuine likenesses. I am delighted with Ly Glenlyon, she is so gay & so simple. There is a great diversity of opinion as to her looks—some say she is beautiful & others that she is very plain. I keep to the earlier.*

Friday, Sept 13 A showery day but not bad enough to keep any one at home. The Prince was satisfied with his usual ½ day's shooting & came home to luncheon having killed 4 brace & ½ of grouse, & one black-cock. The birds were wild but he liked his walk over the hills. The Queen sent me a bundle of heather & I found she had been enquiring for me. When I went to her it was to beg me to make her a wreath of heather. She told me Isidore† was rather jealous of my performances & said '*je ne sais pas si cela tiendra*', & abused my wires; but she says he does not make natural wreaths half as well as I do, which I am proud to hear. The Queen drove afterwards to see what are called the Cataracts of the Garry, & Car & I went about with her pony & gathered very choice bits of heather for the wreath. It took me nearly 2 hours to make but it ended very successfully & was very much approved of. We had at dinner the two Drummonds on guard, one is Ld Strathallan's son; he carried the sword which the Ld Strathallan who was killed at Culloden had in his hand at the moment, & he made many pretty loyal speeches to the Queen about it. They are all strong Jacobites here & their loyalty is as stout as ever. I do not think young gentlemen in England wd like particularly to volunteer to be on guard for three days together in a tent at the door. They declare it is a delightful life & they never were so happy. The Queen is in very high spirits & enjoys the variety from her Windsor life very much. After dinner for half an hour she came to sit in my bedroom & was full of jokes & fun & ran upstairs only just before the gentlemen came out of the dining room.

Saturday, Sept 14 The post comes in at a most inconvenient hour, abt. ½ past 3. One cannot go out till after getting ones letters & the answers only go next day at eleven. At twelve o'clock was the guard mounting & for an hour we had bagpipes & a great many evolutions.

* In 1846 Lord Glenlyon succeeded his uncle as 6th Duke of Atholl, and in 1852 when there was some talk of the Duchess being appointed Mistress of the Robes, Char thought her 'clever & nice but too inclined to giggle.'

† The Queen's hairdresser since her accession and previously hairdresser to the Duchess of Kent. No doubt some connexion with the hairdressing establishment already mentioned.

The day was windy & now & then a mist set in for an hour or two at a time. The Prince did not set out till after 2 o'clock & before dark had killed three stags. He said he saw one herd of more than 1000 & another of 3 or 400. He had a great deal of running & a little creeping & came home excessively pleased; Ld Glenlyon was the only person besides keepers who went with him. Car & I drove the Queen & the little Princess & Mlle Charrier as far as the falls of the Garry & Princessy played all sorts of tricks to show off before me & Car. She was told by Mlle Charrier to have *l'air gracieuse* when she bows to people along the road. She bowed for some time and said '*J'ai eu l'air très gracieuse*', & to do this it was discovered she made a most horrible face.

There has been a question of the Queen's going to the Kirk—for she has a great curiosity to see it. She is promised that the service is to last only an hour & 1/4 & I am sorry to say that it was found that the pew wd do, & there was no difficulty of that sort in the way, & she is to go. Ld Aberdeen negotiated the short service. I am the more sorry for this as the poor little Episcopal congregation is very small indeed, there are only very few old people; the remains, Ly Glenlyon said, of Non priests and Cameronians. I always thought the latter were Presbyterians. It is surprising that all these Jacobites shd frequent the Kirk. There is every variety here, for an odd log church on the road is of the free variety. I pointed it out to Ld Aberdeen who wd like to set it on fire.* In the morning the Queen had a long talk with us about the Kirk, she is very curious indeed to go to it, & tells us we must take care that she does nothing to shock people. She talked over sermons & preachers and evidently alluded to Dr Hook. She likes Archdeacon Wilberforce's sermons better than any one's & thinks the Bp of London's too severe† & likes gentle comforting sermons & not to be frightened & found fault with. I shall be very curious to hear the

* In 1843 a 'non-intrusion' party opposed to ministers being 'intruded' by patrons, broke away from the Established Church of Scotland and claiming the right to defend the spiritual discipline of the Church, formed themselves into the Free Church of Scotland. Lord Aberdeen had fought vigorously on the side of the Established Church.

† The Rev. W. F. Hook, Vicar of Leeds; the Venerable Samuel Wilberforce, Archdeacon of Surrey was made sub-almoner to the Queen in October and three months later appointed Dean of Westminster. Bishop Blomfield held the see of London.

minister here, he never can refrain from making his sermon appropriate to the occasion.*

Sunday, Sept 15 This morning looks very like an even downpour for the whole day & the close carriage is coming to carry us to the Kirk. An even downpour till 5 o'clock. The Queen had given notice she would be at the Kirk & not minding the rain she went. The congregation had not expected her & the church was not crowded; as there is a Gaelic service afterwards they told us it was never full. I think the Queen did not particularly like the service but she was exceedingly attentive. The Prince said it was very like what he was used to in Germany, by which I suppose he meant he liked it. It was quietly & well done. The sermon was concealed in a Bible & read, & the prayers were not bad—but how can one do more than listen, until by the constant repetition of the minister you can guess what comes next. I had forgotten that there is now no sort of Amen at the end. Sitting during the Psalms is quite unaccountable.

The Queen went for variety to sit in Car's room after dinner. The evening was very dull, we guessed words as on Windsor Sundays, but everybody was sleepy & Albert with the greatest exertions could not hold his head up for two minutes together.

Monday, Sept 16 There will be a great deal to draw here for the Queen wants views done for her in every direction.† After luncheon the Queen went to see the falls of Bruar & I not being wanted ordered our ponies & got Sandy McAragh [gillie] the best of all guides, & Ld Glenlyon's servant, & made him take us up the hill of Tulloch on the opposite side of the valley across the Garry which we forded, Sandy leading us one at a time & wading with the water above his knees; in a kilt I suppose that does not matter. Sir James Clark followed on an obstinate pony. The hill was steep & grassy & not at all difficult to get up. I had an order for another heather wreath—it did not succeed to my taste quite as well as the first, the heather not being picked with such care. However the Queen liked it & it was admired by the dinner company, all the men in their kilts.

I hoped we would be ordered to dance reels, the house is full of

* A marble memorial on the wall of the kirk indicates that the Rev. A. R. Irvine had but recently entered upon his ministry at Blair Atholl.

† Several of these sketches are preserved at Windsor Castle.

pipers and it would be so easily managed. There is piping at 6 to wake us; the Queen's piper plays at 2 & the Albert piper at 6, & at guard mounting 2 pipes walk up & down playing for an hour. Ly Glenlyon brought her key & opened her hoards of Jacobite relics—3 miniatures of Pce Charles, his compass which he had all through his wanderings in the Highlands, a lock of his hair in the paper in which he gave it with the date written upon it at the time, snuff boxes &c, Ld George Murray's white cockade.* The Prince brought out his collection to identify his miniatures by these; in the 4 portraits compared, 2 had brown eyes & 2 had blue, so it was not easy to identify the doubtful one.

The Queen had her first ride in the hills & she enjoyed it of all things. She had been sketching a little from the window & wants to try & colour & has a great longing to draw some dirty children & I am to find these & begin, & she is to come quietly & look on & draw them when not observed. Ly Glenlyon wants the heather wreath for a relic & I think I can get it back for her.†

We drove to the Falls of Tummel in the evening. Albert drove the Queen, & Car & I & Ld Glenlyon followed in the pony carriage & four; the road is through Killiecrankie & across the Garry. Going home, at a bridge, the identical spot where we had to leave our leader the day we arrived, one of the leaders kicked & got its leg over the traces, there was a great confusion & kicking but the postillion sat quite firm & we bundled out. Meanwhile two horses left to stand alone took fright & galloped off down the hill passing the Queen's pony chaise. Her ponies did not take fright as they might have done & nothing happened & we went home quietly with a pair.

Wednesday, Sept 18 Another beautiful day. I made one or two slight sketches in Glen Tilt & ran home late to luncheon. The Queen had her 2nd ride on Ld Glenlyon's pony & immediately after breakfast went with the Prince & Sandy to lead the pony to the hill of Tulloch. She was quite enchanted with the drive, straight up the hill & through the turnip field. A skirt has been made to go over her gown & she rides & walks in turn. Sandy was of course as proud as possible of the honour of being her guide— & no one can get him to tell a word about it—'it no for me to tell all that Her Majesty talked about'.

* All these relics are exhibited in the Transvaal Room.

† Charlotte was successful and it is now exhibited in the Banvie Room; the narrow ribbons to secure the wreath at the nape of the neck are still in place.

The Prince was to shoot a fat stag from the window. A few of these were caught when young & put into a sort of park—the others came to them & there is a spot they jump down & cannot get back from, & the park now has a very good herd in it. They are in peace there, no one ventures in amongst them, & they bellow all night in a variety of sounds like bulls & roar sometimes almost like a lion.

The rifle was brought into the dining room & the fat stag chosen. The Queen went to a window of another room & looked out. I saw the poor beast catch up his legs for an instant & then look round surprised & walk a few steps & then die—they say it was well shot thro' the heart. The other stags walked quietly away very little startled & the dead hart was brought round to the door on a horse for the Queen to look at him. It was quite a Landseer picture, all the tents & the Highlanders on guard for a background & the dead deer & the pony standing by him, a number of picturesque kilted keepers, and at the same time came Ld Aberdeen's pack of otter hounds which have been brought from Haddo to shew the Prince. They are the same which Landseer painted,* & the keepers with these dogs are very picturesque too, they carry long black spears & are draped in green velveteen. The poor little Princess was dreadfully distressed at the stag's death. She came down to talk about it very bravely, & said it would have been much better to kill the big one that roars—'let us kill him'—but she burst out crying & could not be consoled. Seeing the deer lifted up shocked her; she said 'his head fell & his neck was no more strong' & she cried bitterly.

Thursday, Sept 19 The Queen sent for me to stay with her while the Prince went to shoot a stag from the window. He wanted her very much not to see it, for the same scene the day before had made her shake & be very uncomfortable. Of course I could not keep her away from the window & she was looking on when the stag was killed. He dropped down dead the instant he was struck. After luncheon the Prince went to the Forest & the Queen sent for me & Ly Glenlyon to go with her to Glen Tilt for there was a chance of seeing a great drive of deer. She waited some time under cover of the wood & saw a number of herds on the heights. They went away in another direction and we waited another half hour, speaking only in whispers, & then

* *The Otter speared*, by Sir Edwin Landseer, R.A., exhibited that year at the Royal Academy.

came a great drove of deer over the ridge & pouring down the hill side in one continual stream. Some were very near the valley when something frightened them and made them turn about & scramble up the hill again. Two figures appeared on the road & the blame was laid upon them—it proved to be the Episcopal clergyman [Mr Walker] & a friend taking a walk; he is in bad odour with the Glenlyons who accuse him of poaching by fishing & of trespassing. Soon after the Prince came down the hill & went home in the carriage with us.

Friday, Sept 20 A beautiful morning & no post to London. I determined to be out early & to have a long drawing morning. I met the little Princess & Aimée coming home & the old pony following saddled & bridled. This tempted me to mount & to go some distance for the sketch. The poor little cockney groom got on rather badly on foot & I told him to follow at leisure. At a gate as he was not in sight I dismounted, went through & got on again. I tied up the pony at a fence and made a sketch but when I got back his nose was bloody & the horses the other side of the railing had been bullying him— & somehow soon after leading him along I let go the bridle & off he was. The rattling of my bag of paint-boxes & pencils kept him going & I had a full half hour's chase till the bag was thrown & he stood still. I found when I got home there was a great hue & cry after me, for luncheon was early & the Queen was to go beyond Forest Lodge to sit with the Prince in one of the lodges—a stone hiding-place—while the deer were driven by. I followed the Queen in Ly Glenlyon's phateon with her & Ld Breadalbane who came on a visit for 2 days. After the Queen had got to her hiding place we were all made to crouch behind a low stone wall—the ground was wet & two or three little showers fell, but in the plaids & cloaks we thought it was impossible to be cold. The drive failed again from the usual excuse of a change of wind; only a few herds passed. All the same it was a very amusing afternoon & we were all very merry behind our stone wall.

The Glenlyons dined & I had to make another heather wreath in a violent hurry. Two capercailzie were brought by Ld Breadalbane from Taymouth. We had one at dinner, it was like an enormous blackcock but rather better. They were in beautiful plumage.

Saturday, Sept 21 I was ordered to be ready by ½ past 10 to go with the Queen & Prince into the Forest—up Glen Tilt to within a mile of

Forest Lodge. At this spot we met the ponies and the Queen mounted Ld Glenlyon's grey pony & had her long shepherd's Plaid apron tied round her instead of a habit. Piles of cloaks & the great luncheon box was packed on moor ponies. The Prince mounted his & I rode the good ugly beast called 'Beauty'. Ld Glenlyon led the Queen and our little procession wound up the side by a zigzag path made for the Duke of Atholl when he was 80 years old. The old keeper Peter Frazer led the way, and the rear were Highlanders leading dogs; just like a Highland sketch by Landseer. We saw a herd of deer feeding & the plan was laid to go round to the back of these.

The Prince went on to shoot some stags, and I remained with the Queen on this peak—it was covered with soft moss like velvet. The Queen was quite delighted with the wild scenery and the Prince was in ecstasies, he got a shot at some stags stalking up to them, but when he got in sight they got away to a distance & he missed them or wounded one. After the Queen had made a little sketch & I had also coloured a little memorandum of the outline of some hills, we got on the ponies & went to meet the Prince, who found a good spot for luncheon near a spring. We spread plates on the heather, & the luncheon box was opened. It is just like a dressing case, and all the bottles & cruets & plates are in one place where they can be used without unpacking. We saw quantities of deer afterwards, & the Prince went along a lower ridge, & Ld Glenlyon led the Queen & me by the upper one to drive down the deer to him. By some mistake we waited on our range for the Prince to get before us, & he waited for the Queen to move on, & a great deal of time was lost, & it was near sunset before we began to go down into Glen Tilt. At a stony crest we put up 2 sets of ptarmigan & quantities of grouse. The Prince joined us half way down & said he had waited an hour for us. He had a few far off shots & wounded a hart which he thought was brought to bay, & complained that the best chance he had all day was lost by using a rifle of Ld Glenlyon's with a bolt he cd not manage. We did not get to the carriage till near dark, & drove back by moonlight. The Queen was not very tired, but it was much too long an expedition for her, & I tried often to get Ld Glenlyon to hasten on. Nothing could be more beautiful than the blue evening hush over those distant ranges of hills at sunset; seen from the height it might have been Greece.

We passed a gypsie fire near the stream, round which was a very picturesque group & we found it to be Ly Glenlyon & Car & all the

Cousins who live at Old Blair, and belong to the Body Guard. Ld Charles [Murray, brother to Lord Glenlyon] caught 2 doz. little trout and they all cooked & ate them.

Sunday, Sept 22 We are just going to the Kirk—Dr [Norman] McLeod, one of the Presbyterian Chaplains, does the duty. Car & I this afternoon mean to go to the Episl Chapel. They all tell us it is a very poor place & has not even a floor.

This was the most beautiful day, the white frost in the morning however, was sharp enough to kill the dahlias! The Queen's Chaplain, Mr McLeod, preached at the Kirk & she went again to it. This time it was crowded to overflowing, more than 1000 people were in it, strangers from Perth & all the country round. The sermon was not bad but not very remarkable for the 'priest preacher in Scotland'. The second Prayer was very good indeed & very like the Prayer book—the first was as usual a sort of profession of faith rather than a Prayer.

After luncheon the Queen & Prince came to our room to talk over yesterday's adventures. She had stood the fatigue perfectly and was able to take two good walks to-day. Ld Glenlyon came to propose plans for to-morrow & he asked me & Car what we meant to do this afternoon. I told him we were going to the Episcopal Chapel—at which Ld Glenlyon flew out into a torrent of abuse against Mr Walker & entreaties to us not to encourage him. The Prince had not got further than the passage & came back to hear what was going on. He defended me going to the chapel & said Mr Walker had better be encouraged to read & preach more & trespass in the Forest less— & added that the Queen meant to send for him to propose a service here next Sunday. On this Ld Glenlyon carried off the Prince & made a great row about this & was exceedingly silly. I have heard since that the Prince told him if he could get his own (Ld G's) Chaplain to do the duty, very well—otherwise they could not mind his feud but must get Mr W.

Car & I went to the miserable little chapel but found it shut up & that the service is alternately in the morning & evening, & this evening was the turn of the Tummel Bridge Chapel, & the morning here.

Monday, Sept 23rd A stag was shot from one of the windows. The poor beast was first wounded, then missed by the Prince & Ld Glenlyon, and shot after a long time by the latter.

Car & I breakfasted with Ly G & devoted about all the morning to looking at the guard mounting, and then at a trial of a keeper called Billy Duff, a savage picturesque keeper with a long black beard who was kept prisoner all night in the tent, having attempted to pass the sentries without the parole for the 3rd time. He had his punishment of a breakfast of bread & water & was not let to carry the Standard at the Guard mounting, but after the reprimand he was released. This playing at soldiers is throughly enjoyed by officers & men.

The Queen wished to see some grouse shooting & she & I followed the Prince the whole afternoon for four hours. He shot badly I should think, but killed 6 brace. Ld Glenlyon & I again had a sort of dispute in few words for he always wants to keep the Queen out as long as possible & I to get her home. She, out of civility, will do any thing proposed & only throws out hints that she wants to be back before dark, & avoid steep places. He understands no hints & I have got a reputation for great fuss & fidgets. All this goes on whenever the Prince is not there. We did get back by 1/4 before 7 which now is nearly dark. The evening was very sleepy.

Tuesday, Sept 24 The Master of Strathallen who is now on guard has a calotype machine which he has set up just above the tents. He has made some very good views of the house & of the people grouped around the tent; Ld Charles leaning against a gun is a very good one. Car & I with the same gun for a background succeeded very well, all but our faces, for we made grimaces in the sun & laughed besides, when the spectators peeped at us. Ld Charles has his two little trout rods & the Prince took a fishing lesson. The Queen drew & we got a group of men, horse, & dogs arranged for her. All the people living with the Glenlyons had come & the afternoon was spent in dawdling about in complete idleness. Ld Glenlyon's temper cannot stand these reverses. I am his *bête noire* & somehow he thinks me a complete spoil sport & the incarnation of fuss, & the Queen is amused beyond anything & she & the Prince laughed the whole evening at various little anecdotes Car has to tell of his complaints against me. Ly Glenlyon is quite delightful & I am very glad to see so much of her.

Wednesday, Sept 25 I drew a bit of the Glen & hurried home to luncheon & found Car in a great taking anticipating a crash with the Glenlyons, for the orders he gave & the orders the Prince gave were directly contrary to each other. The Glenlyons meant to go to Forest Lodge with all their party, & the Prince to go alone with the Queen. Old Bowater & Car were in a great fright & I went to the Queen; it was set straight in a moment & we were all to go—but I promised to keep away the whole party from the Queen if she wished for privacy. Ld G is so tyrannical that he will let no one make plans but himself, & the Queen & Prince are not allowed a view in the matter so they remain on the defensive saying they cannot be out beyond a certain hour, & he arranges all the rest. Now there were two stags which had been brought to bay before daybreak & were lying quite exhausted in the river—waiting to be shot by the Prince & at ½ past 4 the deer in Ben-y-Gloe were to be driven down. We left the carriage near the bridge in the Glen Tilt & the Queen & Prince went on to the first poor stag. Meanwhile the gentlemen who had gone on before rushed down to say we shd be too late for the drive & the whole party went on to the other stag. The poor stag was lying quite still in the water too tired to move. About 80 yards off he was shot & we hurried on; the carriage was the other side & the Queen forded the river to get to it on her pony, Ld Glenlyon leading it & Lord Charles helping & Ld Glenlyon scolding all the way. Ld G insisted on our crossing the ford which we did, the two ponies fetching & carrying the women while the men in kilts rushed into the water & the others scrambled for the dear ponies & dogs, & all rushed helter skelter thro' the water and along the road. The scramble through the ford would have been such a lovely Landseer subject. Poor Ld G who spares himself no trouble waded over both for me & Car & scolded us both all the way across. Everybody who could see or get on a pony was soon out of sight & only Car, me, Ly G & her brother remained & walked quietly along the road. We sat behind stones & in due time everybody came back & told us this drive too had failed. This must have bored Ld Glenlyon dreadfully for he is so anxious that the Prince shd succeed in shooting lots of deer & on this business he had been twice to the Forest Lodge from Blair & back in the course of the morning, making his preparations.

Thursday, Sept 26th Ld Breadalbane sent C Landseer* to sketch for the

* Charles Landseer R.A., elder brother of Sir Edwin, had been a pupil of B. R. Haydon. In 1851 Keeper of the Royal Academy to which he gave £10,000 for the foundation of Landseer scholarships. He had accompanied Lord Stuart de Rothesay on his mission to Brazil in 1825 and there recorded views of the country in watercolour and pencil. (See also p. 170)

Government House, Calcutta, south front; their private apartments were in the left wing

Sketch by Charlotte Canning of her private drawing-room

Government House, Barrackpore, showing Lady Canning's rooms on the extreme left; on the right the banyan tree

Banyan tree, Barrackpore, August 1859, water-colour by Charlotte Canning

Queen. He is to sketch the house & a number of figures in front of it; he is not at all pleased with this subject & fidgetted about a great while doing nothing. About an hour after he came a note arrived from Leitch* who was at the same inn, the Bridge of Tilt, & had waited there 24 hours after announcing his arrival by a card which I never got. Caroline & I took Leitch all about the place to shew him subjects to draw, we walked for 2 hours as fast as we could & came home tired to death. Leitch is delighted with his orders & says he will make a great number of pretty drawings from the subjects I showed him.

The Prince went out deer *stalking* at 7 in the morning & killed 3 stags & was home by 12. The Queen went out very early alone with the Princess, the nursery maid, Footman & Groom. She had a very small shabby pony taken out privately & got her ride upon him quite by stealth for fear of affronting Ld Glenlyon by not riding his pony which frightens her very much, tho' she owns it is without much reason, but he has a wish to trot down the hills which she very much objects to.

Friday, Sept 27th The Glenlyons have had their kitchen & stable burnt down. The sentry found it out & gave the alarm & they all got out of bed & spent the night on the lawn with all their goods. I have heard no particulars yet. The poneys & horses were all saved but a poor dog was forgotten— & burnt.

As soon as the letters could be finished Car & I ran up to Old Blair to condole with Ly Glenlyon & hear all about the fire. Their house had a very narrow escape for the stables, Captn Macduff's office, & the kitchen, were completely gutted. Every scrap of furniture was brought out upon the grass & only the kitchen things & every thing in the office was burnt. The Factor, Capt Macduff, has lost a great deal; all his family papers in an old cabinet he valued very much, indeed everything he & his son-in-law had was packed up & stowed away in this place when the Glenlyons took possession of the house.

The sentry at the door here saw the fire and called out another sentry. Mr Oswald [of Dunnikier] heard the alarm given & ran up as hard as he could & pulled Ld Glenlyon out of bed & got them all up & out of the house; in a few minutes more they might have been burnt.

* W. L. Leitch, watercolourist, had been introduced by Lady Canning to the Queen; his success as a teacher gained him the post of drawing-master to the Royal family for many years.

There was not a ladder to be found & only one little wooden staircase. The guard behaved perfectly well & their discipline told on this occasion for no one moved without orders & they did their work perfectly quietly & well. Ly Glenlyon, the little boy & Charlotte Murray sat out on the grass the whole night in what clothes they had collected & the adventures they had to tell us were very funny to hear when the alarm was over.

The Old Blair party dined & in the evening we had all the Guard & all the best dancers to dance reels in the Hall. There were some excellent performers. James Murray danced the sword dance very well notwithstanding having driven the deer from the top of Ben-y-Gloe in the morning & had a tumble head over heels in running down; all the officers came in the evening & joined in the reels.

Saturday, Sept 28th Ld Aberdeen heard of the arrival of an otter & we all went to the banks of the Garry to see him hunted, Ld Aberdeen himself looking rather disgusted with the performance & assuring us he had never had to do with a bagged otter before. The poor otter was very stiff after living four days in a box & when he was let out of it refused to go into the water & took to the road. He was caught & pulled away from the hounds & carried to the stream & hunted in & out of the holes but he was hardly able to swim. The poor beast crawled out at last upon the stones & was killed in a moment. It excited ones pity very much. After he was dead the keeper held him up on the point of his lance & the dogs followed, jumping up exactly like Landseer's picture. There was plenty to draw in every style, all our friends in their kilts wading abt, Isidore wading across for a good sight, & the Queen on her poney with an umbrella & mackintosh. The wind changed & put a stop to an intended drive of deer. The Prince tried to get a shot near & the Queen went with him part of the way. No pony was provided for me which distressed her very much & she offered me to take hers by turns, which of course I wd not accept so I got on the Prince's, having it led & sitting sideways. We could see nothing & we went no further & the Queen returned home. The sun came out & tempted her out again but this time she was determined to have nobody but me with her & to order a Groom to follow with a real carpenter pony, all the time dreading that Ld Glenlyon wd find her out. At last the Grey came, for the others could not be caught & at the same instant Ld G appeared with the Prince & the little plot was not discovered. The Grey is a very good pony but somehow he frightens the Queen & with Ld G to lead him she gets into such a state that she constantly has to get off to conceal her terror.

Sunday, Sept 29th I was very curious to know what wd be done abt the service. The Queen did *not* go to the Kirk & Mr Walker was not sent for, or the promised Chaplain. Ld Aberdeen volunteered to read prayers & that even was not accepted. The Queen sent word that she dined alone with the Prince. Ld Liverpool said he had a sort of leave to ask all the Old Blair to dine, considering the state of their kitchen, but he thought it was not wished & persuaded me to think we ought not to send to them. With an effort & after consulting Car I thought it best to go straight to the Queen & she at once said they *shd* be asked. I thought it wd be very inhospitable *not* to do so but after all Ld L said I thought it was not allowed. The P does not know what hospitality is & I was never more glad than to get permission to do this cheap civility. We thought the single men wd fare well enough with the officers in the dairy & we asked the 4 Glenlyons & the Drummonds. To-morrow if we dine alone the packing up wd be sufficient reason for not having company. Car & I went in the evening to the poor little Episcopal Chapel.* It has bare earth between the seats & only a board to stand & kneel upon & a pathway paved. The galleries crowd it up & it might hold a number of people but only 12 were there counting the clergyman. The sermon was just after the Collect & a Psalm was sung by the 4 men who are usually the whole congregation. The service was very well done & I am glad to hear that poor Mr Walker is not the bad man he is represented to be. It was too bad of Ld G to prevent the Prince from sending to him. The dinner went off very well & we had a pleasant evening.

Monday, Sept 30th The Prince went out to shoot very early & the Queen sent for me to go with her to try & meet him on his return. We missed him in the wood but were close to some shots that were fired at a number of Roe deer— & he missed them.

The Prince, to make the best of his last day, was out again after luncheon at 1 o'clock & later I followed with the Queen & Ld Glenlyon & Ld Charles. I was told of an immense herd & saw at a distance a hill

* This small church can be seen from the road, banked against the hill and facing the kirk.

that looked as if covered with brown fern, but the brown hill side seemed to move, & on the herd came for nearly two miles. The hill side was alive with them & we could hear their bellowing & the sound of their feet, with a glass we could see them beautifully. From our bird's eye view we could see both Prince & deer at once when they could not see each other & it was interesting beyond anything to watch their stalking—how near he got sometimes without knowing it. Some stags got into the wood & the whole herd was quite low down when they took a panic & turned, flying in columns like strong streams which took a great while to *défiler*. The Prince ran up to get 5 shots but too far to take effect. There were more than 2000 deer. The herd rushed by the drivers but nothing would turn them then. The Prince killed a fine hart in the wood just before dark.

The Queen is so sorry to go away from here; she really has been very happy & the visit has answered very well. The Glenlyons & Drummonds dined. The wreaths I made were always so much admired that I determined to send them each one which they were very grateful for. The Queen gave Ly G a very good bracelet of blue enamel & diamonds & the print of the children, & Albert gave us a little souvenir of himself, the teeth of a stag set like acorns with green enamel leaves.* The great present to Ld G I believe is to be a piece of plate by Cotterel,† & 200£ to be given to poor Capt Macduff in consequence of the fire.

Tuesday, Oct 1st The morning is fine & still & at 9 o'clock we set off.

* A parure composed of stag's teeth and enamel leaves is in the Transvaal room.

† The first Cotterel of several generations of silversmiths (extending to 1777) gained his freedom at Goldsmith's Hall in 1596.

13

Rosenau and Gotha

It struck Georgy Liddell who came into waiting at Windsor as 'very odd', that while 'everything else changes, life here never does, and it is always exactly the same from day to day and year to year'.[1] But Charlotte had plenty to occupy her for within two days of the Queen's return Louis Philippe came to be invested with the Garter and admired the great dinners exceedingly (tactfully held in St George's Hall so as not to bring the Waterloo Gallery too much into prominence), and was 'enough of a *maître d'hotel*' to be aware how well they were served. Driving one morning to Twickenham in the char-à-bancs he had given the Queen in 1843, he revisited the house of his two years' exile, and then proceeded to Claremont (where, again in exile, his last two years were to be spent); here an excellent repast despatched from Windsor Castle earlier in the day awaited him. The Lincolns had been present one evening, 'she looking as handsome as ever & as if nothing had happened' for there had recently been a reconciliation effected by friends which had set Lord Lincoln in a good humour, and she was evidently taking pains to do well. 'She does regular governess work', Char added, '& is up at 8 to give the children their breakfast every day.'*

At the end of the same month Charlotte improvised for the Mistress of the Robes at the Opening of the Royal Exchange. 'You must read all about our Pomp of yesterday,' she wrote, '& pray remember that *I* acted the Duchess of Buccleuch & sat with the Queen in the gold coach drawn by the 8 cream coloured horses. The Procession must have been beautiful.' The crowds lining the

* Their only daughter also came under the influence of opium.

streets ('beyond anything I ever saw') added their cheers all the way from Buckingham Palace when through the thick fog they could distinguish the Queen, resplendent in silver brocade and point lace, diamonds sparkling on satin bows, diamond tiara and coronet on her head, the Garter ribbon looped with diamonds, and on her left arm the Garter of purple velvet.[2] At Temple Bar where the sun broke through, the Lord Mayor met the Queen and headed the procession of aldermen 'who stuck on their horses very creditably', and Char was thankful to learn that they were trained artillery horses, and that each alderman had four men to watch him. On dismounting they were obliged to squat down on the pavement to remove their over-tight jackboots, worn to protect them from mud, but this must have escaped Royal observation for when writing to her Uncle Leopold the Queen commented: 'All the proceedings *at* the Royal Exchange were splendid and royal in the extreme.'[3] The gold plate and gold knives and forks at the great luncheon in Lloyds committee room furnished Char's letters with plenty of material. On the whole she found the new building very handsome but was inclined to disparage the architecture for not being 'of a pure taste but rather like something French or German'.

In March of the following year, 1845, the Queen had received Lady Stuart who wrote an account of her 'Palace visit' to her own mother, at which the subject of the turquoises bought in 1843 was uppermost.

The Queen was *very* kind & gracious, & agreeable, she sent for her Turquoises, to bewail their turning green, which we laid to the change of the Coiffeur's Pomade, & did not suggest the superstition of 'Inconstancy', in the *Bien Aimé* of which Turquoises are supposed to be *tell tales*, and evidently she had no *arrière pensée*, when she said 'I wish I could find a remedy, for it makes the Prince *so unhappy*'! She owned however they were very cheap & could not be *première qualité*. The Prince of Wales had a little cold & was kept upstairs, & she has promised me his Print, as it came out in thanking her for the one I have of the Princess Royal, that she had meant to give me the other—she is the prettiest of the two girls, I did not see the Baby.

Lord Stuart whose health was steadily declining remained quietly at Highcliffe. Charlotte was occupied with her Court duties; in June she attended a fancy dress ball of the mid-eighteenth-century period at Buckingham Palace, where she danced in a minuet opposite Lord Douglas, whom it will be remembered was renowned for his dancing. The next month the Cannings gave a dinner on the marriage of Canning's niece, Lady Elizabeth de Burgh to Viscount Lascelles, and on August 9th the Queen prorogued Parliament, and the afternoon saw her departure for Germany. This was her first visit and was to include a journey up the Rhine in the *Fairy*, her new river steamer, and to culminate in a great gathering of the family at Coburg and Gotha, both places she eagerly desired to see. With her husband at her side to point out the landmarks of his youth, this journey would be one of particular sentiment, for Rosenau, where he had been born, 'the beau ideal of a summer residence, a cottage orné',[4] four miles from Coburg in idyllic countryside, would complete the pilgrimage.

But despite her enthusiasm the visit turned out to be in the nature of a disaster. It was no secret that the behaviour of the Prussian Royal Family and Court in refusing to give what she considered proper precedence to her husband, profoundly irritated the Queen. Furthermore, the custom of herding several hundred deer into an enclosure to be shot profoundly shocked public opinion at home, and that the Sovereign should have been present at the slaughter was a further aggravation.

Charlotte's journal is incomplete, probably by mischance rather than design; a gap occurs as the English Royal party was about to leave Prussia at the conclusion of the Rhine journey, and the journal takes up the account again six days later. The second interruption comes at the end of the Gotha visit; the account of the short stay at Château d'Eu on the return journey is likewise missing.

Saturday, Aug 9 1845 I was ordered to be in readiness to go with the Queen to Woolwich at 4 o'clock, an hour after her return from the H of Lords, & Lady Gainsborough [Lady of the Bedchamber] arrived at the Palace very soon after me—her morning had not been agreeably spent, for by mistake no notice came to her of the hour at which she was to go to H of Lords with the Queen. She understood it as an order & for an hour, *made* a train & dressed & came to the Palace where she was neither wanted or expected— & had only the small consolation of the promise of a scolding to the originator of the blunder if he could be traced.

The Queen & Prince went in their travelling chariot to Woolwich which shows that some new carriage must be prepared for the Foreign journey, for I much doubt her being content with seeing the country from one of the old lumbering coaches. On Board the yacht we found Ld Aberdeen, Ld Liverpool & Sir James Clark. The rest of the suite (only Col Wylde [Equerry to Prince Albert] & Mr Anson) followed in the *Black Eagle*. The yacht is changed in many ways since last year. All the inside wood work painted like a sort of satin wood, a very pale oak, & the deck covered with an oil skin painted like oak planking and nailed tight down—a most un-ship-like fashion of [Lord of the Admiralty] Sir G Cockburn's of which he is very proud. The best change is the widening of the bridges & galleries between the Paddle boxes; there is now a broad platform on each side with a great leather sofa and it is a great comfort to have a solid seat. Ventilation is given to our cabins & 6 inches taken away from one side of each row; I am told the apparatus only carries out the old air & the new is expected to find its way in from under the door & I cannot say I feel much the better for it.

A new & permanent Commander has been appointed. He is full of ingenious devices for the Queen's comfort & besides that the greatest difference is to be seen in the order & management of the vessel. Now everything is done man of war fashion: before it was just like a common passage steamer. Now there are marines & in short it is a new order of things, & Ld Adolphus approves much of the change.

We anchored about ½ past 6 near Canvey island below Gravesend, not far from our old crab-fishing haunts. It was blowing extremely hard & of course we were promised fine weather, but the glass was very low.

Sunday, Aug 10 We weighed anchor at ½ past 3 with a fair wind blowing almost a gale. I spent my morning alone for many staid in bed for fear of being sick & Ly Gainsborough wished to rest between two days of such hard work. The Queen & the Prince appeared as we got near Flushing, both very proud to boast of not being sick. She is in high spirits, delighted with the thoughts of this tour; she walked up & down all the afternoon talking over all the London gossip of this year, above all the marriages, past and future, & certainly her Maids of Honor, & my relations, have furnished plenty of topics in that line. At Antwerp we anchored opposite the Cathedral.

Monday, Aug 11 We landed at ½ past 6 in quite a heavy sea with an awning over the Barge to keep off the rain.* The Belgian carriage took us to the station, & the King's great carriage, which has a dressing room and all sorts of contrivances, was ready to take us to Aix la Chapelle. At Malines the Belgian King & Queen got into the carriage & went on in it as far as Vervier. At the Aix station we found the King of Prussia & his brother [Prince William] & a coach full of Princes.† We had to undergo a very long luncheon at the Burgomaster's, a chorus of amateur niggers performed most beautifully all the time, and afterwards went on to the Cathedral. I had forgotten how beautiful some of the treasures are—Charlemagne's head & arm and other bits in gold cases—the great relics are only shown with so much pomp & ceremony that it was thought unnecessary for the Queen to see them.

This time we were in the Prussian Royal carriage which is far less convenient than the Belgian one, & by this time I was so tired that it was painful to be in company where one might not go to sleep. The train was very slow & the delays were long & frequent & it was just sunset when we reached Cologne. We were once more decanted with carriages to go thro' the town to the Brühl railroad. Private individuals had decorated with flags, flowers, oak leaves, asparagus tops or any convenient vegetable—some long garlands of Weymouth pine made up like a sort of fur with a dahlia here & there had a very good effect, & quite new to me.

Again we went on by railroad for about twenty minutes, and when it was quite dark we reached Brühl—the 50 yards from the station to the Château were performed in carriages. The Queen [Elizabeth of Prussia] & the whole court were at the bottom of the staircase, and they took the Queen up to her rooms at once. Then began our troubles

* Which did not prevent the Queen from being 'amazingly danced about'[5] before reaching the landing stage.

† The ticklish matter of precedence lay ahead.

—of course one was tired enough to be ready to cry, & badly contrasted with all the smart people dressed for dinner in all magnificence, & there was dinner all ready but not a scrap of luggage arrived! There rose a hue and cry for a huge travelling basket of the Queen's, in which lives, I believe, combs, brushes, shoes, stockings, books, sugar plums, writing paper &c. I never will carry it up & down stairs & so I never know how to find it. I described the servant in whose care I had left it (it had once before in the morning at Aix occasioned as much fuss) & I sent 10 people after it & waited an hour in troubling everyone, till a sensible man suggested that something had been put in the Queen's room, & that might be it— & sure enough there it was, and all the contents in order.

Then began out of doors the *concert monstre* [tatoo]—the bands of 40 regiments—about 500 performers to more than 200 drums. I never heard such grand music in my life. 'God save the King' was magnificent; & a most beautiful march by Mendelssohn I shall never forget. After this the luggage arrived & by 10 o'clock Lady Gainsborough & I were ready to appear. The Queen had begged to be excused from going into dinner, but somehow we found her there when we went down, & a round table was added on to the King's table for us. I was almost blind & deaf with fatigue, & not enough practice in German even to guess at the subjects of conversation—happily the dinner or supper came to an unexpected end, & the Queen went to bed & we were released.

This Palace is very rococco—rather handsome. Ceilings like fans & great square rooms 2 storey high, & a very fine staircase—it is rarely used, & therefore very scantily furnished. Ly G & I have each but one room, with a screen to hide everything unsightly—the King & Q were so civil in apologies for our bad lodging that one has no right to find fault, & we have quite as good rooms as everyone else. There is a great muster of Prussian Royalty. The Prince of Prussia & his wife* whom I think rather pretty, but most affected; Prince Frederick (son to the Queen of Hanover†) & a 3/4 witted son [Prince Alexander]. The Duchess of [Anhalt-] Dessau his sister, & a daughter [Princess Agnes]—an uncle, (also Pce Frederick I think) & the sailor Austrian Arch Duke [Frederick].

* Princess Augusta; later to become the parents-in-law of the Princess Royal.

† Her third husband, Duke Ernest of Cumberland, had become King of Hanover at the death of his brother, William IV of England.

Tuesday, Aug 12 The household breakfast was at 9—quite English fashion—good tea & bread & butter & rolls. We had it in a room lined with Dutch tiles of large blue & white patterns unlike anything I ever saw. The project for the morning was to see Bonn & to be present at the uncovering of Beethoven's statue—in honor of which a festival of music had been going on there for days. The railroad took us there at a more rapid pace than our previous journey. After a good deal of pomp & ceremony & signing of papers the Queen walked up on the pedestal & the Royalty went out upon a Balcony trimmed up with velvet. Then some chords were pulled, & down came the covering, & the statue was seen—but lo! he was turning his back to us. It had the most absurd effect of rudeness on his part, and would have been a damper to one's enthusiasm if one had felt like the German admirers around us. The Prince showed all his old haunts to the Queen; every room in the house he inhabited, & had no end of stories to tell. We returned to a four o'clock dinner at Brühl.

The evening proved very rainy & ill fitted for the illumination of the river. At 8 we were to set out, and still it poured. We dressed warmly in morning gowns, went to the railroad, & to Cologne, & then to a steamer moored to the gap in the middle of the bridge of boats. There were so many preparations against the rain, of awnings & velvet curtains, that it was hardly possible to see anything from the stern of the vessel, but below, the cabin was decorated with plants & brilliantly lighted, & tables covered with eatables. Eight young ladies with blue gowns & white dahlias handed about tea & coffee & a sort of pickle. I thought they were orange flowers, or bonbons, & that it was ungracious always to refuse, so I took a pinch of something & to my horror found I had got little fish.

When we were 1st on board the steamer the illuminations were only a few candles or pots of fire in the windows, & we went two or three miles up the river till we were quite outside the town—then we turned, & as we floated down the guns fired & rockets went up, & all the towers were lighted up with red & blue lights & Roman Candles. At last we got to the Cathedral which looked red hot with red lights burning within the tracery; it was quite beautiful—but unfortunately torrents of rain began then to come down. The Queen, & those who did not like to get wet, remained behind the awning & failed to see much, & those who wished to see were thoroughly soaked. Ld Aberdeen's usual remark that all pleasures lasted too long was very true this time. This I ought to say was the Queen's first sight of the Rhine—she is quite German enough to look upon it as an epoch in her life.

Wednesday, Aug 13 Again we had to go to Bonn, this time it was for a grand Beethoven Concert. The music was fine but rather tiresome. A great cantata made for the occasion by Liszt was sung over again for the benefit of the Royal party. The Afternoon expedition was to see Cologne Cathedral. It has got on very much lately & certainly will be the finest Church in the world if the plan is carried out. I think it must even surpass St Peter's, but it is very far from completion.

The Royal family dined in private counting in all to 20—the King and Queen of the Belgians had arrived while we were at Cologne & in the course of the day Solms', Duke of Köten, Württembergs &c. had arrived. At 9 o'clock crowds of people poured in for a concert [conducted by Meyerbeer]—Liszt, Spohr, a very good singer called Jenny Lind, Garcia, & a woman with a beautiful touching voice & a sort of St Vitus's dance. The Queen was tired & went away at the end of the first act.

Thursday, Aug 14 A very rainy morning. Lady G & I had to be up very early to send off our maids & baggage—who travelled with post horses. Again the railroad took us to Bonn & we went on board the steamer the *König* & not the *Fairy*—why I know not. She arrived on Tuesday at Cologne. The plan of a donkey party up the Drachenfels was given up & also a drive to Godesberg, but the weather cleared up as soon as we got under weigh & the scenery was seen to great advantage. The Queen was quite delighted & insisted on sitting all day at the Bow of the vessel. I was ordered to draw all day long & there was no use in making a fuss about it, & 20 or 30 bad little scratches were produced.

The luncheon was on deck at the least interesting part & then we hastened back to Bonn to see Andernach & all that pretty bit—unfortunately near Ehrenbreitstein the rain came down again, but not enough to drive us back to the awning; just as we came abreast of it the salute began, every bit of the rampart was manned & a *feu de joie* fired with musketry & guns—all the forts & Coblentz did the same & the effect was magnificent, more than 1000 *coups* were fired they said, & such a salute never was given before. All Coblentz was along the banks

& the reception was a thing to remember always. They steamed on again & very soon we got to Stolzenfels.

Here the weather showed no improvement and the Queen was kept indoors at the castle, three miles beyond Coblenz, while Char was busy with her pencil and sketch-book. Prince Metternich was among the guests and the Queen found him 'much older . . . and laying down the law very much'.[6] To Char he seemed very old and deaf, 'his wife as uncivil as ever & dreadfully out of shape & strange looking'. On the 16th having bidden goodbye to the King and Queen of Prussia the Queen and Prince sailed in the *Fairy* to Mayence where they put up at the hotel d'Europe, and the next morning accompanied by Charlotte were in their places for Divine Service at the English Church. Continuing by carriage, Wurzburg was the next night's halt, but six o'clock saw them again on the road, Queen Victoria and the Prince in their own chaise, leading; the Ladies and Gentlemen following in another carriage. At the Coburg frontier the King and Queen of the Belgians joined them as well as the reigning Duke Ernest II of Saxe-Coburg, the Prince's brother, and at the Coburg Palace the Duchess of Kent welcomed her daughter. After a short interval the Queen and Prince Albert drove to Rosenau where they slept in the room in which the Prince had been born, leading the Queen to exclaim the next morning on waking: 'It is like a beautiful dream'.[7] While the Prince was oppressed by the 'mass of Royal personages who stream in from all sides',[8] whom Char likened to 'the whole Almanach de Gotha alive', Lord Aberdeen, according to the Queen, was 'pleased "beyond everything" with our dear little country and . . . thinks the people good and comfortable'.[9] [The journal is resumed on the second day at Coburg.]

Thursday, Aug 21 In the evening we went into Coburgh for the Queen to hold a sort of Drawing Room to which all the chief people of the state came and deputations of all sorts. The women were as nicely dressed as one could see anywhere & went through their presentations with quieter, better, manners than one sees at a London Drawing Room. The rooms are very handsome but not high enough, there are no good looking glasses, all in these rooms are made of small panes joined together like a window without any woodwork.

Friday, Aug 22 There was a great annual fête [Feast of St. Gregory] of all the schools who go in procession to a field & play about and dance. We dined in booths in the field & the children stuffed themselves with broiled sausages shut up in hot rolls. That same evening after the usual great dinner we hurried back to Coburgh for a ball. I heard great approbation expressed at the Queen's hearty dancing, & I suppose she enjoyed it exceedingly as she allows herself to gallop, valse, & polk with her cousins, she went on incessantly till the ball ended. Lady Pollington & the desperate valsers are all wrong not to keep their partners straight opposite to them & at a respectable distance. Here they go twice as fast and never look over each other's shoulders as she & Dunkellin do.

Saturday, Aug 23 We went into Coburg early and walked in the public garden and went about the Palace with the Queen paying visits. In the Gd Duke of Baden's room I saw one of the works of the Java Prince Ali who lives at Coburgh like a tame monkey about the house.* Ld Aberdeen was so taken aback the first day to see this black in his Turkish dress instead of handing us coffee, quietly take some to drink himself. When others are not in uniform he sheds his turban & gold & silver & becomes a regular German Dandy with most prussian manners. He has studied painting with great care & his picture of the Duke & Dss of Coburgh with their real black servant & heaps of dead game is a good imitation of Landseer.

The Prince showed us a sort of museum made by himself & his brother as children in some of the garrets in the roof of the Palace. They are rich in autographs & have a great many of Luther's letters. The Queen's next visit was to Princess Hohenlohe & they bethought themselves to have a luncheon of the hot sausages out of the street [*Bratwürste*, Coburg's national dish]. Ly G & I left in an outer room & half dead with fatigue were delighted to get a sort of beggar's share of this meal which was really very good. I went on with the Queen to a

* Born in 1814 at Samarang, Java, 'Prince Ali' (a deformation of his name 'Prince Saleh') studied in Europe to be a painter, became a friend of Duke Ernest II, and lived at Coburg.[10] In the account Queen Victoria gives of the visit, she too refers to him phonetically as 'Prince Sale'.[11]

very German little *château* belonging to the Dukes of Württemberg.*

I cannot describe the sleepiness I underwent in the evening. After the great 5 o'clock dinner at Rosenau & the drive back to Coburgh we sat thro' a German Tragedy—four acts—[Schiller's] *The Bride of Messina*—to me who understood only unconnected words it was dreadfully dull & long.

Sunday, Aug 24 The sermon reminded me rather of the tragedy, but at the early hour of 10½ I was fresh and very much interested to know how the Lutheran service was done. The church [Moritz Kirche] was crowded, women below & men in the galleries. The altar was away from the wall & had candles & a crucifix. First the Clergyman chanted a few sentences, then a hymn was sung, then a very few more sentences, then a hymn, then he came to a little reading desk & read a few verses of the new testament, then a verse of a hymn, then he went up into a pulpit and declaimed with gesticulations a few minutes which someone said was a prayer. Then a hymn again, then a sermon† and a short prayer ending with the Lord's Prayer, then a long hymn & the Minister went to the back of the altar & chanted & blessed the people, making the Sign of the Cross behind the crucifix, then a hymn was sung during which people began to go away. All our party were struck with the same thing, that there seemed to be no praying. No one kneels or joins in the prayer which usually is written and lasts 2 or 3 minutes, & the hymns are supposed to do for Prayers. They are quite magnificent—the whole congregation join & sing in perfect tune. I hear the words are very fine.

The Queen gave Lady G & I the choice of driving or not. We were too happy to get a quiet afternoon. I ought to tell you more of the people I have been with but I have not got on much with many of them. Our drives are usually Ly G & I & Lds L & A in one carriage; sometimes I am with the Queen & Prince & Duchess [of Kent] & at dinner I usually am placed by a very nice little Prince of Baden, or by the Württembergs who are not particularly agreeable. One of them [Duke Alexander], the widower of Pss Marie [d'Orléans] is exactly like the pictures of John Kemble. The other [Duke Ernest] is less tragic either in

* The *Illustrated London News* on the other hand found it to be a 'Twickenham-villa looking edifice'.

† Preached by Genzler, who had officiated at the marriage of Queen Victoria's parents at Coburg in 1818, and had christened Prince Albert in 1819.

appearance or manner but certainly dull. All the suites of these are dull & commonplace beyond description.

Monday, Aug 25 I had a holiday & was let to go & draw all day by myself till the 5 o'clock dinner.* We had to sit thro' a comedy [*Zopf und Schwert*] that evening in the same Coburgh Theatre—I wish how very much I had worked at German for a little longer for I can *hear* every word they say so distinctly that without the least trouble I could even in the opera follow it in the book, but unhappily I know hardly any of their meaning. The Comedy baffled me completely & by the 5th act I was dreadfully sleepy.

Tuesday, Aug 26 We were awakened by a serenade for the Prince's Birthday, a mixture of Hymns and Valses, a hymn with a valse accompaniment, the effect was indecorous certainly but rather pretty. After breakfast the Queen went to a lawn before the house to see a dance of villagers all dressed with flowers and the odd high black hats, green petticoats & black borders, & the men in jackets & black tights. They Polka'd very well & valsed & did a wonderful sort of *sauteuse* turning round in 2 steps. All the carriages and horses were gone to Gotha & again this afternoon we were left to amuse ourselves.

After dinner the room was cleared out for a concert and we heard a great deal of the Prince's & his brother's music & perhaps you will think me a courtier when I say the Prince's was very pretty. The Queen was in despair at leaving Rosenau which she was quite delighted with—they feel Coburg more their own country than Gotha which was inherited only in '26 when the family of the Dukes of Gotha became extinct in the male line. I had the whole complicated story of it explained to me by the Prince but I do not undertake to repeat it.

Wednesday, Aug 27 We left Rosenau soon after 8 o'clock. The Queen travelled with the Prince & the Duke & Duchess [of Coburg] in a light open carriage which soon left our heavy coach far behind & as Ld Liverpool has abandoned our carriage for ever for the sake of more space with Sir James Clark, Col Wylde & Mr Anson, we revelled in the space he left.

We very soon left the frontier of Coburgh & passed thro' a number

* Char made two watercolours and one pencil drawing of Rosenau (Windsor Castle).

of towns of the Saalfeld Duchy which were ceeded by Coburgh when they inherited Gotha. All these ci-devant Coburgh towns received the Queen with great pomp and we generally caught her up whilst the Burgomasters made their long orations. We stopped to dine at Meiningen at 2. The palace is like an immense Irish barracks and all the best rooms are at the top, 3 storey high. The Duke [brother of Queen Adelaide] & Duchess of Meiningen presented all their people to the Queen & then came a dinner which lasted at least two hours giving time to each person to eat & digest every dish before the next arrived. It was provoking that this long delay made us arrive at the beautiful country only just before sunset. The last stage was from Schmalkaden, a place Ld Aberdeen told us he had been in with the Allies just after Leipzig, & had seen the road strewn with wounded & dying.*

The woods & hills were beautiful but it so soon got dark that we saw very little till we got to Reinhardsbrunn—once a convent but rebuilt in an odd Gothic style by the late Duke. It is very well furnished & very comfortable & well kept but must be only a summer place. A procession of miners came by torchlight to serenade, they wear an old fashioned dress with little leather aprons behind to slide down, *seated*, into the mines. We were all dreadfully tired & glad to go to bed immediately after tea.

Thursday, Aug 28 We had a quiet morning & were able to draw & walk about.† It is a very pretty place and the grounds are nicely kept & there are gay beds very full of gaudy & common flowers. The old step grandmother‡ arrived quite early to breakfast with the Queen and to save herself from a first meeting with all the ceremony of the entrée into Gotha. This Entrée was done with great pomp late in the afternoon. The Duke rode in full uniform by the side of the Queen's carriage which also contained the Belgians, and the Duchess went on to be at the Palace door to receive her. There were crowds of people & speeches & garlands & showers of flowers and at last the Queen arrived at her journey's end—the old Duchess's house [Friedrichsthal]. The old grandmother is nearly stone deaf but very much *au fait* of

* The Battle of Leipzig, 1813, at which Napoleon suffered defeat at the hands of the Allies.

† Two large watercolours (Windsor Castle).

‡ The Dowager Duchess of Gotha was the second wife of Prince Albert's maternal grandfather.

everything going on. She doats on her grandchildren, especially on Albert & her delight at having him & the Queen with her is excessive.

They dined alone with her & Ly G & I found our way up to the great Schloss [Friedenstein] where we are quartered. It is an immense place nearly as big as the whole town, the rooms are large & waste, very little furnished & low but some have very fine ceilings. There was an immense dinner in the evening but very soon after all the people dispersed & by 9½ o'clock we were back again in our rooms.

Friday, Aug 29 Soon after breakfast the Queen & Prince & their brother & his wife walked up to the castle & wandered about in it & recommended Ly G & I to come too. They went to look at the Chapel in which 'our late father', as they call him, is buried for the present, & the rooms he lived & died in.

This vast building contains all sorts of collections of curiosities & the Prince showed some of these. Strange to say a suit of clothes of the late Duke is treasured up in a cupboard. The ways in which sentiment unexpectedly breaks out are very amusing & this veneration of the Duke's old clothes seems to come quite naturally from people who praise him from morning till night.* The Prince and the Dss of Kent seemed quite overcome when they went into his rooms & the Chapel—but still they went in public to the rooms & let a crowd of people follow.

The annual feast of the rifle shooters [*Vogelschiessen*, Popinjay shooting] was going on all this week and the Queen went to the shooting house to see it. Here at Gotha the women wear gigantic black bows with loops of broad ribbon hanging behind a yard long, & strange plumes of black feathers on the top of the head; it looks very old fashioned & dignified. As usual our path was strewd with flowers & smelt very bad from rank french marigolds & dahlias crunching under one's feet.

In the evening the Queen held a court & all Gotha was presented.† During dinner we had an alarm of fire, the window curtain of thin muslin was demolished—this at the top of a quantity of over fatigue upset poor Ly Gainsborough who was obliged to go out of the room

* The late Duke Ernest of Saxe-Coburg-Gotha, father of Prince Albert, was disagreeable, extravagant, and licentious.

† Later the same evening the Queen was delighted to see again her old governess, Baroness Lehzen.

in a wretched state, & next morning had to be very much bored with enquiries after her health—the Duke begging to know how she was after her very bad *access* of the night before. *Excess* it sounded like at first, but I found it out to be his English version of *accés* or *attaque de nerfs.*

Saturday, Aug 30 The great *chasse* had long been prepared for that day, & like all other days since we got to Coburgh it turned out to be beautiful. We had a very long drive thro' the woods beyond Reinhardsbrunn and at last came to a road newly cut thro' the trees which led to a sort of shooting cottage, called the Hunter's Rest [Jagersruh] on a lawn high up on the hill at the foot of the highest peak of the range. We had a *déjeuner* there & went afterwards to the appointed place prepared for the *chasse.* Three hundred men besides had been employed beating the woods for ten days to drive the deer to this spot & to enclose them in about 1/4 of a mile of wood walled round with canvas; this was divided into two parts. We walked across part of it to a little temple built of fir & heather; the poor stags were still in the other division of the enclosure & the shooters were stationed in different little turf forts, four or five guns together. Then a signal was given & an army of *chasseurs* instantly threw down the canvas wall between the 2 halves & about 50 stags & hinds rushed in. They were most of them very large & had finer horns than one usually sees in Scotland. Then everybody fired at the poor things who were driven in & out of the wood & up & down the hill till all were killed—it was a piteous sight, much the worse from the bad shooting, for most of the poor beasts were dreadfully wounded long before they were killed. Fifty-five bodies were brought to the side of the path at last—I had guessed that perhaps 6 had been shot & was astonished to see the row of corpses. A great mob of people stood on the hill behind so no doubt the reporters of the *London News* have illustrated & described every particular.

Sunday, Aug 31 I went to Church [St. Augustina] with the Dss of Kent & found the Queen already in the pew. The hymn in the *Huguenots* was sung—the same as 'Our God is a tower of strength',* Lady Gainsborough was still ailing and got a whole holiday & I was wanted

* Luther's hymn '*Ein feste Burg ist unser Gott*' occurs in Act I of Meyerbeer's opera.

for the drive, it was a very long & dusty one & the *bût* was to see two old *châteaux* [Tentershausen, Melsdorff]. I was with the Queen & Prince & Duchess in a low open carriage & had a specimen of the pelting they undergo every drive from showers of garlands & great wet dahlias &c., a poem or a speech at every village.

After dinner for a Sunday evening's amusement there came an extraordinary calculator who multiplied 11 figures by 11 figures in a minute & read off a line of 20 figures on a slate at a glance, remembered them & worked long sums on them without ever looking at the slate again, & proved all his calculations at length. He is a remarkably dull man in other respects.

Monday, Sept 1 After the courier was despatched we got Ld Aberdeen to go with us to see a collection of pictures open in a wing of this enormous palace. The custode yelled in our ears descriptions in German of each picture, shouting the louder the less we understood. The great *Liederfest* was to be held, & before that the Queen had to receive an immense number of Princes, the Gd Duke & Duchess of Weimar, 7 or 8 Saxe-Altenberg, the Princess of Prussia, Prince Charles [of Prussia] & his wife, the Saxe-Meiningens, some Ruddstadts I believe, & I forget how many more. The singing feast was out of doors; two great booths contained the court & the 3000 singers. They were too far apart and one did not hear very well.

The dinner was in the large room with caryatides & very magnificently done & in the evening there was a small ball. The K & Q of the Belgians made their adieux preparatory to their journey to begin at 5 in the morning in hopes of reaching Cologne in 2 days.

Friday, Sept 2 This is our last day at Gotha & the Queen is getting very low at the end of her holidays drawing so near. When Lady G & I went to wait for the Queen in the morning we were found by the old Duchess who took us to her room & said all kinds of amiable things & made us each take away an ivy leaf in remembrance of her. All our pretty speeches were lost upon her for by no screaming cd one make her hear. The Queen succeeds better & her account of the old lady's deafness was that it was less than the Duke of Devonshire's & not much worse than the D of Wellington's. A very fine drawn distinction I think. The good old lady was dreadfully startled by a *gentilesse* of Ld Liverpool's—he sprang forward to pick up Ly Gainsborough's parasol & his heels went up in the air & he came down backwards on his head at her feet, full length on the floor!

The whole party of Princes & relations were met together at Reinhardsbrunn for dinner; I was begged by the Queen to draw which I was obliged against my will to do, & made a bad scribble which like all I have done this journey, she intends to paste into her book. These beautiful days all end with bitter cold evenings & we got back frozen with cold which had to be thawed with my private stock of tea. Since that we have ended the evening at a great ball at the theatre.

Sadly out of spirits at leaving Gotha on September 3rd, the Queen travelled to Frankfort where King Ludwig I of Bavaria, and Metternich ('in unusual force'), were received to dinner. Sailing up the Rhine in the *Fairy* to Coblenz, the train took the party on to Antwerp and from there, embarking in the *Victoria and Albert*, they continued to le Tréport. The landing, effected at low tide, was staged on the beach, Louis Philippe's barge being exchanged for a horse-driven bathing machine which dragged them across the sands and which amused Queen Victoria prodigiously. The visit lasted only until the next day, and back at Osborne the Queen noted in her Journal: 'Dined with our people, & afterwards looked at the beautiful sketches Lady Canning made, during our Tour, which are all so like the places.'[12] The following day Charlotte went home to Grosvenor Square.[13]

14

Tinted Statue of the Queen

From Windsor Castle on November 9th 1845 Queen Victoria wrote to condole on Lord Stuart de Rothesay's death.

My dear Lady Canning,
I must write you a line to express in the Prince's & my name our sincere sympathy on this melancholy occasion. Though your poor Father's state of health for the last year must have prepared you to a certain degree for this event,—still when the *blow* comes it is always unexpected, & always as severe,—even if you had been led to fear it—for some time past.

The end had come slowly at Highcliffe, and to Charlotte who had been with her mother during the last painful week fell the duty of writing to her sister. No detail was omitted for she rightly judged that Louisa would be desirous of knowing every particular. Lord Stuart's death certificate gives the secondary disease 'Apoplexy, three years' as the cause of death; the primary disease was not known. Nevertheless he was regularly dosed with emetics, sent for drives twice a day, blistered with an ointment of castor oil and ammonia, and after a full hour of frightful convulsions the doctor again placed 'the blistering stuff', and bathed his head with cold water. It was too late to bleed him and their only comfort was to join in prayer. By this time Canning had arrived and Charlotte and her mother took it in turn to wash and to change their clothes, but they were so tired from watching that they kept falling asleep. When the end came, peacefully at the last, Charlotte could feel 'that no human power could have done good. I never expected or never hoped for recovery or a much longer life. I think Mama did—but she has borne the blow with perfect patience & very religious strength, & has much comfort in the memory of how very well she did her duty.'

Indeed Lord Stuart de Rothesay had not been a model husband, but his wife had never doubted his affection for her nor his fondness for his daughters. From now, until her husband's appointment took her to India ten years later, Charlotte was her mother's chief support in financial problems and others connected with Carlton House Terrace and Highcliffe Castle.

But Charlotte had a graver heartache than her father's death to contend with. Till now her marriage had been quite outstandingly happy; an account is given of how Canning's friends would 'chaff' him for such devotion to his wife that he could not bear her out of his sight, but at about this time he had become absorbed in a love-affair with a woman whose influence prevailed for many years.[1] In this crisis and throughout the testing years ahead, faced with the desolation of this painful circumstance, Charlotte countered by never discussing it nor appearing outwardly disturbed.[2]

When she was not in waiting she was a good deal at Highcliffe taking in hand the garden, planting trees, putting peonies in a clump of ilex and a herbaceous border along a sheltered walk, seeing to the domestic staff, raising a subscription for the local parson, visiting the village school, and on Easter morning 1846 after packing the jaunting-car full of maids, setting off with Canning in the fly to Christchurch, where finding evergreens used for church decorations she hastened to reassure Aunt Caledon that she must not think 'it was out of Puseyism for certainly no tendency in that direction appears'. Most of the summer she was at Osborne, the move into the Queen's newly built house not yet effected. One of her occupations was to give drawing lessons to the Queen, who on enquiring '"What shall I do now?", "Do you think I should add some green?", "Is that blue enough?", did exactly as she was bid'.[3] In July the rain was incessant. 'I never saw a more complete "Highcliffe" day & the poor dear old Duchess of Gloucester is expected & ought to be crossing in this gale &

torrents of rain. She has never been in the Isle of Wight in her life & looked forward with delight to the expedition.'

Lady Stuart was at Tyttenhanger when she heard from Char that the Queen intended to go to Highcliffe and immediately set out to prepare for the visit. Charlotte had recommended removing the loose covers, putting down some carpets, 'plenty of flowers, a little ornamental china from the organ case, & a *little* tea or luncheon if possible'. Writing at the same time to the housekeeper there was the additional order of 'a few bottles of *Seltzer* & soda water', asking also that the lapis lazuli inkstand should be put out & some of the best table covers. 'The reason I wish this done', she continued, 'is that I think it not unlikely that some day the Queen may be sailing about', then fearing that the news would animate the entire village, added that though there was no harm in being prepared she did not much expect the Queen 'to be sailing about'. Meanwhile Lady Stuart had arrived and enquired for more precise details. 'It will be quite a flying visit', replied Char, '& I cannot the least tell you when, perhaps not for several days. I think it very improbable that any luncheon shd be wanted but if it is, I had meant that it should be sent from here, & that we shd only permit hot potatoes.' Seltzer water was again urged, and tea. She hoped her mother would not propose that Canning should be there, 'his hair wd stand on end at the bare idea'. But 'pray let there be a fine bouquet of flowers in the ugly dark French vase' for it looked particularly well standing close to the piano in the vestibule. The drawing room should be the 'inhabited spot to sit down in (only we shall never stay long enough to sit)'. Finally Charlotte reminded her mother that the *Fairy* moved 'so fast, so noiselessly, so without smoke, that she might easily take you all by surprise', but that she was easily distinguishable by her 'yellow funnel (sandy colour), the sides of the vessel black & a little gilding. The Standard always at the mast head & *no paddle boxes*. She is low & very long & has 3 very small raking masts. You may be sure it will never be the *1st fine day*!—it is never till the *2nd* that that sort of thing is planned. I am afraid this leaves you no peace of mind.' The puzzle of luncheon tormented Lady Stuart and a further note from the Isle of Wight again emphasized the need of Seltzer water. 'If you do give a luncheon remember *cold beef*, that is always in favour. *No mutton*. Chickens, prawns & sand eels. No *onions*. I think a *gâteau napolitain* wd be good as it keeps, but with all this I doubt the necessity of *any* luncheon. Seltzer water is the great necessity under all circumstances. Some hot water & milk in a bed room for washing off dust perhaps may be wanted.' Playing for safety Lady Stuart seems to have stocked up with beef, for in the next letter her daughter lamented 'your *Beef* is a load on my conscience!'* Deluded, perhaps by wishful thinking into believing she had sighted the *Fairy*, Lady Stuart was rebuked by Charlotte whose superior knowledge of navigational winds led her to exclaim: 'How could you possibly think the steamer on its way after such a night of gales—remember it must be *Northerly* or Nth E wind & settled weather which I am sure has not been the case—for the chance of landing up the beach.' Following on the worry of the luncheon was now the worry of the landing. 'The Queen likes the thought of landing on the Beech in a northerly wind, & she says she once went about in flies at Weymouth', but what she was allowed as a girl would hardly be suitable now. 'That I think would never do', though some means of transport from the sands up to the house on the cliff would have to be devised. Of greater concern was the possibility of the Queen being mobbed on the beach. 'That would be a dreadful scrape for she likes everything done so very quietly & as the landing must be *very ungraceful*, I shall feel so guilty if there are some 1000 spectators. Of course it will be known that I told.'

Char's notes arriving in quick succession dwelt on fresh obstacles. The weather was bad ('just the climate for tropical germs'); the arrival of the Duchesse de Nemours (the Queen's cousin) to stay; the Hohenlohes expected, the Abercorns arriving. With such activity afoot Charlotte still found time to send over a

* This letter no doubt made the round of the Aunthood, for here Lady Stuart inserted: 'We had Beef & *gâteau napolitain*, but not much waste in our week's consumption as there are de *beaux restes* still.'

request for the book of Charles Landseer sketches,* and the present-day publisher of the highly-priced volume of these drawings in facsimile might be forgiven a shudder at the recklessness with which she ordered their despatch.

Dearest Mama, Seeing a bad drawing of Charles Landseer's reminded me that I had often wished to borrow the Brazillian book to show. This wd be a convenient opportunity & as the evenings are rather dull I think if it could be lent for a few days it wd be very welcome. My servant would ask for it at the Southampton station if you would send it on Tuesday directed to 'Southampton Terminus. To be left till called for'.

After a fortnight of day-to-day expectancy Lady Stuart was told that drives to show 'the back of the Island will have their turn before Highcliffe, & if that ever takes place at all now I shall be quite surprised'. The summer passed without the expedition being made. However the information that there was a 'hue & cry for a house for the Queen Dow [Adelaide]' raised Lady Stuart's hopes of a tenant for Highcliffe, but no sooner raised than crushed when she learned that it must be close to Osborne, 'this rural retreat', as Char named it to her grandmother. 'If we were much used to state anywhere at Court, I should think this was an imitation of Trianon. Whatever it is, it perfectly enchants the Queen & Prince & you never saw anything so happy as they are, planting their trees with the 5 babes playing around them', and when Lady Lyttelton and Char were called upon to plant a tree each in their own honour, 'I was proud & chose a tall oak & she had a Deodar Cedar'. The 'flitting into the new house' was completed, and the Italianate villa (astonishingly characterised as 'rather on a Londony plan') was commended for its comfort and fine views. Ten days followed at Windsor where the Queen and Prince and the Cannings indulged in a skittle match, and in early October Char was home. By the end of the year she and Canning were in Rome for a five-month visit.

A new Pope, Pius IX, had been elected in the summer and

* See p. 144, note.

Charlotte had several opportunities of seeing him at public ceremonies. At midnight Mass at Santa Maria Maggiore on Christmas Eve, though likening it to a 'theatrical performance, but with that multitude of wax candles in little glass lustres & the beautiful dresses it cd not be otherwise', she thought he did his part so very well & looked dignified, nor had she ever seen a better countenance. Charlotte had two pleasant commissions from the Queen. In the first she was unsuccessful. 'I am in hopes of finding a pug dog with the help of Mme Potemkin [wife of the Russian Minister to the Holy See] who procured Lady Gainsborough's. There is not one to be had in Rome but Bologna is said to be a good place for them.'[4] Her second duty was to pay a call on Gibson at his studio. In 1844 he had visited England and Queen Victoria had commanded from him a statue of herself. Both as a likeness and as a work of art Charlotte had no misgiving in praising it to the Queen.[5]

It is universally allowed that no modern portrait statue has approached it in merit. Mr Gibson has revived upon it the ancient practice of colouring the border of the robe in pale blue & red. I think he has done this very judicially, so as to relieve the cold white of the marble without attracting the eye too much. He has also tinted the sandals & tassels & parts of the tiara with pale yellow, but this appears to me to be less successful & Mr Gibson is very desirous of gilding these parts, or rather of inlaying them with thin plates of gold, as used to be done in some of the ancient statues,—for ordinary gilding does not preserve its colour:—but he does not venture to do this without receiving Your Majesty's sanction both for the work & the additional cost. The statue is quite finished & ready to be sent home & Mr Gibson is most anxious to obtain Your Majesty's permission to exhibit it at the Royal Academy.

To this the Queen replied from Claremont ('this *so* very dear old place') on January 10th 1847:

The account of my Statue has *delighted* the Prince and pray say everything kind & complimentary to Gibson—(who is such a good and amiable Man) about it—from us.

You will be interested & pleased to hear that Winterhalter has been most successful in the *Family Picture*, wh is universally admitted by all those who have seen it, to be one of the finest Modern Pictures painted, both as to composition & colouring, & the likenesses are most striking. It is in the style of a Paul Veronese, & has not at all the appearance of 'a Family Picture' wh is so seldom an agreeable thing. He has likewise painted a beautiful little Picture of our eldest Boy in his Sailor's dress wh is excessively popular . . .

I have made great progress in my Drawing since I saw you, & I am sure you wd be surprised & say as Leitch does: 'I can hardly believe Y[our] M[ajest]y has done these.' He is an excellent Master & I recommend him whenever I can . . .

I perceive that I have forgotten to give you an answer about the 2 questions relative to the Statue. We are most ready to allow it to be exhibited at the Royal Academy; we do not wish Gibson to inlay any gold on the Diadem; the little colour he has already placed wld I shd think be enough. We are very impatient to see it.*

Edward Lear had a studio in Rome and the Queen opened her letter to add a vignette of Osborne 'which I have had done after one of Mr Lear's Drawings & wh I beg you to give him, & to tell him of my perseverance in drawing'.

Charlotte's letters abounded with news of friends, the Torlonias ('who have more pretty things than in any house I have seen but some glaring bad taste besides'), the Dorias, Borgheses, the great Roman ladies in their diamonds; of their English friends ('quite full of fine arts & antiquities & quite different from themselves in England'), Malmesburys, Shelburnes, Mme de Flahaut ('receiving every night & by way of collecting society more than anyone else'), the Duke of Devonshire ('economising but still he brings his cook & gives recherché dinners'), and while she observed reprovingly that 'our friends & companions are very apathetic & live a kind of society life which seems to me a great waste of time here', nevertheless during Carnival the Cannings gave a great supper to many of their friends and with the Malmesburys and Shelburnes hired a balcony on the Corso to see 'the humours of the Carnival'; their box of confetti weighed 1200 lbs. Lord Malmes-

* When it reached England in July the Queen wrote again: 'Gibson's statue is very fine but we cannot quite approve the face; everything else is beautiful.'

bury was able to congratulate himself on finding the most agreeable and clever people of his acquaintance in Rome, and 'the Shelburnes and Cannings are remarkable for both qualities'.[6]

A round of country-house visits, mostly in Scotland, occupied the summer, and when Canning was sent on a diplomatic mission to Madrid for a few weeks Char joined her sister at Curraghmore. In mid-December she was on her way to Osborne. 'I had in the train an odd fidgety man who got out 4 times making various excuses about his servant. He came on the *Fairy* too, to my surprise, & proved to be Prof Sedgwick who was invited to look after springs & wells.'* This gave her an opportunity of sounding him about the landslips at Highcliffe. 'He is an incessant talker & such an odd looking man, that when he was muffled up in the corner of the railway carriage & twirling his thumbs, a panic seized me he perhaps was mad. Luckily he asked a sane question in a common voice & I was easy about him.' At Windsor Castle for Christmas, the Queen gave Charlotte a blue enamel bracelet with a ruby and diamond clasp.

* Professor of Geology at Cambridge.

15

Family Betrothals

Charlotte had now turned thirty. Her life was set in a pattern which was to continue for some years. Her husband and immediate family were her first preoccupation while solicitous concern for her ageing grandmother and aunts and numerous cousins found expression in nearly every letter. But her duty to the Queen determined the shape of her life.

In February 1848 two pleasant days were spent at Cuddesdon on a visit to the Bishop of Oxford where each successive night fourteen or fifteen distinguished men dined, but Char admitted to being 'very ignorant who they were and what were their particular merits'. The days were spent in Oxford, the colour of the first day being 'Broad Church & University Reform & the second day High Church'. Most of the names were unknown to her but she was glad to find 'pleasant Dr Acland a physician, & son of Sir Thomas' among them. There was also a 'quite young Chemistry Professor, a Mr Maskelyne, who was very full of Photographic information but on the whole I heard nothing & learnt nothing, for such a mass of black coated people all sticking together in the middle of the room talking to each other told one nothing at all, & the single individuals dragged up to be introduced to me talked of the weather & any stupid thing'. Her next letter, also to her mother, written a few days later carried very different news. With unexpected suddenness revolution had broken out in Paris and the French Royal family were in flight. Queen Victoria had every room in the Palace prepared to receive any numbers that might come, and her anxiety for the Duchesse de Nemours was very great. On February 28th Char heard that the National Guard had declared in favour of monarchy which would, she noted with relief, 'make them more convenient neighbours than that horrid democracy we feared'.

The first visit to Balmoral occurred that autumn and she hastened to acquaint Lady Stuart with some unusual details.

It is not very pretty near the house but there are beautiful views near & great variety of drives. We have tolerably good weather but very cold & all the party here are in winter garments & all day long we are allowed fires, a comfort I never expected. It is a very small house & wd be comfortable for a few people & a due proportion, but now with *eight* at dinner every day besides the 3 children & their governess, there are *60 servants*. What these do & who they are I have no guess for the proportions are unlike any other establishment. Housemaids were altogether forgotten & two had to be *improvisé*-d who had never played the part before.

She sent a message to her cousin Car Cocks that the 'luncheons were quite in a new style. All together, Queen, P, children, Gentlemen & Ladies & the children's governess—this was an enormous novelty, you will see if Car does not think it very wonderful indeed'. Much of her time was absorbed in sketching views (nine of them are now in Queen Victoria's albums), but her thoughts were with her sister in Ireland where the famine was at its worst, and Louisa's letters were read with keen interest by the Queen.

Towards the end of September and while staying with Lord Aberdeen at Haddo House, Charlotte wrote 'of a very kind thing the Queen has offered us. It is to give us the Stud House at Hampton Court'. This was a house in the Home Park ('quite in the flat') where George IV had established his stud from 1812–20, and which the Queen now offered the Cannings thinking they might like a country house, but they were not to scruple to refuse if it did not suit. The Cannings were in a dilemma, unwilling to turn down so gracious an offer, yet aware of certain disadvantages.

I am not sure that it wd suit us much for at what time of year wd one ever live there. I have always preached against villas & Saturdays to Sundays out of town— & it is far for a drive. Yet I do not much like refusing— & for a month now & then it might be pleasant. I feel sure you will advise to accept.

Meanwhile Canning in London had been to look at the house and Charlotte hurried off another letter to her mother.

I write rather in haste to say I hope you have been very discreet about what I told you of the Stud House & have not mentioned it for I think we shall not accept. Canning went to look at it & to enquire about expenses & it seems to take a great deal to keep up, certainly 5£ a week. The place too is very gloomy & damp for autumn & winter which wd be the chief time one wd want it besides early spring, for in summer a villa life is so very inconvenient & wd entail so much company in our spare rooms that I am sure we shd find it very ruinous—it holds a number of people. The answer must be concocted for to-morrow.

The nature of the reply is evident from the following letter written from Windsor Castle on October 11th 1848:

My dear Lady Canning, I thank you much for your 2 kind letters, by the last of wh I see that the Stud House wd not suit you. Our only regret is that it has not been in our power to afford you the comfort of a country House which we shd have been so glad to do—but we quite comprehend your reasons for not taking it . . .

It was quite a *crève coeur* for me to leave my *dear* little 'Highland house', & my *dear beautiful* Highlands & their excellent & attached Inhabitants, & I live much there in *thought*.

At the end of the year a thoroughly Victorian romance was coming to a head. It concerned a Lady-in-Waiting to the Queen, none other than Char's first cousin Car Cocks and a son of the 11th Earl of Devon, the Reverend Charles Leslie Courtenay, Canon of Windsor and domestic chaplain to the Queen.* Lord and Lady Somers were inflexible in forbidding the match and the Queen was active in forwarding it. Writing from Osborne in December to report Car's arrival 'thro' storm of wind & rain &

* It was of this same Mr Courtenay that a member of the Household protested to the Queen at his calling himself (correctly as it happened) 'the Hon & Rev', and earned the reply 'It is a matter of perfect indifference to the Queen what he is called.'[1]

such rough weather', yet managing to get through her two soakings quite well, Charlotte also referred to the arrival of the Nemours. The Duc had been ill with lead poisoning from the water at Claremont where the French Royal exiles were now installed. 'The poor man looks quite like death just as you would imagine of a slow poison to look, quite blacked & blue & yellow. His wife was not the least hurt by it & is as fresh & handsome as ever', but by the next letter their company was beginning to pall. 'We have the Nemours here still & I cannot say they are much improved but rather the reverse for they are both so very dull. She is very pretty & nice to look at, but besides having a tiresome voice she has nothing to say & everybody's mouth is shut by the number of topics we are all scrupulous of broaching in their presence.'

The court moved to Windsor for Christmas, but crossing from the Isle of Wight was 'so *very* cold on board the *Fairy* that the Queen was quite willing to stay under shelter in the Wind house all the time, otherwise one wd have been nearly frozen'. Canning was invited for Christmas and went shooting with Prince Albert, and the year 1849 started happily with Louisa's arrival on New Year's day, staying until Char's waiting ended on January 4th.

Once back in London Charlotte was in a better position to watch the development of her cousin's courtship who was also home at her parents' house in Grosvenor Place. Mr Courtenay's lack of money was the impediment but by degrees finding there was a 'goodish something', Lord Somers seemed ready to reconsider his decision, but matters moved slowly, everyone being so discreet & well-behaved. Charlotte sent what information she could to Windsor. 'I have written a little gossip to Ly Lyttelton to stay the poor Queen's stomach for there was nothing positive enough to write directly to her, & I thought she must be in too much suspense.' By return 'Ly Lyttelton writes me that the Queen is very impatient to know more & Mr Courtenay was looking his part well, very pale & interesting & preaching good sermons'. It was almost superfluous to add that Grandmama Hardwicke 'takes the romantic side which so naturally belongs to her. Is she prepared not to find Mr C good looking—I know she & Aunt Caledon both will like him for he is so very sensible & straight forward & has been devoted to Car in that well-behaved way for so very long, past *6* years'. The Queen's known predisposition to the match prompted a happy ending.

Windsor Castle
Feb 7th 1849

Dear Lady Canning,

I hasten to answer your letter just recd, & to say that I am (—I meant to say), *we both are*, very glad to hear that the difficulties are overcome, & that Lord & Lady Somers have consented to dear Car's marriage with Mr Courtenay.

As they really seem so attached to one another, & as Car's happiness seems really involved in its taking place, I am much rejoiced to think that *I* have been able to bring this event about,— & thus to show my sincere affection for dear Car, tho' I cannot but grieve over the prospect of losing her. It is 11 years & ½ now, since she came to me, & that is a long time.

All now ran smoothly. In her journal the Queen noted that Mr Courtenay had accepted the living of Bovey Tracey and that the marriage was settled.[2] A few weeks later at Buckingham Palace she saw Charlotte to arrange about the wedding,[3] and on June 20th it took place in the Palace chapel. Down went an account of it in the Queen's journal.[4]

We stood close to the altar . . . The Bishop of London officiated, but was so agitated that he began the service without the Bride & Mr Courtenay had actually to stop the service! . . . At the conclusion of the service I embraced Caroline & then left the Chapel followed by the Bridal couple. We went up to the Diningroom, for the signing of the Register of *our* Chapel, signing *our* names as witnesses . . . We went away immediately after receiving our favours. Caroline was a little overcome when we spoke to her . . .

Next month the Queen had occasion to write from Osborne on another matter.

Dear Lady Canning,

You let me know the other day that Macdonald, the Sculptor was to be in England, & that he understood that I wished to be informed of his arrival. This is quite true, for 2 years ago I wished him to make a Bust of the Prince. However *Marochetti did one last year*, & we therefore do *not* at present wish to have another done; but we wish to know if Macdonald has not got any Busts—*not portraits* but fancy heads,—as he excels so much in Busts. Could you ask him whether he has any, or whether he was in the habit of making *fancy* Busts?

We have drawings of 3 Statues of his wh Gibson sent us: the celebrated Ulysses & his dog,—Hyacinthus,—& a reclining Nymph. I am very curious to see *your* Picture; Winterhalter hopes it is successful.

This place never was more beautiful, & more enjoyable. Really quite Italian weather.

The portrait of Charlotte was commissioned by the Queen from Winterhalter and was painted during that summer; on its arrival at Osborne on July 31st it was passed as a good likeness. Macdonald was unable to accommodate the Queen with fancy busts but a little later a wider search was set on foot in Rome, Gibson undertaking to 'go through the studios of the best sculptors here to see if they have statues of youthful male figures for a baby's rooms. I fear that I shall not find many of that kind just now for the sculptors have not modelled new fancy subjects . . .'[5] Two years previously the Queen had been much pleased with Theed's statue of *Psyche* which she placed in the drawingroom at Osborne, but another two years were to elapse before Macdonald's *Hyacinthus* was bought as a Christmas present for Prince Albert.

In early September, staying with the Ashburtons at a shooting box in Scotland, Charlotte complained that the small house 'was stuffed very full of people & *very* bare of comforts. The worst is there are no tubs—this with millionaires for one's host'. Carlyle was one of the guests but seems to have made less impression than the cabbage roses which were at their best, and the strawberries and cherries just ripening. Drumlanrig Castle, which followed, offered more congenial hospitality.

Arriving at Osborne in October soon after the death of George Anson, Prince Albert's private secretary and his only very intimate friend in England, Char found him 'so cut up, he looks quite altered & low. The Queen sobbed & cried all the afternoon & for three days they have dined alone & we have hardly seen them'. Following hard upon this loss was the great anxiety for Queen Adelaide who for a time was 'in shivering fits & fainting' and quite in 'a dying state'. The Queen came up from Osborne to see her, and spending a night at Buckingham Palace on the way to Windsor, gave Charlotte her orders.

Friday Morg. [*Oct 12th 1849*]

Dear Lady Canning,

As we intend to dine *alone* tonight, you might tell the Maids of Honour (when you see them at B. Palace) that they were at liberty also, to dine at home or with any of their Relations in wh case, I shd dispense with *your* coming to dinner. Of course if you find when you see the M. of Honour at B. Palace that they have no relation with whom they cd dine with *tonight,—you wd* come to dinner, but you are at liberty to *disperse* whenever you like, *after* dinner.

Ever yr's affly V R

The Queen continued quite low with worry and Char noted that they had nothing but Household dinners, and though slightly better she thought it improbable that the Queen Dowager could live many days.* To Eleanor Stanley, also in waiting, 'the dulness of our evenings is a thing impossible to describe';[6] on an earlier occasion while the Queen was looking the other way she detected a Lady-in-Waiting giving such a yawn that she thought it must dislocate her jaw.[7] Canning was invited for a shoot at the end of November and by mischance grazed the temple of one of the Household who moved to catch a wounded bird; Canning immediately fainted, thinking he had hit the Prince of Wales whom the Queen had brought out with her.[8] Gossip attributed his fainting fit to a stormy interview he had had with his '*chère amie*' and which had considerably annoyed him, fearing it might come to the knowledge of Her Majesty.[9]

'What a week of horrid events we have had', Char wrote to Lady Stuart on July 1st 1850, for the Queen on leaving Cambridge

* Queen Adelaide took a turn for the better, but died on Dec. 2nd.

House had been struck just above the eye by a young madman, and arriving a moment later, Char saw him being marched off by a policeman. A very few days later Sir Robert Peel died from the result of a fall from his horse. Charlotte counted it a dreadful blow to the whole country, and while she found the Queen and Prince looking dreadfully low, his widow was almost distracted and was now 'quite in a stupor'. She herself had not escaped injury, for earlier in the year she had had a bad 'overturn' from a carriage, and Lady Lyttelton found her very nervous, with symptoms like those of a slight concussion of the brain.

Char's affection for the Aunthood kindled her interest in each cousin's marriage, and when Sarah Savile had married a mere second son (when Char had hoped for an 'elder son') she could not think it wrong to wish that the elder brother would have no heir—since he had bad health any progeny would have every chance of being very sickly—so that Sarah's would eventually inherit. Now her cousin Lord Eastnor, Car Courtenay's brother and Uncle Somers' son and heir, was engaged to Virginia Pattle. It was hardly a connection to be desired, nor did it commend itself to Lord Somers. The Pattle sisters, of whom Virginia was the sixth, were the daughters of an Anglo-Indian of wealth, and having been brought up in India were said to converse together in Hindustani. Unlike two of the sisters, Julia Cameron and the assiduous Sara Prinsep who entered that year into her reign at Little Holland House, Virginia was remarkable for her beauty, but for force of character she was probably their peer. Eastnor being volatile in his affections Char was delighted at the prospect of his 'being *fixé* after fluttering about so long', and hoped his inclination to settle would compensate for her want of fortune or a *beau nom*. She had heard that 'the Pattle is as clever as she is beautiful & she is certainly a very well conditioned girl & has never had a word said against her of flirting or rushing after fashion or admiration'. There was however the insuperable affliction of the Christian name which was apparently either a shade too indelicate for Victorian sensibilities, or else its affinity with the continent whose countrymen were still assessed as vulgarians, was too close. 'Oh that she had another name', Charlotte sighed, and particularized the name by underlining it. However the parentage, though not remarkable, was respectable although her upbringing had been a little disquieting. The Metternich son, Richard, was found to have been a great admirer, as was Hügel (father of the philosopher), 'a fat walleyed Bavarian or Saxon I forget which', and Char hoped she would do well 'without adorers but she has certainly been unwholesomely accustomed to them & has seen them in an easy pleasant footing quite unlike what is usual in the society of ball-going young ladies, but I believe it is an infinitely worse preparation than dissipation for a quiet dull family home. I hope tho' she *is* a good creature & will do very well & we must all help & support her & try & get her into a quite new line of company'. After the first meeting Char wrote enthusiastically: 'We have seen *Virginia* Pattle, she is very nice & has perfect manners as well as beauty', and with Uncle Somers reconciled she seemed to suit everyone to perfection. Her beauty, recorded more than once by G. F. Watts, was not of the conventional type. 'She now & then looks perfectly lovely & at other times I see why it is possible that she is not admired by some people', and by contrast, in Charlotte's estimation, she made Eastnor 'look too frightful'.

The Queen had become so enraptured with the Highlands that there were now few journeys abroad in the Royal Yacht, and though Char thought the two days that the Queen and four children spent at Ostend in late August 1850 'dull enough & it is a very nasty place to spend even so few hours in', yet she found such a glimpse of abroad rather amusing, besides putting the yacht into favour again. In early October the Cannings were staying at Haddo House helping Lord Aberdeen entertain the Duchess of Kent who liked her visit and was very good-humoured and easily amused, but sadly sleepy. On the railway journey to Liverpool she aroused such enthusiasm as effectually to bar the way to all refreshment rooms and Canning was obliged to get them two papers of buns by climbing in and out of the train over the buffers. After many postponements the Eastnor marriage had taken place and the honeymoon spent at Highcliffe. Soon after the couple's arrival at Eastnor Castle the Cannings joined them, and Charlotte was quite astonished by the beauty of the country and found the house very handsome, which together with the village, farm and church, resulted in the 'perfection of a rural English home'.

A glimpse of Charlotte at Windsor Castle in the new year, furnished by the seventy-five year old Duke of Somerset, reveals her playing a game in the evening and appropriating all his counters. 'Lady Canning won all my fish, and I said she cheated.'[10]

The public census was still sufficient novelty to make 'the most amusing commotion in most houses' in the spring of 1851, and on March 31st Canning sent a model paper in his best hand, Charlotte insisting that her own profession be added. 'Peeress & Lady of the Bedchamber which looked very grand, & Peer & Privy Councillor for Canning. I had the advantage of a year in age which felt quite a deception for to-day is my birthday, but we thought it right to put down as 33 last birthday.'* Two days later, pursuing her duties and in Court mourning for the Queen of the Belgians, she feared she was 'going too much like a bride to Court to-morrow but the Queen orders us all into white. Luckily I was provided with a complete silk worn last year & still perfectly clean, so this time I go for the cost of new ribbons'. She always enjoyed a 'cheap contrivance' to save on her dress allowance; later in the year with two grand Court affairs in sight (again in mourning, for the Duchesse d'Angoulême) she devised a 'beautiful moiré antique train made out of the petticoat of my Fancy dress with all the gold picked off', in which she must have cut a handsome figure amid the splendour of the Garter ceremony.

* The census paper lists a household of nine servants: butler, under butler, footman, housekeeper-cook, lady's maid, two housemaids, a kitchen maid, and a steward's boy.

16

Miss Nightingale

The summer was ushered in with all the excitement of the Great Exhibition, but to Louisa Waterford it presented a particular problem. The Queen had sounded Charlotte with regard to Lou accepting the position of Lady of the Bedchamber. This kindly intention—compensation perhaps for Canning's imperfections (if the Queen knew of them)—must have put Louisa in a great fright. The sisters would have made a memorable pair with their arresting looks and grace of manner and carriage ('those two sisters . . . so genuine and charming'[1]), but Louisa's disposition was a retiring one and marriage had not overcome her shyness. Charlotte was the intermediary.

July 9th 1851[2]

Madam,

On leaving Your Majesty I went to Louisa and as soon as I could find her I informed her of Your Majesty's gracious intention. She was more gratified and flattered than I can express at learning this mark of Your Majesty's favour and lost no time in communicating with Waterford, but he is at present in Ireland and probably not at home: I fear it will still be three or four days before she can hear from him . . .

Lord Waterford reacted with vigour, and it requires no effort to guess at his form of expression.

10 Grosvenor Square[3]
July 12th 1851

Madam,

It is with extreme regret that I have it now in my power to reply to Your Majesty & to inform Your Majesty, that my sister has this morning received a letter from Lord Waterford, by which to her great sorrow she feels precluded from receiving the distinction Your Majesty so graciously thought of conferring upon her. Lord Waterford is most deeply sensible of the very high mark of favour Your Majesty contemplated bestowing on my sister, and is sincerely grateful for Your Majesty's kindness, but from his letter it appears that his objections to her assuming duties which must occasionally withdraw her from home & from Ireland seem to be so decidedly expressed, that my sister does not entertain any hope of being able to shake him.

It would otherwise have been a great happiness to her to have so many opportunities of being near Your Majesty in being attached to the Royal Household.

I trust Your Majesty will permit me to express my own sincere regret and to add that my sister & myself have been much distressed at learning that a rumour of Your Majesty's kind intention has been heard in several places. We are unable to account for this as with the exception of my mother & Lord Canning there is no one who has received the slightest intimation of it from us.

I have the honor to remain
Your Majesty's
Dutiful humble servant
C Canning.

Windsor Castle
July 13th 1851

My dear Lady Canning,

I recd your letter just before we left London.

It is with much regret that I learn from you that your Sister's duties as a Wife will prevent her from becoming one of my Ladies.

Let me thank you for the part you have taken to bring about,—what you & your Sister would have seen with pleasure;— & pray express to her my concern at this result.

Though a rumour has—(inconceivably) been heard, relative to Lady Waterford's possibly succeeding Lady Portman,—I should wish all that has passed to be considered *strictly confidential* & not as *if any formal offer* had been made to your Sister.

With the Prince's kind remembrance,

Ever
Your's afftely V R

Queen Victoria returned from Balmoral for the closing days of the Great Exhibition accompanied by Charlotte who was confident that there would be 'plenty of curious stories of discontented exhibitors. Canning has had complaints from a robe maker who had invented a way of making clergyman's gowns not to slip off their shoulders, for which he expected a medal'. Queen Amélie and the Princesse de Joinville were guests at Windsor Castle after a month's travelling in Scotland which had delighted the one but not the other. 'The Pss de Joinville thought it all detestable & I believe even here made no disguise of her feelings, but as she pines for heat & south the Queen could just forgive such a feeling in her, tho' in any one else she wd have considered it high treason to say a word against Scotland.' Charlotte's time had as usual been employed in sketching; one of these she thought successful enough to give the Princess Royal for a birthday present. From Osborne came a letter of thanks for 'such a pretty picture of the dear Dee. I shall hang it up with the one of Osborne which you were so good as to give me on my birthday last year, and shall prize them much as your painting and keep them long for your sake'.

Charlotte had become very fond of the Royal Children, the youngest, Prince Arthur, having 'the Royal look I have heard Grandmama talk about which I think she said was remarkable in the Queen when she was a baby'; the Prince of Wales she found very touching in his affection for his tutor and his sorrow at losing him. 'His little notes and presents which Mr Birch used to find on his pillow were really too moving.' The six eldest children presented a play at Windsor Castle in January 1852, in German verse, 'interposed with little choruses sung by the little creatures in parts'. She found they acted with spirit and without the least awkwardness, 'the P of Wales was a poor boy whose only possession was a cock, he sold it for food for his starving mother, P Alfred a rich elderly man in cocked hat, brown coat'. In the summer of the same year Charlotte was present at the christening of the eleven-year old daughter of the Rajah of Coorg, for whom the Queen was godmother. 'She was in her Indian dress and not all white as it ought to have been. A tight sort of under gown with short sleeves & white muslin & gold draperies. I never saw so graceful a little creature, such beautiful poses & movements', and in this same dress Winterhalter depicted her, decked with ropes of pearls and holding a Bible as witness to her christianity.

On their new yacht *Fair Rosamund*, the Cannings and Lord Shelburne sailed from Cowes to Vigo in July, and having set their hearts on seeing Santiago de Compostela, made the journey by night in a diligence drawn by eight mules, while admiring the beauty of the country bathed in the light of a full moon. Back in English waters the Cannings sailed to the west coast of Scotland and since the flag was flying from Brodick Castle, Isle of Arran, dropped anchor to visit the Douglases. The Duke of Hamilton had died the previous month; always an eccentric, he had left instructions for his embalmment and only the previous year had enquired of his doctor to whom he should entrust the task should he die when the doctor was absent. A bird-stuffer or a chemist had been the prescribed alternatives until the King's Apothecary (a State appointment) had been determined upon. Recently the Duke had climbed into his Egyptian sarcophagus to assure himself that the lengthening alteration had been successful, and his last drives had been made for the purchase of a great quantity of spices. 'No one can say he did not think of death', was Charlotte's laconic comment.

It will be remembered how in the past Hatty Cocks' health had been a source of worry; now as the wife of Mr Wegg-Prosser her faith was causing equal concern. Leaving Arran the Cannings landed on the island of Cumbrae where the Prossers were living in a cottage close to the Collegiate Church, recently established by the Episcopal Church in Scotland and run on Tractarian principles ('quite in the St Barnabas style & I shd think beyond it'). Charlotte, whose opinion of Mr Prosser was not very high ('weak & obstinate too, besides a sort of silliness throughout'), hoped it might satisfy him, but Hatty showed disquieting signs of going further still. Char's opinion of English Roman Catholics was that they were stiff and formal (—'always rather *guindé*'—), giving as an example the twenty-year-old Sir John Acton ('a very grave youth who would grow younger in time'), but on the whole she thought 'the *ménages* do best to go or stay together', but she was sure *the* step had not been taken, and if 'Hatty "goes" I shall be amazed & very sorry & will blame her more than most people for she so thoroughly knows the subject & has been so very *sound* in her opinions all this time & not the least inclined to foolish vagaries'.* A further irritant was the family's mania for saying everybody was getting so much better and never mentioning the reverse; in this case Lord Somers' health was at issue. News of his death reached Charlotte at Balmoral and though grieving for Car Courtenay and the misfortune of having her sanguine disposition which had mitigated her awareness of her father's state, she felt that he had been so suffering that it was a mercy to be taken to a happy rest.

It was to be a year of deaths, though of more general interest was that of an unknown John Nield who unexpectedly bequeathed—though at the outset it was considered 'an impudent hoax'—a large sum of money to Queen Victoria. 'The gt fortune did not seem to make much effect', Charlotte learned. 'The Queen only said—how very odd.' The death of the Duke of Wellington was a severe shock, the Queen and Prince feeling his loss exceedingly. 'The Queen says she cannot feel how things can go on without him, & I only wish I could recollect all the true & kind things she said shewing how worthily she appreciated him. The mourning she wore for him a week was taken off to-day.' Through some kind of mismanagement Charlotte failed to attend his funeral. 'I cannot at all get over not having been to St Paul's. I was not the least helped & I was not told to manage for myself either, or I could perfectly have done it & I shall all my life regret it. Everybody whose opinion I respect says it was the finest & most impressive thing that could be conceived.' The Prince himself told Char that the music was almost too much to bear.[4]

At court, at the beginning of 1853, the marriage of Napoleon III was the chief topic, and though 'I don't think it thought wise *here*', Char was of the opinion that he had done a sensible thing, observing that 'a Royal alliance comes to no use in adversity & in

* Hatty eventually embraced the Roman Catholic faith.

prosperity the Emperor can do without it'. She remembered having seen Eugénie de Montijo at a ball in white with a dress of bows & tags, very fair hair & skin & dark eyes. Good delicate features, a little formal & a pretty figure, not tall or short. She was the right age and clever. To Grandmama Hardwicke it was as good as a fairy tale.

The birth of Prince Leopold in April took Char to the Palace to collect what news she could. She learned that he was large and healthy* and that chloroform had been given to the Queen for the first time, but she hoped that the rumour that he was to be called George was untrue. At about this time, and on Ruskin's recommendation, she and her sister called at Holman Hunt's studio to see his *Light of the World*, not yet completed but abounding in apt symbolic meaning.

This was the last pleasant event Charlotte would chronicle for some time to come. Disturbances, eventually leading to war between Russia and Turkey, provoked general unease. Eliza Canning, staying at Highcliffe, was in great distress and indignation, and lamented not being at Constantinople but Char considered it a blessing she was not, for 'helping Stratford to calm himself' would have worn her out. March 1854 saw the start of the Crimean War, the British fighting with the Turks and the French; Russia the common foe. At Balmoral in October news arrived of the victory of the Battle of the Alma; almost simultaneously arrived also Lord Aberdeen, 'most bellicose & in haste for more victories'. A few days later Char told her mother that the 'Government sends out a band of nurses to Scutari & Miss Nightingale is to head them. Her family have consented & there can be no one so well fitted as she is to do such work. She has such nerves & skill & is so gentle & wise & quiet, even now she is in no bustle or hurry tho' so much is in her hands'. Charlotte was in a position to gauge the effectiveness of the appointment for as chairman of the committee for the Institution for the Care of Sick Gentlewomen in Distressed Circumstances, she had engaged

* The Prince suffered from haemophilia. 'His other names will be George Duncan Albert . . . Duncan as a compliment to dear Scotland.'[5]

Florence Nightingale the previous year as Superintendent to reorganize their new premises at 1 Harley Street.[6] It had been a testing time for both. Criticism was levelled at Char for employing a gentlewoman without the permission of her parents, while for Florence Nightingale it served as an apprenticeship for the greater work ahead.

To Charlotte fell much of the responsibility for interviewing nurses for Scutari with all the accompanying difficulties of selection. 'I doubt if *Lady* Scripture Readers will be accepted, there are so many such volunteers and only *really* useful people are taken.' A few of them must have trickled through for later Char referred again to the Scripture Readers 'who had to be kept away from pertinaciously choosing to read the Bible to Roman Catholics & violent tracts, instead of to Protestants, thereby causing irritation. They had to go'. The nuns seem also to have dabbled in much the same pursuits. 'A few I believe were rather for converting',whereupon they were at once lodged in a convent and turned over to nurse French soldiers.

A visit to Paris resulted in the Cannings being commanded to St Cloud to be presented.

The Emperor & Empress received us both together in a drawing room at a corner looking towards Paris. She is certainly exceedingly pretty & graceful, it is an odd face with eyes rather too near together but they are of a beautiful shape & she has a very short upper lip & good skin, & it is very real beauty of its kind. I always knew she was not what *we* call tall & she is half a head less than me. The Emperor is very short & broader than I thought. He & Canning sat on one side and talked of graver subjects, & she & I on the other & much lighter in our topics. The Empress asked after no end of her English friends & now & then launched into gossip & a shrieking voice & great animation. She must be very amusing when at her ease. The *dames d'honneur* & the *grande maîtresse* were sitting in another *salon* like people in an English country house & *aides de camp* going about from room to room. The quantity of rooms & good furniture & good flowers beat our English Palace terribly, even at Windsor for an audience we shd have to take people thro' a shabby dark corner.

Back at Windsor Castle just before Christmas, Charlotte found the Queen knitting a comforter for her cousin the Duke of Cambridge, whose 'tendency to low fever' prevented him from pulling his weight in the Crimea. But there was a large consignment of woollens ready and the Queen was grateful for 'Aunt Caledon's mits, & she was delighted to count up 100 pair'. Lady Stuart was kept busy also.

Dearest Mama, Will you do a commission for the Queen in the way of choosing some books. A French book & an English book are wanted to be added to some Christmas presents for the Governesses, so will you order the carriage & go to any bookseller you like. *Any* book if nicely bound wd do. An illustrated Sévigné or any modern book with or without prints—or annuals, but not too trashy, or a nice book of any kind. Please send the parcels with 'for the Queen' written outside, & let the shops know that what are not taken will be sent back. The Ballads they have. It is not a whole present but a book is always given in addition to others.

'Not,' Char added as an afterthought, 'Martin Tupper's *Proverbial Philosophy*,' as that had presumably been had the previous Christmas, but '*Stones of Venice* might do for one, or Mrs Jameson's *Paintings, Sacred & Legendary Art*'. The commission was successful and the Queen sent her thanks; Char knew only that a governess had been the recipient of *Voyage en Zigag*. On Christmas Eve 'the Christmas Trees are all preparing & we assemble in the corridor at 7 to receive our presents—it is a *very* disagreeable ceremony', but leaving open her letter she finished it up '*after* the Christmas Trees', and wrote delightedly of her very pretty bracelet, a book of poetry & a very nice velvet pocket book.

Anxiety for the Crimean War continued very great, though the Queen was sanguine as to the final result. In the spring of 1855 Charlotte was again in the 'thick of lady nurses', interviewing and choosing. At the installation of the Emperor Napoleon III as a Knight of the Garter in April she attended Queen Victoria, and in the painting E. M. Ward later made of the ceremony she is seen slightly to the right of the Queen, bearing her train. A few days later she earned a rebuke from Lady Stuart for not wearing mourning for a death in the family. 'Of course I knew the poor Archdeacon was yr cousin once removed,' she replied, '& it is not a sin of ignorance that I am not in black at Court, but I hope it is pardonable for I felt so very stingy.' By going in white and violet and black velvet 'which is faint mourning', her mother's sense of propriety was satisfied.

17

Lord Canning's Appointment

The first indication of a matter of great moment to the Cannings occurred in a letter from Charlotte to her sister at the beginning of June. 'What did you think of the news Mama told you?' Canning had been Postmaster-General since 1853, but now with Lord Dalhousie's imminent retirement from the Governor-Generalship of India, his name had been put forward as a successor. The power of appointment belonged to the East India Company though it was usual for the Government to be consulted. 'I cannot yet tell you what answer is to be given,' Charlotte continued, 'but there are really no reasons, but one's own feelings & dislikes against it & I *think* it will be that we go, but I don't know & will not take any part in the decision but only be ready to follow like a dog. If it was only for *one* year I wd delight in it—but 5 is terribly long. Nothing is worse to think about than taking leave of poor dear GM when it wd be *certainty* of goodbye.' Canning was undecided and went to his friends for advice. Lord Malmesbury advised him to refuse,[1] but on June 16th after a final talk with Lord Aberdeen, he accepted. 'You will not be surprised I think,' Char wrote to her mother, 'I feel sure it is the right decision for tho' C never is in the habit of distressing himself by looking back to what might have been, & wd not have done it, yet I think many an occasion might arise when the contrary decision wd really be a cause for regret.'

Of her own feelings there is little to go on, other than the dread of so lengthy a separation from her family. Louisa, perhaps sensing an emptiness in her sister's life, thought it would cause a 'want to be supplied wh will be *the* right thing for her', and in later years Char herself wrote of the monotony of her London life. There is no evidence to support the gossip still circulating after the death of both Cannings, that it was in order to break up Canning's love-affair that he had been appointed to India.[2] The Queen herself expressed surprise at his nomination. Few letters survive from these last months in England as Charlotte was a great deal with her mother, and Lou had come over from Ireland to join them, but when at Balmoral in September she observed that 'the Prince of Prussia & Princess Royal are going on very happily on very comfortable terms & taking very kindly to each other & much together'.

The end of November saw the Cannings' departure. Since the opening of the overland route through Egypt it was possible to sail to Alexandria and continue by train to Cairo and on again from Suez by ship to India. The steamer *Caradoc* was put at their disposal, and with Char's two maids, West and Rain, and other staff, they were to embark at Marseilles in early December after a few days in Paris. At the beginning of the month E. M. Ward had executed two preparatory sketches of Charlotte for his Garter ceremony picture. They both reproduce a shapely head gracefully poised on the long neck; dark brows draw attention to the markedly intelligent eyes. She was plumper now than at the time of her marriage twenty years earlier; yet the artist has nevertheless interpreted something of the swiftness of motion which seems to have characterized her movements, and has conveyed the impression of strength tempered with grace. Of her character the most unlikely person (because as spare of praise as of money) was perhaps her most fervent champion. Dunkellin's younger brother, the future Marquess of Clanricarde, to whom Canning's property passed at his death, was exceptionally miserly and unloved, but he regarded Charlotte as the only good woman he had ever known.[3]

The Queen's farewell, taken at Windsor, must have saddened Charlotte but she left no record of it. Only the entries in Queen Victoria's Journal mark the end of Char's thirteen years of service. 'Nov 22. After our breakfast we took leave of the dear Cannings, with great regret. They start on the 26th.'[4] On that date Lady Stuart de Rothesay wrote dejectedly in her diary: 'Char and Canning took leave of me at 6½', and Char noted down: 'Took leave of Mama in her bed, & left Grosv Sqre at 1/4 to 7.'

The Cannings stayed at the Hotel du Louvre in Paris. 'We shall be off to-morrow morning by the 9 o'clock train,' Charlotte wrote on December 2nd. 'This would have been our real last Goodbye if you had come & I grudge all these days very much I might have had with you & Lou, but you would have been very tired & very cold here.' They both had colds caught at the newly opened hotel where the glazed roof over the main staircase shut out nothing but rain, and though Charlotte had only a few bonnets to collect yet she found that 'the want of any kind of anti-chamber quite spoils these apartments which otherwise would be charming, but it is so inconvenient not even to have a place for the *laquais de place* to wait & to have all the shop people at once in the salon'. She described an evening at the Tuileries to her mother.

It seemed very odd to go there to this new dynasty. They live in the Pavilion de Flore & the Imperatrice has two drawing rooms very smartly done up with modern tapestry, silk & bronze, not much to my taste & very gaudy. The chairs & sofas are arranged as in common living rooms & rather comfortable. The dinner was in the Galerie de Diane. I sat next to the Emperor & C next Eugénie. The plate was all silver and suddenly after being rather surprised at seeing meat *on* the table a crab on a cover caught my eye & I remembered *your* service; all the other covers by that time had disappeared. The Emperor afterwards said to me he did not know if I remembered some plate that had once belonged to my Father which he now had. So he evidently thinks a great deal of it. I think the arms are rather altered for that sort of frosted *écusson* was not under my crab, only engraved arms. After dinner the evening was very long notwithstanding many attempts to make it not formal, seeing drawings & the famous lace flounce the wonder of the Exhibition. It was bought for Eugénie & it was that she wore for the *clôture* on a high cerise velvet. It is of Alençon & quite wonderfully fine. This with its stiff inside was brought down & exhibited in the side room next door—a pretty sitting room of her own where the Emperor takes people to talk at leisure. She came in herself to show her gown & was rather missy in disturbing the conversation with Lord Cowley. She is strong & well now & still very pretty, her round petticoats conceal her state very much.*

At Malta a few days later Char was reminded of earlier visits on the *Gondola*; this time, instead of the bleakness of the lazaret, they were guests of the Governor at the Palace of the Knights. The stay at Alexandria was short, but it seemed to Charlotte more characteristic of the East than Constantinople. The magnificence of the palace prepared for them in the Turkish quarter, the sumptuous meals, the supply of new combs, brushes, toothbrushes, even tooth powder, in all the rooms, quite astonished her;[5] to Canning the questionable luxury of a towel with a six-inch deep surround of gold embroidery was like wiping ones face on a Field-marshal's uniform.[6] Cairo however proved more absorbing still. They were lodged in a palace belonging to Ismail Pasha 'its garden opens upon the Nile, I really believe near the spot where Moses was found', Charlotte told the Queen. 'I cannot describe the gorgeous & enormous rooms—the centre saloon is 155 ft by 60 ft & furnished with all the gold papers & damask & ormulu & clocks & lustres that Paris could supply as suitable to Egyptian taste. We found it difficult to prevent the servant from lighting 700 candles in one room the first night . . . A number of black slaves . . . are constantly about, & whenever we move 4 men in the Egyptian dress with silver sticks & bells go before us shaking them.'[7]

She paid a visit to the wife of the Pasha, a Circassian whom she likened to Lady Conyngham [mistress of George IV], 'very tall & handsome, that size & sort of beauty, but softer'—and to his sister, 'once the cleverest & wickedest woman in Egypt', now dying on a brass bedstead in a bundle of old clothes.

I came away very sorry for all these poor caged birds who do nothing but smoke the livelong day. They had great *luxe* in their pipes of amber mouth pieces with very fine jewels, & gold vases of sweetmeats studded with diamonds, & all the slaves dressed with velvet jackets & silk &

* The Empress had tried, without great success, to revive the lace-making industry by placing large orders. The Prince Imperial was born in March 1856.

gold trousers & long sort of coats with tails that would trail on the ground but are tucked up. They are all Circassians & have fine eyes but are not otherwise handsome. I believe they marry them to servants & are really in much the same condition as well behaved maidservants in anybody's house. The sight of all this gives me not so much any feeling of a very improper state of things as of the cruelty of condemning the poor creatures to such a life of imprisonment. Then those wretched black creatures who attend upon them! That is the horrid & degrading part of the custom. The Harem has now & then travelled by the railroad & I asked them how they liked it, but it does not seem to suit their tastes or amuse them. New fashions creep in, the last is of three years date, & all the long plaits of hair were cut off & short thick hair cut square is the rage. But you will be tired of hearing of these wretched people & I have to pack for the steamer.

To Queen Victoria, who had been no further than Coburg, it seemed a dazzling tale.

Windsor Castle
January 25th 1856

Dearest Lady Canning,

Your first *very* interesting letter of the 19th Dec. from Cairo has given me the greatest pleasure & I thank you very much for it. *How very* wonderful all those Oriental luxuries & customs *must* be, & how like a *dream* it must all appear to European eyes! If it was not for the heat & the *insects* how much I should like to see India, that most luxuriant Country full of such wealth & I am sure intended some day to become civilised & to hold a different position in that respect, to what it has hitherto done!

The circle at Tyttenhanger must have been impatient for further descriptions of Charlotte's life—so very different from hers at Windsor Castle—and the account of life on the steamer going up the Nile and of the little Arab child on board whom she stuffed with oranges and cake, would have diverted them. The Cannings had two interpreters with their party, of whom one, a Christian of Syrian extraction, not often parted from his wife, consoled her in his absence by writing several letters before his departure of different dates and left them with a friend to be dealt out at convenient intervals. He was fat and awkward and dressed in the 'old Turkish turban & petticoats which he continues to catch up & exhibit his white stockings & fat legs & *caleçons* in a manner of strangely indecent appearance'. Christmas day was spent at Keneh in tropical heat and except for the hour of reading the service in the cabin which was reassuringly familiar, all else was new and strange. Thebes was reached that night by full moon, and the temple—'as old as Moses, probably of Abraham's time'—was again visited the next day. They were constantly on the watch for crocodiles and the first they saw were as 'green as verdigrised bronze' lying asleep on a bank near Assouan; the strange birds and wild fowl were so diverse that 'an English traveller declared he had seen three scarlet geese as red as grenadiers' coats', which though not believed were taken to be flamingoes.

Back at Cairo she hastened to tell her mother of the last stage of the Nile journey.

Yesterday was the great sight of the sights of Egypt. The Pyramids! We were mounted at Ghizeh on beautiful beasts. Mine a white ass of Yemen with smart caparisons & all the gentlemen on Arabs with velvet & gold housings. We crossed a tract of young wheat as usual of that dazzling green I have never seen elsewhere, & the cleanest of crops in that wonderful garden mould. White clover called Bersema too, that looked so excellent a meal in its fresh state & is given to all the beasts here. The Pyramids look enormous when far off & then strangely diminish, for *all* seems so near in this clear sky. I watched three or four of the party begin their ascent each helped by three Arabs pulling them up the tiers of stone. I arrived with the full intention of going up, then the scramble rather alarmed me. But as C told me to do as I pleased I started & was helped up charmingly by the Arabs for a little distance, perhaps 100 ft. Then arrived C at the same resting place, he had a great dread of looking down from a height & he thought the sight of me being dragged up the stones over his head so very horrid & the prospect of going down so much worse, that I actually offered to turn back if he pleased, & he joyfully accepted. I minded it so very little & found the clever way the Arabs had of lowering me down so easy, that I have never ceased regretting that we did not persevere.

Now on board the Indian frigate SS *Feroze*, the Cannings left Aden in the middle of January, and though Charlotte observed that in retrospect their 'long, pleasant, cheerful journey' was not to be compared in exertion and trouble to a journey to Rome by land, yet with the vast unknown continent of India opening up before her, and while reading all she could of its history, it is not surprising that she was overwhelmed by all there was to learn.

At Bombay where the Cannings stayed over a week Canning was received with all the ceremony of a Governor-General. Lord Dalhousie was only awaiting their arrival at Calcutta before taking his own departure, so that after a fairly hurried stop at Ceylon, and at Madras, the *Feroze* steamed into the Bay of Bengal, perfectly timed to anchor in sight of Fort William, Clive's Calcutta fortress commanding the river, as the clock struck half-past five on February 29th 1856. Charlotte must have been on deck most of the day for the slow approach up the Hooghly River among the sea-going ships and the graceful masts of the traders was not to be missed, nor on the right at Garden Reach the large houses of classical design, stuccoed and prosperous, each in its own garden, deployed along the river bank.

When the ship anchored just below Fort William a message was brought on board that according to custom Charlotte must land alone.

C of course agreed to whatever was proposed, but I don't think he admired the arrangement much more than I did, & it was not a pleasant addition to such an affair to have to make my public entry by myself. I did not feel at all good-humoured about it, I own. I had my choice whether to land before or after C, so I pocketed my grievance, & settled to land first, & see him arrive, instead of following after, quite privately when the crowd had dispersed, & all his show was at an end.

This was nominally still the cold season, so that instead of resting in the cool of darkened rooms, the crowds had come out to see the arrival at the Chandpal Ghât, the landing-stage almost on the threshold of Government House. Charlotte landed first with one of Lord Dalhousie's ADCs.

I walked through an avenue of triumphal arches, with flags & hundreds of spectators on each side, up a road of red cloth to our own little barouche, which looked surprised at itself, with four horses & Eastern postillions in dresses of red, black, & gold, & running grooms to match, & an escort of four of the body-guard. I put the A.D.C. opposite to me, & was taken along part of the road prepared for C through an avenue of troops, till I turned off through an arch into the garden, to the private entrance.

Immediately on Canning's arrival he was sworn-in, and with the guns firing to proclaim Charles, Viscount Canning in the office of Governor-General of India, Charlotte, at his side, entered upon a page in history.

PART TWO

18

Government House

During her first year in India Charlotte's preoccupations were mainly domestic. 'I am sure I shall like being here', she told her mother after the first week. 'It will always be full of interest, but just at first it is *flat* to be such a fish out of water, to see nothing, to hear nothing, & understand nothing.' Many things combined to make those first months discouraging. Her letters, though in no sense complaining, were chiefly devoted to accounts of the monotony of her life in Calcutta, the oppressiveness of the climate, and—a sore trial—the awkward disposition of the rooms in Government House, resulting in an entire lack of privacy. A further difficulty was the inadequacy of the furnishing, for Lady Dalhousie had been dead three years (fourteen years earlier Charlotte succeeded her as lady-in-waiting) and the establishment was lacking the most elementary requirements of plate and linen.

By any standards the house would have been considered one of outstanding magnificence. Its situation, carefully chosen at the beginning of the century by the Governor-General, Lord Wellesley, commanded an unrivalled position in the city; only the garden and low surrounding balustrade separated it from the adjacent *Maidan* [grassy plain] thus yielding a view of a very 'English appearance', Charlotte wrote to the Queen, 'like the flat part of Hyde Park & the high houses on the north side'.[1] The exterior had been designed by an officer in the Bengal Engineers, Captain Wyatt, nephew of James Wyatt, from Robert Adam's plan for Kedleston Hall, Derbyshire. The three-storeyed edifice was built of brick covered with plaster, umber in the Cannings' day (as it is today) and better suited to the glare of the tropical heat than the dazzling whiteness of the intervening years. An imposing flight of steps led from the driveway to the great north portico in the main portion of the house, while the semi-circular south front, its dome supported by a lofty colonnade, overlooked the garden which though small ('like a London square') was well stocked with Cape jessamine 'as high as shrubbery laurels', clusters of roses, oleanders, and double hibiscus.

Linked to the central building by curving galleries were four massive square wings, the Cannings occupying that on the south-west where their rooms on the first and second floors were shaded on the south by a roofed-in columned verandah. On the first floor Lord Canning had his study, handsomely proportioned; the rooms adjoining were those of the aides-de-camp, private secretary, and the waiting room. Above, and still within the shade of the verandah, but boasting its own delicately fretworked balcony, were the private apartments, the windows to east and west shaded against the sun by green wooden hooded shutters which in the monsoon provided additional protection from the heavy slanting rain. Charlotte's private sitting-room was here though 'being *au second* makes one feel like recovering from a long illness', and the wild birds nesting in the capitals of the colonnade 'fifteen of the brightest, sleekest green parroquets with pink rings round their throats' kept up a perpetual screeching. The variety of parrots sent for her to see was a source of pleasure: 'I never saw such beauties—rich brown, with sky-blue epaulettes, red heads, violet throats, crimson stomachs & tails'; and when Canning could not resist buying a pair, the smaller was described as having a '*veste* & *culottes* of *gros bleu* & crimson, like velvet'.

The arrangement of the reception rooms was a source of constant worry. 'I am tormenting myself with plans how to live in this house to best advantage', Char exclaimed, owning that it was the strangest plan of a house and the most uncomfortable. The great marble hall used as a State diningroom occupied almost the entire space of the first floor in the central building, its southern end forming a drawingroom which, though newly furnished with red damask chairs and 'very handsomely done', was more properly a passage room connecting the two south wings, and with nine doors and nine windows Char despaired of creating an atmosphere of dignity and repose. She therefore chose her private drawingroom in the south-east wing and proceeded to 'chintz it' (blue stripe and rosebuds on a white ground which she used in succession year after year, for it suited the walls so well '& gives colour tho' so full of white itself'), adding plants and a good selection of books which seem 'never to have been seen in this house before. I believe the rooms were as bare as the Gallery at Buckingham Palace'. By the time her miniatures were hung and prints of her friends and the Royal Children disposed about the room, an oval portrait by Swinton of herself displayed on an easel, and blue Sèvres conspicuous for its quantity, she felt it to be the most civilised room in India. The arrangement of the furniture was conditioned by the punkah, a canvas-covered frame suspended from every ceiling, providing a gentle current of air when pulled back and forth by a rope. Chairs were placed strategically to profit from this passing draught. In her bedroom Charlotte thought she would never submit to it, but after a few weeks she found (though shocked at herself, as she told the Queen,[2] for her lack of compassion for the men employed) that it now never occurred to her 'to think of the punkah-man pulling at his rope. I believe they go to sleep & when awake do not mind'.

The heat was a deterrent to any activity, even to drawing in a room darkened all day by shutters. 'It is provoking to feel so utterly useless, when C works like a horse. My personal life is absolutely uneventful. Putting dimity in a drawing-room, or a new mat, is about the principal event I can look forward to.' An account of the manner in which they endured the heat is given by Lord Canning the month after their arrival.

By shutting up every chink of window from 7½ A.M., and the venetians outside, and by keeping heavy mats hung up against the outer doors into the court and garden ('compound' here called) just as you see them in Italian churches, we manage to keep the air inside the house pretty cool all day long, and, with the punkahs going, one's room is very endurable. But any attempt to go out, even in a carriage, makes one gasp, and dissolve immediately, and an open window or door lets in a flood of hot air, as though one were passing the mouth of a foundry. At 6 P.M. windows and venetians and doors are thrown open, and in comes the strong wind, blowing one's paper off the table (which is performed by the punkah at other times) and making the chandeliers swing, and their glass drops jingle, all night long. But even at night, if one gets out of the draught (which we never do, for we dine in a gale which blows up the corners of the tablecloth, and sends the bills of fare and lists of the tunes across the table, unless a fork is put on them; we sit in a gale, and we sleep in a gale), one becomes what Shelburne would call *nadando en sudor* in an instant.

Yet she found her absolutely monotonous day passing wonderfully fast. Of her husband she saw little for he started work at six while she rode at that hour in the cool of the morning and their breakfast together, with the temperature already too hot for her to take more than a glass of iced water, was always hurried over for him to get back to work. Except for luncheon at two o'clock with the staff, she would not see him again until evening when she might cajole him into taking a drive 'round & round the course bowing to all the *beau monde*, & part of the way at foot's pace', though as his work increased this form of relaxation became rarer, and she herself considered a drive a 'slow dowagery affair', and preferred a hard gallop until too hot to bear any more. Despite the climate her health did not suffer; she reassured her mother that they both stood it perfectly and that she was never better in her life, though she feared she would grow thin and soon be a skeleton and very yellow, 'like everybody here'. The poor children were like tallow candles. By October her maid was taking in the body of her dress a full four inches.

The two English maids were settling well, and enjoyed having people to work under them:

Rain greatly delights in the command of the two tailors who work for me; a third even comes in to help, & they get through beautiful neat work in a wonderfully short time. They do not embroider: a 'chicken-wallah' comes for that, who works as well as the Irish. Another man, called a 'pen-wallah,' comes every day to carry all muslins away to be ironed: so you can imagine that the maids live like ladies. All the same, I am delighted to have brought *two*, for I do not feel at all inclined to be at the mercy of an old woman & a young one, whom I have to do a certain quantity of housemaid's work, which I positively refused to have done by men. These two creatures go about with silver bangles & anklets & armlets, & are twisted up in white muslin, sometimes with orange borders.

Alone the washing of chintz presented unexpected difficulties, and since Charlotte was for ever hearing of the superiorities of Ceylon where they were said to wash, mangle, and calender to perfection, she thought of sending over a *dobie* [washerman] to be educated. In the house her lack of privacy from servants was trying, and she rather felt the loss of a heavy-footed English servant. 'I am not sure that I do not regret creaking footmen. These gliding people come & stand by one, & will wait an hour with their eye fixed on one, & their hands joined as if to say their prayers, if you do not see them, & one is quite startled to find them patiently waiting when one looks round. The showing up of visitors & taking them away & all that sort of footman's work, is entirely done by aides-de-camp, which is a horrid bore. I have such scruples at giving them so many journeys up & down, & it *is* indeed far pleasanter to have a creaking footman in livery.' Nor could she accustom herself to seeing the native bodyguard sentries, 'dressed in red like an English cavalry soldier & probably covered with medals', fanning themselves with hatchet-shaped palm fans.

With the advance of summer came also the rains and the insects. In a letter home Charlotte told of cockroaches as big as mice which ran along the floor side by side like pairs of coach horses, or would spread their wings and fly at her, and the red ants were so numerous that the legs of tables stood in saucers of water. On the dining-table insects were in such quantity that small silver covers were put over glasses to protect them, but she and Canning felt privileged in having behind them two men at meal-time whose duty it was to flap horse-tails at the insects. In her bedroom one night with five bats flying and squeaking and lizards running across the floor, she had only her mosquito net for protection. The rains brought troubles of another kind. Canning wrote of 'having to condemn dozens and dozens of gloves, and ones shoes get furry with mildew in a day, and the lining of one's hat is covered with a sort of eruption. Books, too, have to be wiped all over once a day, and despatch-boxes not opened for some time assume the appearance of a bottle of curious old port—white and fungus-y'. Charlotte also lamented the loss of her favourite yellow-white gloves from Lewis, but as they turned nankin colour with the damp she begged instead for 'the common white a *little* bluish', and to send them always wrapped in blue paper. The state of pens and ink and writing-paper she often found quite deplorable. 'There is a man whose sole office is to go round & look after everybody's writing-table throughout the house, so it ought to be all in a state of perfection, but the damp ruins everything. I have some tin boxes with false bottoms & quick lime underneath a grating & in these I keep photographs & drawing paper, & the air in these boxes has not a particle of damp; so dry it is that it feels like another climate when one puts one's head in. I mean to put my new ribbons in one of these.'

At right-angles to Government House, on the north side and in its own garden—rendered doubly beautiful by the massive trees marking its boundary—stood the spacious old Cathedral church of St John. A fine classical building, its high windows opening from the north and south aisles on to colonnades, and at the west door the carriage drive leading from impressive gates at the east end still sweeps beneath a large square porch shuttered by green venetian blinds. Although it was a stone's throw from Government House Charlotte was obliged, when she attended church, to go accompanied. This was not the only hardship. 'I never heard a worse preacher. It isnt easy to keep my old habits & twice to Church on Sunday I see will inevitably be knocked on the head. For Passion week I have tried to get to Church, but it is such an affair. I dragged an Aide de Camp there & my equipage is always the carriage and four, & four body-guards, & runners, & a jemahdar [head servant] by way of footman! It is a great

Lucknow from the top of the Great Imambara, water-colour by Charlotte Canning

Bullock-cart carrying troops up-country during the Mutiny, lithograph by G. F. Atkinson

Fort of Agra and the Taj

The Nepal Temple, Benares. Water-colours by Charlotte Canning

plague but C is all for following precedents, & my personal independence is quite at an end.'

More than once since her arrival in Calcutta Charlotte had referred to the expediency of having suitable ADCs on the staff. 'You have no idea how essential it is to get gentlemanlike good sort of Aides de Camp, for I foresee that they will be my constant companions for the next five years. They tell me I must take one out driving with me; I doubt if I can stand that. Just imagine fishing out Captain Anybody from a regiment & going driving along the Serpentine every afternoon with him.' The selection seems to have been invariably suitable and even later when young Johnny Stanley, second son of the 2nd Lord Stanley of Alderley, joined the staff and came very near falling in love with her, she was amused and delighted by him. Meanwhile she set about the task of seeing to their bungalows at Barrackpore, the British cantonment fifteen miles upstream from Calcutta, founded in 1775. Here the Governor-General had his country house, not so impressive in scale as that of Calcutta, and though at first she found it 'too English for me to appreciate properly, being quite a matter-of-course-looking place like Sion, or any park or villa anywhere', Charlotte became immensely attached to it despite lack of accommodation, and other inconveniences. Government House stood close to the river in a great park with an ancient banyan tree beside it, and immediately in front of the house Charlotte contrived to recreate a part of the Highcliffe garden. She also moved the landing-stage closer, providing alternative means of conveyance from Calcutta, though from her account to Queen Victoria it seems to have had an overriding disadvantage. 'Boating is not quite a pleasure, for one's senses are cruelly offended by the numbers of floating bodies of Hindoos who travel up & down with the tide till they entirely disappear. This holy river is thought the happiest of resting places but a mean propensity to economy in the wood of funerals causes many bodies to be launched into the water when hardly scorched. What would English Sanitary Boards say to these practices!'[3]

The wide view from her rooms across the grassy river bank

and down the broad sweep of the Hooghly was a perpetual pleasure. As she watched the boats and river-craft passing towards Calcutta in the solitary days of that first year, when Canning was immersed in work and she had no intimate friends to whom to turn for companionship (her position precluding anything but acquaintances), she must often have reflected how one day she too would sail home to the loving affection of her family where she and her husband might rediscover the intimacy they had lost. Had she been told that before that day broke she would lie by this same river bank not many yards from where she stood dreaming of home, never again to see the familiar landmarks of her own country, she might indeed have suffered a pang of sorrow; but that which her duty and her abiding love for Canning required she would with God's help perform, regardless of the consequences.

The park and the ground beyond were a great feature of Barrackpore. Immense, dark and mysterious in the twilight, at all times romantic, it also suffered the criticism of appearing too English. 'The Park is carefully planted with round headed trees to look as English as possible—more so than I approve of', Charlotte informed the Queen, 'and I am glad when Bamboos & Cocoanuts & Palms have crept in. All the apparent chestnut, elms and ash prove quite unknown on nearer view.'[4] But its charm was already potent. 'The luxuriant growth in the jungly ground outside, of dazzling green during the rains, is more beautiful than I can describe & I always think of the Palm House at Kew which gives a faint idea of it. I wish I knew the plants better but there is so little power of being out in real daylight & I cannot often indulge in very early rising as it is the thing that knocks me up.'[5] The unfamiliar shrubs and trees, the long grasses and the brilliancy of the flowering bushes here as elsewhere in India, were a never ending source of delight and she quickly learned to distinguish the mango, the peepul, the tamarind, the white poplar. The park yielded further enchantments. The pleasure garden; the menagerie inhabited by a giraffe, a tiger and cheetah, bears, even a rhinoceros, and flying squirrels; the aviary where the collection of exotic water birds, flamingoes, white egrets and 'the blue Chinese bird with a great *huppe* on its head like the bird in the fairy tale' lived in graceful arcaded structures. Built over water tanks, classical and gothic in design, over grown with creeper and slightly decaying, these lent an added romance to this curious locality. On the other side of the park was the elephant stud which Charlotte described to her mother.

We had a ride on the great elephant. It was very striking, when we were quietly going out just before sunset for our evening walk, to see the whole elephant stud, eight in all, drawn up in their howdahs and trappings to be looked at. The two largest came to eat bread out of our hands, and made their salaams to us. They are the most sensible gentle monsters. A little one is trained to play tricks and rear; his duty is to carry the silver ladder on state occasions. They are only used in camp and for state visits to native princes. We were tempted to mount and ride to the menagerie. I was delighted to look well into the trees & be on a level with their flowers, but one has a constant panic of being swept off by the branches. The driver sits behind the ear: then comes the howdah for two, & a servant sits behind. When the elephant kneels for one to get off, the ladder is about ten or twelve steps high. I believe one ought to trot along at a great pace: we only walked, & jolted very much.

Within doors matters were no better than at Calcutta. The furnishing had been sadly neglected although Lord Dalhousie had seen to one room, but red damask and velvet pile carpet were not much to Char's taste, besides being another passage room. She admitted to the Queen that the house was 'rather shabby for Lord Wellesley's grand projects were not sanctioned from home after he had finished Government House & intended to reproduce it here. I amuse myself with attempts to make this house comfortable & enliven the drawing room by decorating it with framed sketches, & Your Majesty's last gifts of portraits are surrounded by recollections of Osborne & Balmoral & all my favourite spots at home. The plan of an Indian room is odd & not in English ideas of comfort. This, for instance has 13 doors with panels like venetian blinds & 3 windows opening on a verandah. Matted floors, white walls, ceilings of painted beams exposed to view, that the ravages of white ants may be instantly discovered.'[6] To Lady Stuart de Rothesay she wrote enthusiastically: 'I am getting so fond of this place, & I believe it would look rather nice even as an English country-house, so marvellously is it improved by 450 yards of rose-chintz, a great many arm-chairs, small round tables, framed drawings &c & flowerpots in number.'

The bungalows which required attention were those for the ADCs and guests, and were dotted about the park, their thatched roofs—which remained until 1863—showing at intervals among the trees near to the river bank. They bore little resemblance to their twentieth-century counterpart being small, graceful one-storeyed houses, usually umber in colour, with an enclosed verandah on all sides but the south which was left open, the high rooms opening into each other to catch any passing breeze. Many necessities were lacking and Charlotte, hoping the day would arrive 'when every A.D.C. will have his bungalow here furnished with new chintz & a Minton jug & basin', set about making a list of purchases from home, together with instructions to her mother, and requirements of her own.

Squat china candle sticks for bedrooms to which glass shades could be put. Will you enquire & send ½ a dozen pair if they exist, of the same common stuff as the crockery; if the glass shades are there so much the better. I should not dislike also to have a ½ dozen common inkstands to match & pen-trays (*allumette* & little candlesticks would be useless here). Six neat shaped things—vases—that would hold good large bouquets would be nice for the guest bungalows, all of the same white & blue edged pattern, if a good shape exists. I am sure Goode can get it all from Minton easily. A couple of vases of some good strong colour I should like in the style of the 3 little boys supporting vases. These two last items *I* could pay for separately. Also one more little solitary *déjeuner* & tray of a neat pattern. This is all so confused that I recapitulate on the next page. The reading lamp requires more consideration than anything & I should like something very good for the eyes & well shaded & well defended from the draughts & punkahs. Pray consult authorities as to this. Every lamp & candle not shaded blows out.

Government House

Overland

Chintz in all 360 yards, 9d or 1s or 1/6 *at most*
Not *more* than 4 patterns to furnish Bungalows
6 table covers not *less* than 2 yards width
2 table covers not less than 1 yard & ½ wide

Long Sea

400 yards chintz of 2 patterns not less than 9d or more than 1/6
400 yard lining about 4d *not* calendered

Staffordshire ware

30 *sets* of washing stand crockery, soap dishes, tooth brush duties and *Chambers all with covers*
Tiles for hot water kettles, large size
18 hot water jugs
18 sponge basins
6 extra large jugs & basins
All white bordered with dark blue edges & of very neat forms easily kept clean
1 doz small teapots *Rockingham*
1 doz smallest size milk jugs
1 doz sugar basins with covers
1 doz very small slop basins
2 doz breakfast cups
2 doz plates
6 inkstands & pen trays
6 flower vases
6 pair low candlesticks with shades of glass
All white blue border.

Private order

1 high blue glass
1 pair vases, coarse china
1 small single *déjeuner* (cheap)
2 Reading lamps with shades & arrangement to prevent blowing out by the punkah
A sutherland table I should rather like that folds up.

Charlotte suggested that this order should come out 'by long sea' (round the Cape—a term familiar to earlier generations of Anglo-Indians) instead of by the shorter, partly overland, route. Greatly welcome as were letters from India, Lady Stuart de Rothesay must sometimes have received them with misgivings.

19

'In Courtly Style'

Within a few days of the Cannings' arrival in Calcutta Lord Dalhousie, the outgoing Governor-General, and his daughter Lady Susan Ramsay, gave a ball at Government House. This was to introduce a large proportion of Indian society and was a very splendid affair.

Monday was the great ball. He [Lord Dalhousie] advised me to have all the company brought up to me & introduced, & this was done, & I think it answered very well. After they had all arrived, we went into the ball-room, where there is also a throne. There are pillars all down it, and it is really very handsome indeed, &—with the draughts & punkahs—quite cool, & not full with 600 or 700 people. The supper was magnificent, every one sitting down in the marble hall under the ball-room, at five large tables. Some Amherstia flowers decorated the middle vases; it is a most beautiful plant. All the old people danced. They seem to think it quite strange that I do not.

Lady Canning in her late thirties was still a beautiful woman; sadness and anxiety, though no doubt apparent to her intimates, had not yet begun to take their toll, and the journey out had provided a measure of refreshment after the painful leave-taking. While her bearing was one of dignity her gentleness of manner was often remarked upon, and a graceful carriage, a countenance at once intelligent and refined, and a willingness to be amused, made her an object of general esteem.

On this occasion however there was a dissonant voice. Among the guests a young American, a Mr G. F. Train, had received an invitation; eighteen months later in his book *Young America Abroad in Europe, Asia, and Australia* he published a description of the evening. Although palpably affected by the glitter and splendour of the assembly his account strikes a jaundiced note.

I had been most fortunate in my arrival here, first, because the excessive heat of summer has not commenced and, secondly, because I am here at that most interesting period in Indian history when two Governor-Generals are opening the doors of Government House to hospitality and the enlivenment of balls and parties. My invitation says 'To meet Lady Canning' and I am told that the entertainment will be on an extensive scale, as the city is full of civil and military servants from all parts of India . . .

My card of invitation said 9 o'clock, and at ten my carriage was at the door; I thought I was too early, but I found myself late. The entrance, in fact the several entrances, through the several gateways to the palace had a most imposing appearance, both sides of the well-made road being lined with lamps of cocoanut oil, blazing from every post in the grounds. At the main doorway there were some two hundred servants squatting in rows in the large entrance hall, dressed in more than all the colours of the dolphin or the rainbow. I could not but notice their peculiar sitting posture, like so many pelicans on a beach. Walking through the lower hall, passing at every turn the Sepoy guard, we were shown up a long staircase and ushered into the reception-room [ballroom], without having our names announced, a contrast to such entertainments in London, where your name is passed from mouth to mouth. On enquiry I found that it was not the custom, and hastened through the outer hall to see the dancers, whose numbers fairly crowded one of the largest halls I ever witnessed.

Lord Canning, in a stiff black state dress, stood at the head of the room, in front of the chair of state—a native officer standing on either side—with what I supposed was the mace of office. The new Governor seemed fairly lost amid the blaze of chandeliers, whose dazzling brightness reflected from the prismatic glass made my eyes ache so much that I lost half the enjoyment of the evening. Lady Susan Ramsay, the daughter of Lord Dalhousie, was on the right, leading off, with all the gaiety of youth, the first quadrille. The daughter of the Commander-in-Chief [General Anson] was in the same set, and received particular attention from the elegant aide-de-camp by her side. Neither of these young ladies need look for her portrait in the 'Book of Beauty'. Lady Canning did not dance while I was present, but reclining in courtly style upon the regal chair, received court from her honoured lord and the several distinguished civilians and the military officers present. The formality of her reception was freezing, for that aristocratic bow was worse than an electric shock. Her dress was of white tulle, over a white satin skirt, looped up with red roses, with a head-dress of red velvet and pearls—not, in my opinion, elegant; but the blaze of diamonds compensated for what was wanting in taste. She still possesses the marks of early beauty, but time and the dissipations of her exalted position in London have diminished the attractions of youth.

Later I saw a significant movement of the great leaders towards the stairs, all pairing off with punctilious ceremony, and following on I found myself in the supper-room [marble hall], a room even larger than the saloon, the tables arranged after the shape of three-fourths of a square, with a long one in the entrance aisle adjoining, and seats and plates for at least fifteen hundred guests; and yet there were many who remained without a place, myself among the rest, for I was too busy noticing the movements of those around me to look out for Number One.[1]

Charlotte, hearing of this passage after the publication of the book, showed no indignation and simply related the facts: 'I had hardly any voice & I could not attempt to speak to many, so you may hear again of the "freezing aristocratic manner" Mr Train, the American, attributes to me in his book of travels. I want so much to see it for only the extract about me is in the papers. By the way "the regal chair" was a red sofa I shared with Lady Susan Ramsay & Mrs Anson, & the ball was the one given by Lord Dalhousie on our arrival. Do read the book and do not believe in the bad taste of the toilette he describes.'

She had a good eye for dress and was thankful that the wardrobe she had brought with her had arrived in the 'most perfect preservation, & proves to be very suitable, though I might be a little hurt at my "elegant simplicity of dress" being remarked in a newspaper, when I thought I was the finest of the fine'. Though she considered that 'muslin for ever & ever is the only comfortable thing, & white looks certainly best', she nevertheless sent commissions throughout the year to England. 'Your ribbons are excellent & perfect as to colour. I think it would be well to have a dozen yards of moderate width for bonnet strings or bows & a very broad white sash every now & then, about every two months, with gloves from Lewis.' Occasionally the execution of the errands was unsuccessful and Lady Stuart de Rothesay was not exempt from reproof.

Of presents I thank you so very much for the green velvet wreath—the prettiest shape possible,— & some blackcurrants I am a little puzzled to know how to put in. Of commissions, thanks for the beautiful choice of sashes. Colours look so sick & washy here that the bright blue & pink did one's eyes good—pink ribbon turns very soon to blotting paper colour. I like 2 muslins better than the 3rd, a lilac, & the little stands for the dinner table do very well, they are rather too small but can be used, I think. The only thing quite unworthy of your taste & I saw from your description that you did not really like them, are those gilt dresden vases. I cannot say I like them at all & I never care for a bargain for the sake of a bargain. I have put them on consoles in a distant part of the room & they look as if they belonged to the house. If ever you see a very pretty Parian thing for flowers I should sometimes like it or a pair of them.

As time elapsed Charlotte managed to overcome the awkward behaviour of most of the English society which in the beginning she found perplexing.

The plan here is for every one to come very early, long before they are asked, and no one to go till the greatest lady gets up to take leave, then all the others come up & bow in a flock, & off they go, & are all cleared away in two minutes, the A.D.Cs handing the ladies. The A.D.Cs also receive the ladies and hand them in, but some shy ones still touchingly cling to their husbands, their natural protectors, & look very absurd dragged up by two men.

Though Charlotte declared she thought there would never be 'the least approach to "society" in this house', she hastened to reassure her mother.

It is quite a mistake to suppose that the society here is *bad*. Even flirting is very rare & of the mildest description, & I really believe hardly any woman but *me* goes out riding without her husband. It is really a very proper place; its greatest sin is its intense dulness, with some frivolity—

of a dull kind too. People here are not inclined to toady; on the contrary, they are rather independent & more like republicans; but still the influence & example of the Governor-General is very great, & 'Government House' is looked up to as the authority for everything to a degree which is astonishing. People, you say, tell you that I have done good & have influence. I am not in the slightest degree aware of it, & not conscious that I have done anything but lead a more idle & selfish life than I ever did before in all my days, but that it should ever be *said* rather shows what I mean of the way this establishment is the centre of everything. Gossiping & evil-speaking is very common, I am told; so if there is bad to tell, it comes out soon enough. No one is intimate enough to gossip to me, so I cannot speak from experience.

Taking the entertaining seriously, she judged that instead of allowing everyone to come and call, a reception, and several dinners for thirty a week, would be preferable. 'We have had two dinners of thirty—a sprinkling of grandees & a mass of official & military. The thirty-dinners are so much more manageable than the fifties that we shall keep to them: we can speak to all the people and remember them; they are so dreadfully shy, & one's wretched topics never are the least added to.' She was aware that people were diffident of approaching her and that they 'look around when I go & sit by them & not one man has ever voluntarily spoken to me since I came to India, except General Anson & Sir John Colvile [Chief Justice]. All the others I have to send for, or if they look tractable to beckon to come & speak to me & the ladies look terribly afraid. I shall have to go my rounds like the Queen after dinner, only standing for one second is evidently thought quite indecorous here.'

The rooms were huge and the dining-room table of immoderate length. 'The large cloths do very well indeed', she wrote home on receiving a welcome consignment of goods (for till now there were only cotton tablecloths '& not a particle of linen in the house'), 'but don't imagine we are not "up" to the dodge of joining two. Why, our table at its full length requires two long cloths or perhaps *three* of eight yards', and proceeded to explain the necessity for such a long table. 'People always sit in armchairs at dinner all over India. I am the only person who does not, & now when I dine out I find people do me the attention of putting a small chair. The arms shut in one's crinolines & petticoats & one feels quite buried in them & one's elbows unnaturally hunched up & a general appearance of clothes out of their place in a way I greatly object to—but this all explains why dinner tables for 50 or 56 people are far longer than in England. The rooms too are large, more than 50 ft by 20 or 30 is the size of all the rooms in the wings that are called small.'

The Queen's birthday on May 24th was celebrated by a great ball. Canning though unwell 'not only came "in state", but stayed till half-past two, & was not really the worse. The ball was a grand affair—C gave the Queen's health. I sat next to him, for I am rather for putting myself into prominent places on these state occasions. Lady Dalhousie came in later by a side entrance with an A.D.C. That would never have suited me; I would rather have stayed away altogether; so I came in with C in what seems to me my proper place. The new-mounted tiara came in appropriately with a white tulle gown with Brussel's lace, & a bouquet of magnificent real double-pomegranate to give one spot of colour. C wore his smartest Cabinet Minister's uniform, which made such a splash of gold that we were quite fine enough'. At the conclusion of each dance the dancers walked round 'as at a country ball in England', Charlotte noted with delight.

At Barrackpore things went rather better despite Charlotte's first lament at 'this exceedingly ill-*monté* house; the dinner, with its cotton table-cloth and Bohemian glass & candlesticks looks exactly like a *table-d'hôte*', and by degrees the dinners improved though by November Charlotte was sighing 'we are rather barbarous still'. To their many visitors however Barrackpore offered an agreeable interlude.

'I am afraid they must be very dull at home for they make the most of their visit here, & arrive at about ten in the morning, & some even at eight, to rooms vacated at six, which would distress housekeepers & housemaids in civilised countries'.

Laughingly she remembered how in England she used to wait at inns & railway stations, rather than get to a country-house before six in the evening at earliest! We can lodge one guest in the house, all the others are dotted about in the park in twos & threes in the bungalows—thatched cottages, where each person has a bedroom, dressing-room & bathroom. They are fetched backwards & forwards in a sort of covered chair, called a *tonjon*, or by some a "John Pon", which name delights me.

On Sundays there was their own church which Charlotte was able to attend 'at ten o'clock & again at 6 o'clock—a neat little church, & attentive congregation of officers & wives, Mr Nicholson preached useful earnest sermons'. A further cause for satisfaction (though not openly expressed) was that the custom of short sermons had always prevailed at Barrackpore.

There appeared to be few duties which Charlotte by virtue of her husband's position was called upon to perform. Within a month or two of her arrival she inspected the School for Native Girls, all dressed 'like ghosts in white shrouds'; one child in particular acting out a story captured her attention, 'the most amusing thing I ever saw, there was such expression in the child's face, eyes thrown up, gesticulations & little stamps'. Dr Kaye, Principal of Bishop's College which had been founded as a residence for European missionaries and for the instruction of the Christian doctrine, gave her much valuable information concerning 'S.P.G. Mission doings', but her most interesting experience was her visit to the school for High Caste Hindoo Girls. 'The Hindoo men', she told Queen Victoria, 'have a proper value for education but its great enemies are the old women who think it quite improper, & that only dancing girls ought to know how to read & write.'[2] She wrote diligently to the Queen and it is evident that her letters were appreciated.

Buckingham Palace
June 22nd 1856

My dearest Lady Canning,

Over & over again I had intended to thank you for your two kind & most interesting letters . . . but I am now determined to delay it no longer, the more so, as I fear I shall get no other from you, if I don't write. I am now anxious to tell you that I wish *you* would write to me every six weeks—whether you hear from me or not as it seems else so long not to hear from you. I must likewise remind Lord Canning that I have *not* heard from him yet;—his Predecessor used to write to me sometimes every two or three months, sometimes not so often—sometimes much oftener when any thing was going on—but always from time to time giving me a short account of the state of the Country —of our relations with the Native Princes, the finances & improvements,—so I hope I shall soon hear from him . . .

Our eldest girl's prospects have *since* her confirmation *on the 20th* of March—no longer been kept secret, though as *the* marriage is *not* to take place till *after* she is seventeen—it will *not* be officially or publicly announced till shortly before the time. We have had Prince Frederic William staying with us since the 21st of May, & the young people are extremely attached to each other & very happy together & *he* wonderfully in love! . . .

The great event now looked forward to with much joy & impatience—is the return of my *dear* Guards [from the Crimea],—which is daily expected & who after being first inspected by us at Aldershot, will be received in Triumph in London . . . I send you *two* very good Chromo-lithographs of ourselves—from Drawings done by Winterhalter at the same time when he made the Princess Royal's,—a Lithograph of little Leopold & a Lithograph *just finished* from a sketch Winterhalter did this spring of Victoria in her *first Court Dress.* The Prince wishes to be most kindly named to you.

In replying to this letter on August 8th Charlotte, gratefully acknowledging the permission to write every six weeks, declared: 'It will always be a delight to me to remember the last fortnight I was at Balmoral when I saw the Princess Royal & Prince Frederich William almost in their first acquaintance & have had the advantage of knowing how amiable he is & how fitted to make her Royal Highness's home a happy one, like that she will leave.'[3] It was left to the Princess Royal writing from Balmoral to answer in 'dear Mama's name', and to describe many of the improvements at 'this Place which has so many charms for us all'. The old house had gone, the new tower was in place. 'I think when everything is finished here there will not be a more beautiful place in the world.'

Florence Nightingale was staying at Birkhall and though 'pleasing and attractive', the Princess Royal judged her to be 'very thin, and people say that she looks aged since she has returned from the East', but never having seen her before this was a point she could not determine.

A collection of insects promised for Osborne Museum consisting of centipedes, tarantulas, scorpions and 'insects like dry sticks & others of the mantis sort, exactly like leaves' had at last been assembled. They were obliged to go the long way home for the overland route would have shaken them to powder. 'I fear the Princes will think I have forgotten.'[4] When they finally reached Osborne the following year the Prince of Wales and Prince Alfred hastened to send their thanks. Prince Alfred, aged twelve, had recently returned from a winter at Geneva and a visit to Gotha, and the engaging manner with which he concluded his letter: 'Though I have not been quite as far as India, I have seen a good deal', must have afforded Charlotte a smile.

In the middle of June there had been a welcome addition to the Governor-General's staff with the arrival of Canning's nephew, Lord Dunkellin, as his Military Secretary and ADC. 'Dunkellin arrived', Char reported, 'prosperous & merry & bearded & red. We talked by the hour & it is very pleasant to have him.' His own view of Calcutta was critical, but since he was described by a contemporary as a 'typical *viveur*, immensely popular, very dashing',[5] it is not surprising that he found the society 'bad and stupid',[6] and looked elsewhere for his amusements.[7] But his pleasure at seeing the Cannings again was very real, writing home that 'I thought Aunt C in great blow' and though Uncle C had 'thinned and looks pasty', he did not think there was much the matter with him.[8]

With what relief the family at home must have read of Charlotte's growing contentment: 'I am growing to like India, & am now thoroughly accustomed to it.' Though it was still very hot the air seemed lighter and she could stay out a full hour before breakfast, and at Barrackpore could 'potter about the garden as I might in England. Four or five servants follow me & one will hold up a scarlet umbrella with gold fringes, like one in a pantomime'. But so accustomed was she becoming to this mode of life that she hardly observed it. At last with cooler weather the punkahs were taken down and—'a very wintery sign'—officers were appearing in 'black cloth continuations', people were buying merinos, and a spaniel belonging to an ADC was wearing a winter suit at night.

The year ended with news from Lady Stuart de Rothesay of the death of Princess Lieven, friend of so many years. 'One to be missed, perhaps, more than regretted but I do regret her. It takes me back almost to my first ball, & to *your* first ball, & all the political interests of so many years of my life.' But it was her daughter whose absence she regretted, and writing on Christmas Eve she allowed herself an exclamation of longing, 'Oh dearest Char, to think of the second Christmas since we parted having come round'.

Left. Countess Canning in the dress she wore for camp marches. *Right.* Earl Canning. Photographs taken in Calcutta, 1860

Khyber Pass

Valley and Fort of Kangra, Himalayas in the background.
Water-colours by Charlotte Canning

20

India, 1857

The year 1857, remembered henceforward as one of massacre, bloodshed, and bitter internal strife, opened inauspiciously in Calcutta with a race week, and fearing her family might consider this a dissipation Charlotte was swift to reassure them that she had done her duty by Church at ten o'clock on New Year's Day; indeed she had always kept to her English habits and never rode or went for a drive but on weekdays. Her occupations followed their usual couse. New arrangements for entertaining predisposed her in favour of two small balls and a buffet, no 'sitting-supper'; also a large dinner followed by 'a regular drum' which though getting off to a bad start with all the women seated stolidly in rows while the men stood like waiters behind them, soon developed satisfactorily. Missionaries, Baptist missionaries from Burma in particular, were of concern, also mission schools and charity institutions. With the cooler January weather there was greater opportunity for sketching and it was now that she started on the important series of drawings of rare flowers and trees, most carefully observed and minutely recorded, which were sent home to be mounted and to prevent spoiling by damp. Today her dazzling intensity of colour reflecting the vegetation of the East in all its magic brilliance and delicacy remains undiminished, and these studies are a pitiful reminder of that fateful year when Charlotte's mind, ravaged by uncertainty and care, sought distraction from the fearful tidings which each day brought.

At the beginning of February there was a pleasing circumstance in the belated arrival of Christmas presents by long sea.

The little almanack is very good & wonderfully cheap; as to the little books to give away I do not think they will be of much use for I must always give rather better things than those. When I give to the Orphan Schools it is to their libraries & not to the individuals, or if I give prizes they have to be solid well bound books. A few of the *illustrated* Poets you have sent may do well for that sort of thing. The 19th century Poets is a charming book. The papier maché books from Christchurch are rather pretty but I think I shall end by giving one to Rain & one to West.

Now for your gifts to C. I do not think he can find a moment for writing so I must thank you for him for the most charming green *papier* Almanack that ever was. It is a really useful & comfortable thing to have & green *papiers* are more wanted here than anything. The little ink stand has met with some damage & puzzles us, but we suppose its merit to be to stand sometimes on one end sometimes on the other, but may it hold ink with no other sort of inside? We have an artillery A.D.C. whom I shall consult on the habits of such articles as this 'mortar'. I have got Lou's drawings; it may be a shame to say it but I think in the finished drawing Lou has lost a little of her spirited style & there is a little degree of cramped Pre-Raphaelitism which is quite unsuitable in water-colours. In oils any amount of cramped finish may answer but I think not in water-colours. I think Ruskin is rather spoiling Lou & I shall be glad when she takes a little to her old way again. Do preach small oil pictures to Lou *if* she will finish up so much, but let her water-colours be slight & free & yet rich in colour.

With regard to some good Buhl furniture offered by Lady Stuart de Rothesay, but refused, Charlotte reflected that it would be curious to see handsome furniture again after the 'horrid whatnots & chiffoniers' with which she was surrounded. Meanwhile she was in need of three hundred and fifty yards of muslin for drawingroom curtains which were to come overland, with a duplicate order by long sea. A further commission of a bottle of *eau de Hesse* from the rue Neuve des Petits Champs, in Paris, to help save her hair from turning grey, was the cause of a disaster.

You will be sorry to hear that the packing of your goods is never quite what it ought to be & this last box has been deluged in Eau de Hesse. It ought never to have been sent in the stone *crûche* for the shape alone would make it unsafe & packed in a box with heavy things it was quite certain to break. It ought to have been put in a tin case, soldered up is safer than the stone *crûche*. Then the artificial flowers were not made fast to the sides of the carton & all laid together in a sort of ball in the middle thumping upon one flower which was duly fastened. The stereoscope came well, only the bottom glass cracked which does not matter & the glass pictures for it quite safe because they were firmly packed between two bits of wood. But Lou's photograph of herself had got so bent that there is a crease on the pasteboard which makes a mark all across one side (it is very pretty & like), it should have been between two firm cards. The Hesse spared all that & only spoiled the outside paper. As to my flowers [drawings] which go to you by this mail I shall be glad for you to keep them for I consider them as C's property, but you can do what you like with them meanwhile & charge the carriage of the box to us—it will be a heavy expense.

At the end of 1856 the Queen had lost her half-brother Prince Charles of Leiningen, son of the Duchess of Kent by a previous marriage; she sent many particulars of his fatal illness.

Buckingham Palace
February 24th 1857

Dear Lady Canning,

. . . I was sure you would kindly feel for me & dear Mama in the heavy affliction which befell us in November in the loss of my *dearest*, *only* Brother whom you remember the picture of health & strength. He had a paralytic seizure similar to this last fatal one in November 55 from which he had recovered—to a great extent at least—tho' we have since heard that he was very far from well & had frequent threatenings. From the time he was seized with this last fatal attack there never was any hope—tho' we in imperfect knowledge of the actual case hoped during nine long—cruel days. But there was complete paralysis both of the limbs (except his left arm) and of the internal principal organs—with almost entire loss of speech—tho' not of consciousness. A real recovery was hopeless & therefore we feel God took him in mercy—but to dear Mama & us Sisters it has been a heavy blow & has left a *great* blank.

Dear Mama bore up with great resignation & her health has not suffered materially, tho' her nerves have a good deal, & she has hardly come out at all of an Evening as yet,—at least very seldom. She is *now* still at Frogmore . . .

Here there have been some very melancholy events. Poor Lord Ellesmere's illness terminated fatally on the 18th & the frightful accident poor Lord Harewood had out hunting nearly a month ago, since which time he lingered between life & death, likewise came to a fatal termination on the 22nd. These are very sad events—embracing such vast family connections that the mourning is immense.

. . . Knowing how *worthy you* are of Photographs I send you two of Victoria which are extremely successful & very much liked. We have a good many of them coloured like miniatures & nothing could be liker.

Now with the Prince's and our Children's kind remembrances to yourself and our's to Lord Canning believe me ever,

Your's affectionately V R

Poor Mrs Bradshaw's death is also very shocking. She was my former Maid of Honour Fanny Devereux. . . . She has left *five* little children.

The first sign of anything amiss was briefly mentioned by Charlotte on February 11th and concerned the unrest among Sepoys, caused by greased cartridges which they were obliged to bite or tear open with their teeth to load the newly-issued Enfield rifle. The grease was said to be made of the fat of cow and pig, contact with which ran counter to Hindu or Muslim faith. The East India Company's army in British India—the Bengal Army—though in general commanded by British officers, consisted mostly of Sepoys whose loyalty had never been questioned. But it was not alone the army which showed signs of restlessness; the Government in Calcutta had failed to observe that reforms, annexations of territories—Oudh in particular—and fear of Christianity being made compulsory, led to growing discontent among the people of all classes. Rumours, quickly flaring up, were circulated and spread, fears kindled, superstititions, such as the ending of British rule in this, the centenary of Plassey, were rife; morale was low. There was the 'odd mysterious' sending of chupatties (small scone-like biscuits) from place to place, commented on by Charlotte, each man making twelve, keeping two and sending on ten to the next man—inexplicable, yet perhaps an omen. Undercurrents of subversion and mutiny were manifest throughout Bengal and the North-West Provinces.

The first severe outbreak occurred in the 19th Regiment forcing its disbandment at Barrackpore which was now under the command of General Hearsey, a man 'of plenty of nerve; being a great boaster & talker one is surprised to know what sense & coolness he can show'. His knowledge of Indian natural history was prodigious and for 'a *short* time is not a bore, but the tremendous noise & laugh of this enormous strong old man would be too much for long'. The disbanding was an anxious business carried out successfully as Charlotte noted on her birthday, with the temperature at 91°. A week later she added reassuringly that the incident at Barrackpore was 'over & all quiet'. Her next duty was to write to the Queen.

Government House. April 9th 1857[1] . . . The disbanding went off quietly and the General of the Division, General Hearsey, who is most fluent in Hindostanee made the men good useful speeches. Lord Canning's general order will be read by this time to all regiments and I trust the matter will be set at rest.

The excuse has been the use of some Minie cartridges unfortunately greased with *Beef* suet, the obnoxious cartridges were withdrawn, & sepoys told to find grease for themselves, but the notion that their caste was to be broken, & that they must become Christian, spread widely. At least that is the pretended grievance & many most ridiculous stories were invented in support of the rumour. One being that Lord Canning signed a bond to Your Majesty that he would make them all Christian in 3 years. There was quite a panic as the day for the arrival of the Regiment approached, but the disbanding ended quietly tho' in presence of two disaffected Regiments, one very bad one [34th], the prime instigator of the misdeeds of that disbanded . . . Sepoys are the most tractable good people, but any fear that religion or caste shall be tampered with, can always excite them to every possible folly. I do not think the matter is quite at an end yet . . . but with proper precautions there is no cause for further anxiety.

Four weeks later the Mutiny had broken out.

Government House, Calcutta, May 19th 1857[2]

The mail will take to Your Majesty some very sad accounts of the strange and terrible outbreaks in the last 9 days at Meerut & Delhi . . .

The Cannings had now been in India just over a year. 'The anniversary of our arrival', Charlotte wrote on March 1st. 'It is difficult to believe it is a year, & yet I always feel as if it was a lifetime.' Notwithstanding the monotony she found a great deal to interest her. Powerless to avoid being overheard by sentries, punkah-wallahs, and servants, in a house of open doors, she had now overcome her shyness and sang and played the pianoforte; another point gained was her attendance at St John's which was done 'quietly & alone, which is very comfortable'. Canning's work had multiplied during his first year in office. The war with Persia in the early part of 1857 provoked by the infiltration of Persians into Herat, the 'Key of India', constituted a Russian threat and further reduced the Indian economy. A serious annual deficit and an increased Indian Debt at the time of Canning's arrival had made the country's finances an overriding problem. Furthermore, changes of administration in the Indian Army were needed and various measures required legislation. By the time of the outbreak of the Mutiny Canning had never yet left Calcutta and Barrackpore. Unsparing of himself, Charlotte could scarcely prevail on him to take air and exercise; at great speed and alone he might occasionally be observed walking round and round the gravel path of Government House wholly absorbed in some problem that awaited him indoors which would keep him up until the small hours. By nature a reserved and silent—some might say ungracious—man, cautious to a degree, slow to act, he was resolute for justice. 'A cultivated man of patient thought and perseverance, of most impartial and yet inflexible mind', wrote a contemporary, 'his great defect was want of decision in time of emergency; but this irresolution and vacilation were undoubtedly the result of high conscientiousness, of almost morbid scruples, which on some occasions during the Mutiny were extremely perilous.'[3]

Overtired, unable or unwilling to husband his strength,

weighed down by anxiety and overwhelming responsibility, often surrounded by incompetence and jealousy, lacking the necessary military force, harassed by the Press and European community in Calcutta and at home denounced for leniency and incompetence by a large section of the public, and with the Government demanding his recall, he nevertheless remained firm in his conviction of where his duty lay. 'As long as I have any breath in my body', he wrote to Lord Granville (Lord President), 'I will pursue no other policy than that which I have been following; not only for the reason of expediency and policy . . . but because it is just. *I* will not govern in anger. Justice, and that as stern and inflexible as law and might can make it, I will deal out. But I will never allow an angry or indiscriminating act or word to proceed from the Government of India as long as I am responsible for it.'[4] So noble a declaration, matched by his actions, belonged to a man of inexhaustible courage; to Lord Curzon (a future Viceroy), writing later, he appeared 'endowed with the vesture of real greatness', his qualities having 'conferred a measure of immortality upon his name'. It is a paradox of the whirligig of time that the epithet 'Clemency', flung at him by his hostile countrymen, should have enhanced the name made illustrious by his father.

The story of carnage, suffering, and faith, during the months of rebellion is too well-known to afford repetition. In England where the shock was overwhelming, Lord Malmesbury noted that when the *Observer*, reported: 'That with vigour and energy we may still keep India', a friend remarked: 'A fortnight ago we should as soon have thought of losing Manchester as India'.[5] To Charlotte, constantly beside her husband encouraging him with undeviating loyalty and bearing the burden of his unpopularity whilst it seemed to affect him not at all, these were agonizing months; for the chasm between them had not been bridged. 'By the side of Canning we see the gentle and tragic figure of his accomplished wife, her youth and beauty ebbing away under the appalling strain, her happiness, though not her devotion, shadowed by a cloud, the blame for which had been exclusively his.'[6] The massacre of Cawnpore, siege of Lucknow, the vain expectation of the fall of Delhi still in rebel hands; the deaths of military leaders, Havelock, Wheeler, Sir Henry Lawrence, Anson, Barnard, Neill; the daily reports of disease, starvation, treachery; these brought her very low but never to despair. Transport ships steaming up the river to Calcutta bringing reinforcements renewed her spirits. A dauntless courage upheld her. She caught a low fever which left her 'achy and sore all over' but managed to throw it off observing that 'they call it cold. *I* call it bilious'. The Queen's letters expressing sympathy helped to sustain her.

Buckingham Palace
July 5th 1857

Dear Lady Canning, I had long intended writing . . . when I received your last of 19th May with all the sad & alarming news of the insurrection at Meerut & Delhi. It is an anxious moment but we have great confidence in Lord Canning & in General Anson & trust to hear soon of the fall of Delhi. Still I fear that there is a dangerous spirit amongst the Native Troops & that a fear of their religion being tampered with is at the bottom of it. I think that the greatest care ought to be taken not to interfere with their religion—as once a *cry* of that kind is raised amongst a fanatical people—very strictly attached to their religion—there is no knowing what it may lead to & where it may end.

Here everything is going on very well . . . My Uncle the King of the Belgians is here . . . with his . . . daughter who is to be married already on the 27th to the Archduke Maximilian who was here also, about ten days ago & is a charming person. *Our* bridegroom is likewise here—since four weeks but the marriage will not take place till the middle or latter part of January.

I am stronger & better than ever I was, since the birth of our little Beatrice who is a very pretty, strong child. I hope very soon to send you Photographs & also new Lithographs of some of our Children. Winterhalter has just painted a beautiful Picture of Victoria; it is wonderfully like & a beautiful work of art . . .

Here there have been many sad deaths, beginning with my dearest Aunt Gloster who has left a *sad* blank never to be filled up! . . . We are expecting the Visits at Osborne—1st (I believe) Prince Napoleon for a night— & later the Emperor & the Empress of the French, quite a private visit. The Queen of Holland is also coming over to travel about in England—so you see we have no end of Visitors.

Hoping soon to hear from you again, dear Lady Canning & with the Prince's and our Children's kind remembrance, believe me always

Your's affectionately V R

I think you may like these little Photographs. Our's are from *nature* and that of dear Aunt Gloster after Winterhalter's Portrait.

The rebellion was confined to the Bengal Army of which not more than a quarter of the Sepoys mutinied, but the small available British force and the immense distance it was obliged to travel from Calcutta to reach Benares, Allahabad, Cawnpore, Lucknow, and Delhi the main objective nine hundred miles away, made the hurried movement of troops and equipment in pitiless heat one of severest difficulty. The lack of horses resulted in bullock carts being used; this was a speedier method than marching since they covered two and a half miles an hour, but being without springs, and unable to carry more than one hundred men a day progress was wearisome and slow; in the plains the heat was so fierce that for five hours in the middle of the day there was no movement at all. 'Fast travelling dâk carriages, little vehicles drawn by one horse', as Charlotte explained to the Queen,[7] were an alternative but here the maximum was twenty-four men a day; the river was the slowest means of transport for until the rains began in the third week of June it was scarcely high enough to be available to steamers. At Simla, General Anson, Commander-in-Chief, moved down from the hills collecting men at Ambala, preparing to march on Delhi, but was struck down by cholera and died at Kernaul. Cawnpore had fallen on June 26th; for three weeks General Wheeler had led its garrison of less than four hundred men against three thousand rebels. On being forced to surrender, the women and children were promised a safe journey down the Ganges to Allahabad by Nana Sahib, the rebel leader, but once in the boats (in which there were no oars and the rudders were tied[8]) they were fired upon at point-blank range and mown down. Those who escaped, about one hundred in number, were held until General Havelock advancing with his force was within a day's march, and were then slaughtered and thrown down a well. Sepoys refusing the task, Mohammedan butchers were brought in to finish the massacre.[9]

On July 20th Charlotte wrote to the Queen:[10]

The sad news of the fall of Cawnpore after the sad death of Sir H Wheeler & the massacre of the garrison has proved too true, but no details are known. The horror of the story is now redoubled by hearing that all the poor women and children in the Nana's hands were put to death on the approach of General Havelock. The horrors committed by this man are too dreadful to relate. He has murdered every fugitive.

She hoped that the well and the surrounding ground would be consecrated and a memorial erected to sanctify the spot. The proposal, which was adopted, of a white marble Angel of the Resurrection was her own, but in its execution the sculptor Marochetti unfortunately deviated slightly from her original conception and the result was not entirely satisfactory.

Following the deaths of General Anson, and of General Barnard, also from cholera, General Grant had been appointed temporary Commander-in-Chief, and General Havelock a veteran soldier with great knowledge of India newly arrived from Persia, was put in command of the troops moving up from Calcutta. By many he was thought too outdated in his methods and Charlotte noted that 'he is not in fashion, but all the same we believe he will do well. No doubt he is fussy & tiresome, but his little, old, stiff figure looks as active & fit for use as if he were made of steel.' Taking Cawnpore on July 17th he continued to Lucknow hoping to reach there within a week and relieve the heroic siege in which Sir Henry Lawrence, Commissioner in Oudh, one of three brothers distinguished for their service to India, had been killed.

'The death of the brave Sir Hugh Wheeler is not the only one of your Generals that Your Majesty has now to lament', Charlotte continued in her letter of July 20th, 'for I grieve to say that Sir Henry Lawrence has died of his wound. He received it in a sortie which failed thro' the treachery of his native artillerymen & cavalry & he had to retire into the fortified Residency & died soon after. He is a most dreadful loss. He was all that could be described as most brave & chivalrous & most remarkable for talent & energy, as well as for goodness & generosity. His defence of Lucknow had been so spirited & the worst of it so nearly over, that his death at such a moment seems doubly sad... There seems every reason to hope that General Havelock will arrive in time... Numbers of sufferers from up country arrive in Calcutta. Ladies & children who have wandered about for weeks thro' dangers & horrors one wonders they could survive, & even now not knowing if their husbands still live. Many of these poor things are almost naked or clothed in rags. The moment a subscription was opened here it filled at the rate of 800£ or 1000£ a day...

On August 10th a further letter was directed to the Queen.[11]

I cannot write to Your Majesty all the horrors we have to mourn over. The Cawnpore massacres were the worst of all & little has yet come to light. Two officers and two sergeants have been heard of who escaped from the boats by swimming & some drummer's families. Poor little scraps of journal, one by a child, & a letter from a lady to her mother with verses of 'Farewell' were picked up in that house when they were murdered. The sight of those rooms makes strong men faint—the bodies were never seen. All were already thrown down a well.

We hope General Havelock has got to Lucknow. He began brilliantly after crossing the Ganges; with his *1600* he defeated *13000* & took 15 guns that day... the thought of the crowd of helpless people & the brave little garrison of the Lucknow 'Residency' must urge him on. And the men are real heroes!

Obliged to relinquish his attempt to reach Lucknow, Havelock at Cawnpore awaited the arrival of General Outram with reinforcements. On August 24th Charlotte wrote again.[12]

The great anxiety now is for Lucknow & the thought of it haunts one day & night. General Havelock's attempts to relieve it were most gallant! his little band repeatedly defeated great and large numbers of the enemy but his force was too small to bear this constant & harrassing duty, with unceasing exposure & much cholera in his camp. At last he recrossed the Ganges to Cawnpore (on the 13th I think) having beaten the enemy the day before & no attempt was made to molest him. The sickness at Cawnpore has been very great I regret to say.

Sir James Outram has been heard of from Dinapore, he commands that & the Cawnpore division & will strain every nerve to collect enough force to make an attempt to save those poor people in Lucknow—so there is still a ray of hope.

The Residency buildings are strongly fortified & they alone are now held. There are many wives of officers and civilians and numbers of children who crowded there from all parts to take refuge. They must already have had a time of great suffering & anxiety & one must indeed earnestly pray for their rescue.

I am sure Your Majesty has felt deeply for all these sad events—and I trust I do not err in writing so often & at so much length . . . Your Majesty's gracious expression of confidence in Lord Canning is most cheering to him & most gratefully appreciated.

At last on September 5th Havelock, with the brutal and ruthless General Neill, was able to set out for Lucknow where for three months the besieged had been enduring the worst of sweltering heat and monsoon, without sufficient ammunition, food, or medicine. The heroism of this small garrison in the Residency opposing a very superior numerical force established the siege of Lucknow as an epic in British history.

With these cruel engagements taking place in the north (in June and July alone almost thirty towns mutinied), a prey to sleeplessness and anxiety by night, and by day racked with uncertainty and horror, Charlotte continued nevertheless to show an outward calm. In May the Cannings had given their ball for the Queen's birthday, 'everything was exactly done as usual. It was a dowdy ball I must own, for the gowns looked limp & faded as their owners— & all the beauties gone'. An escape for change of air to Barrackpore, where the park had never seemed 'more dazzling in colour—like the greenest young wheat & emeralds', had made her 'really hungry & we thought the mango fish deserved their reputation. They are like smelts with a roe & come up with the tide & are either fried or done in a kind of water zouchy with unripe mangoes & capsicums'. But she was not away for long; the great ships bearing European regiments were at last steaming up the river to Calcutta and their officers were awaited with eagerness at Government House before moving up country. The arrival of the kilted 78th Highlanders

(Seaforth) created a singular impression for none had ever been seen in Bengal. It was said that 'the Lord Sahib has sent for a regiment of Demons, who wear no clothes: the last must have been an addition, for certainly no Indian ever wore a quarter as many'.

The European population in Calcutta was apprehensive of local mutiny and begged that Lord Canning should allow them a Volunteer Defence force, and their first patrol in 'neat blue flannel uniform with red facings & with sola helmets' had reassured them accordingly. Charlotte could only suggest that 'if it does no good, it need do no harm', but she could not have foreseen that on a Sunday a fortnight later—'Panic Sunday' as it so graphically became known—a rumour of a Barrackpore mutiny sent the entire defence guard into flight.[13] More serious was the disarming of the native bodyguard. 'These men have all been at least 13 years in the Corps', Charlotte told the Queen, '& all have medals & clasps. They were very often tampered with & tho' not mistrusted it was thought safer to disarm them. General Grant wished it, & Lord Canning with regret agreed. It is right to be very cautious. The fanatical mania comes on so unexpectedly & frightfully.'[14]

When the following letter reached Charlotte she noted down: 'I had the kindest letter from the Queen full of sympathy towards those who have suffered. I must tell it to everyone for it is so warmly expressed'.

Balmoral
September 8th 1857

Dear Lady Canning,

I have to thank for several kind & interesting letters . . . That our thoughts are almost *solely* occupied with India & with the fearful state in which everything there is—that we *feel* as we did during Crimean days & indeed *far* more anxiety, you will easily believe. That my heart *bleeds* for the horrors that have been committed by people once so gentle—(who seem to be seized with some awful mad fanaticism [for that is what] it is there cannot be a doubt) on my poor Country Women & their innocent little children—you, dearest Lady Canning who have shared my sorrows and anxieties for my beloved suffering

Troops will comprehend. It haunts me *day* & night. *You* will let all who have escaped & suffered & all who have *lost* dear ones in so dreadful a manner *know* of my sympathy;—you *cannot* say too much. A Woman & above all a Wife & Mother can only *too well* enter into the agonies gone thro' of the massacres. I ask *not* for details, I *could not bear* to hear more, but of those who have escaped I *should* like to hear as much about as you can tell me.

I feel for you & Lord Canning most deeply! What a fearful time for you both, but what a comfort for Lord Canning to have such a wife as he has in you,—calm, and pious & *full* of trust in *Him* who will not forsake those who call on Him. The distance & the length of time between the Mails is *very* trying & must be harrowing to those who have (& *who* has not amongst the gentry & middle Classes in England—Great Britain I should say?—&c) relations in uncertain & dangerous places? . . .

The deaths of Sir H Lawrence—Sir Hugh Wheeler & Sir H Barnard (the latter an old acquaintance of mine who seemed to be doing so well with his small force) are most grievous, & the loss of Sir H. Lawrence irreparable. The retribution will be a fearful one, but I hope & trust that our Officers & Men will show the difference between Christian & Mussulmen & Hindoo—by sparing the old men, women & children. Any retribution on these I should deeply deprecate for then indeed how could we expect any respect or esteem for *us* in future?

Those Troops (Native) who have remained faithful deserve every reward & praise for their position must be very trying & difficult. The accounts of faithfulness & devotion on the part of servants are also touching & gratifying. I cannot say *how* sad I am to think of all this *blood shed* in a country which seemed so prosperous—so *improving* & for which, as well as for its inhabitants, I felt so great an interest. We are *not* desponding—but we are *very very* anxious to impress the Government here with the *immense necessity* of providing a sufficient Reserve of Troops to *feed* those sent out—& to *prepare* for the *worst*—& Lord Canning may rely on our urging this *unceasingly*, for without it—I am sure, we cannot hold India . . .

Pray thank Lord Canning very much for his last kind letter; I will not trouble him with *one* now—& I consider my *writing* to you to be for him also. The Prince wishes to be most kindly named to you both. I cannot say *how* anxious he is about India, or *how much* he feels the necessity of *every* nerve being strained at home. God bless you, dear Lady Canning—we have great confidence in Lord Canning and wish him *all* possible success in his arduous task.

Ever your's affectionately V R

The last sentence would have touched Charlotte most particularly. Later, in replying, it was this she emphasized. 'I believe Lord Canning will himself express the gratitude he feels for Your Majesty's gracious words expressive of confidence in him. I well know how cheering & encouraging it is to him in all his difficult & heavy duties & cares to be assured of such support.'[15] As a diversion from her continuous anxiety she was glad to be charged with an errand for the Princess Royal.

Government House, Calcutta[16]
Sept 25th 1857

I have sent off a box of India muslin &c . . . from which choice can be made for Your Royal Highness's trousseau . . . I hope Your Royal Highness will employ me again for I know how much Indian things are admired abroad. I have ventured to send a little parcel containing two little packets & a square of embroidery which I believe to be intended for a shawl, but which I hope Your Royal Highness will accept as a little remembrance of me & use in your own sitting room at Berlin as a Table cover. I know that Your Royal Highness's room will be filled with sourvenirs in needle work & I would have begged to be allowed to add my share to that of my former colleagues if I were more skilful so I must hope this will be allowed a place instead.

This was only momentary relief. To her sister she confessed how she longed for the time when her head would not be full 'day & night of fighting, & guns, & murders, & counting up marches & roads & distances', and after a longing thought of Highcliffe she checked herself: 'But I do not wish to go now & see you there: I should like first to see all straight again here.' Homesickness was not to be tolerated. 'I never wished the Governor-Generalship to be offered to C, & I think we did very happily at home, & I hated leaving all my own people & friends. But I did not at all object to leaving my monotonous London life, & I took great delight in all the novelty of impressions on coming to a new country. Of late, it has been painful, & anxious, & terrible; but I do not know anything I should dislike more than to be told that C would not have two or three or more years here, so that he might see India again prosperous, & on the way to good order, though fifty years will not put it back into the same state in which it was, so far as attempting to civilise & give liberty, & our English ideas of blessings to the country.' Besides, she was entirely preoccupied with immediate events. 'Our agony is for Lucknow' she cried.

21

The Queen's Confidence in Canning

Good news was at last at hand. The day of Charlotte's letter to the Princess Royal saw the relief of Lucknow. Havelock and Outram on a second attempt had entered the city, but still lacked sufficient force to rescue the garrison and civilians and lead them out of the Residency to safety. With the arrival of Sir Colin Campbell the new Commander-in-Chief (later Lord Clyde), Lucknow was at last evacuated on November 17th. In March of the following year the rebels were finally dispersed.

On September 20th Delhi had fallen. The news, so longed-for, so often rumoured and as often denied, found Charlotte supervising some garden improvements at Barrackpore where she had gone early in the morning accompanied by Sir Colin, who was waiting for troops from England before moving up-country. After breakfast as she was watching the building of a new balustrade on the terrace and wishing that the kind was known in England 'made of plastered pottery & brick, so much better & cheaper than cement', a telegram arrived directed to 'Lady Canning and Sir Colin Campbell'. 'I knew it must be good news & it was: "Delhi has fallen!"'

Government House, Calcutta[1]
Oct 9th 1857

Madam,

There is nothing doubtful in the good news of which I trust Your Majesty heard the beginning by the last mail and the completion by this.

It is with heartfelt joy that I congratulate Your Majesty on being once more in possession of Delhi, and on the relief of Lucknow.

With grateful hearts we thank God for permitting such enormous difficulties to be overcome & the happiness of these events, after such intense longing for them for months past, is far beyond words.

Lord Canning has now a grateful duty in cordially thanking Your Majesty's brave soldiers who have so gloriously conquered in this unexampled struggle and have triumphed over obstacles such as never were attempted in this climate & in this country before.

I well know how much Your Majesty & the Prince will rejoice! & so will all England.

The little army relieving Lucknow has been too small to attempt to keep open the road to Cawnpore and to take possession of the city, but now . . . a force is hastening up with all speed to reinforce General Outram & to complete what he & General Havelock have begun so well. They did not arrive a moment too soon for besides scarcity of provisions, one shudders to hear that mines were found, stretching far within the works, ready to be loaded, & another day might have been too late to save that devoted garrison . . .

The death of General Neill is a sad drawback in this success, & I am sure Your Majesty will lament the loss of such a brave good soldier . . . He was from Ayrshire & is described as a most quiet silent man, a thorough soldier, & with a will of iron . . .

There is more enmity in Lucknow than was expected, or else the Sepoys are very successful in keeping the town & country people away from communicating with our troops . . . There are extraordinary anomalies in this struggle, for Sir J Outram mentions no less than 10 chiefs in Oude who have protected Europeans.

. . . The soldiers inflicted tremendous retribution in Delhi, & private letters begin to tell of enormous slaughter of men, but they always spared women & children I am glad to hear & they also say so many men are killed, or have fled, that none remain to be seen in the town. The Headquarters are in that Palace said to be so very beautiful & where there is still a Peacock throne. There was a great dinner of officers & Your Majesty's health drunk till the walls resounded with the cheers & the soldiers took it up & even the Goorkhas joined.

England by mid-October was acquainted with Lord Canning's 'clemency' order regarding fair punishment for mutineers. To a revengeful majority (similar to the diarist here quoted) the resolution was 'simply babyish! Lord Canning may be a very kind man (black man his brother, and so forth), but he ought to know that you cannot quell a savage mutiny and reconquer half of India by using kid gloves and rosewater'.[2] Convinced of her husband's wisdom Charlotte could write almost objectively to a friend: 'I do not know how unpopular C may be. The burthen of all abuse is always the same—leniency to the natives!—& that means an accusation for which recall in irons would be a faint punishment.' Nevertheless the Queen's unfailing confidence in Canning was her great support.

Windsor Castle
October 22nd 1857

Dear Lady Canning,

I cannot tell you *how* thankful I am for your writing to me so regularly by every mail or what a pleasure & satisfaction it is to me to receive your letters which (without flattery) are universally considered as the *best* which are received from India, & I hope you will continue writing to me by every mail as long as Affairs are not restored to what they were, before this dreadful mutiny . . .

Thank God—the accounts are much more cheering & those of Lucknow are a *very great* relief. The continued arrival of Troops will I trust be of great use, & that no further mutinies & atrocities will take place. As regards the latter I should be very thankful if you & Lord Canning could ascertain *how* far these are true. Of course the *mere* murdering—(I mean shooting or stabbing) innocent women & children is very shocking in itself—but in *civil* War this will happen, indeed I fear that many of the awful insults &c. to poor children & women are the inevitable accompaniments of such a state of things— & that the ordinary sacking of Towns by Christian soldiers presents spectacles & stories which if published in Newspapers would raise outbursts of horror & indignation: Badajoz & St Sebastian I fear were two examples which would equal much that has occurred in India and these the Duke of Wellington could not prevent— & they were the acts of British Soldiers, not of *black* blood. I mention this not as an *excuse* but as an explanation of what seems so dreadful to our feelings. Some of these stories certainly are untrue—as for instance that of Colonel & Mrs Farquarson who were said to be sawn asunder and has turned out to be a sheer invention, no such people existing in India! What I wish to know is whether there is any *reliable evidence* of eye witnesses—of horrors, like people having to eat their children's flesh—

& other unspeakable & dreadful atrocities which I could not write? Or do these not rest on *Native* intelligence & witnesses whom one cannot believe implicitly. So many fugitives have arrived at Calcutta that I'm sure you could find out to a great extent how this *really* is.

I am delighted to hear that that most loyal excellent veteran Hero Sir Colin Campbell is well & that you like him; I was sure you would, for it is impossible not to do so— & we never for a moment credited the shameful lies of disagreement between him & Lord Canning. If he is still with you say everything most kind to him. I am glad to hear that he does not share that indiscriminate dislike of all brown skins which is very unjust—for the Inhabitants have, it appears, taken no part in this purely Military Revolution— & while summary punishment must alas! be dealt out to the mutinous sepoys—I trust he will see that great forbearance is shown towards the innocent & that women & children will not be touched by *Christian* soldiers. I hope also that some rule may be laid down as to Ladies in future living in such an unprotected way as they have done in many of those stations & that at the first alarm they will be sent away to places of security, for really they must be dreadfully in the way & it must be so paralysing to the Officers & Men if they have their wives & children in danger. Sir Colin talked to us of the bad system of 'Bungalows' when he was going to start for India.

Recruiting is going on quite wonderfully lately; last week *2165* Men were obtained! The Militia have come out very readily & the Country has again shown the very best spirit. Generally it is not at all animated by a spirit of revenge or violence against the people of India with the exception of a few newspapers who hold very unchristian language.

. . . As I write to *you* & Lord Canning is so busy I will not write to him also & beg you to communicate what I have said to you to him. He may be sure of my warmest support & approbation.

We came back on the 17th from the dear Highlands with the greatest regret having had the finest weather possible. We stopped for one night at *Haddo*. Lord Aberdeen is well & takes the liveliest interest in you & Lord Canning but is not at all gloomy in his views. The poor King of Prussia is *very* ill; he has had a sort of attack of apoplexy & it is feared his mind may not recover—bodily he is better . . . Little Beatrice is very pretty & a dear, good little thing.

Now with the Prince's kind remembrance (he is as you will imagine *much* occupied with India)—to yourself & our's to Lord Canning believe me ever,

Your's affectionately V R

I send you some Photographs of Balmoral & Osborne which I think will interest you . . .

To Her Majesty's enquiry as to the extent of atrocities Charlotte was able to reply that evidence 'shows slaughter & extermination to have been in all cases the object of the mutineers, & there is not a particle of credible evidence of the poor women having been "ill used" any where. The horror of the massacre cannot be exaggerated & the dreadful mutilations & insults perpetrated upon *dead bodies* have given rise to most of the dreadful stories. When one thinks in what a happy peaceful state of things the massacres first occurred, where there had been no fighting to exasperate, no injury to revenge, it seems as if demons had possessed those men . . . It will always be a mystery of horror . . . Details I hear of the emaciated appearance & filth & misery of these poor women at Cawnpore have filled me with more pain & horror than anything I have heard except reports of the worst insults'.[3] She was able later to send the Queen[4] an extract from a person unnamed, relating to a Mrs Patrick Orr and Miss Madeleine Jackson, held as prisoners in the Kaiserbagh Palace at Lucknow; an English child was with them wasting away. 'At last a doctor was bribed to send some medicine to the baby. The bottle arrived and around it was a leaf of a large English *Bible* and one of the Verses was to the following effect: "Fear not thou that art in Captivity and in distress, for I am the Lord thy God and I will pity thee". At this time all hope had fled—and they only expected death at any moment—but from the instant they so strangely received the leaf of the Bible they rallied, and a few days afterwards they were liberated by us. I have looked in my Bible for the Verse, but cannot find it in the exact words.'

But the anguished days were passing. The presentation of colours to the Calcutta Volunteers, undertaken by Lady Canning, was an exhilarating interlude. The force consisted of six hundred infantry, one hundred and eighty cavalry, four guns, and privates made up of 'gentlemen & clerks & shopkeepers, English or East Indian (which is the polite term for half caste)'.[5] Together she and Dunkellin composed her speech, 'or by rights', she explained, 'he wrote it & I docked off a few words here & there'. The function took place on October 20th and the next day she described it in a letter home.

Yesterday was a *journée bien remplie.* All intervals were employed rehearsing my speech. I hoped to get thro' it well. At 5 the ceremony was appointed to take place and a little before we started on horseback with a cortège worthy of the Queen herself! for I had no less than *five* Generals and staff all in full uniform! An immense concourse of people were assembled about ½ a mile off on the *Maidan* and the volunteer infantry, artillery, & cavalry in line. We rode along the line 2 & 2 & then to the centre & I advanced alone to a spot between two drums on which the four colours rested.

I thought I should not be much alarmed & I gave the flags to the ensigns without my horse swerving or moving the least & I bravely began my speech, but after the first two lines I felt I was *in* for it & away went the words out of my head & I stammered a second & found I must put in an original end to that paragraph. Then happily I remembered the second part & it ended well, but it was very awful. I had pinned a copy of the speech into my pockethandkerchief but quite forgot to take it out & thought anything was better than to fumble for it in the middle. I think not more than five people knew how badly I did it, I don't think the rest could hear but I shouted it out as loud as I could. Here is the whole concern & the speech written off by heart, so well do I remember it now:

'Calcutta Volunteers! I have great pleasure in presenting you with these colours. The readiness with which at a time of trouble & anxiety you came forward & sacrificed your leisure, your ease, & the comfort of your homes in behalf of the safety of the public, & the zeal with which you have applied yourselves to the study & discharge of your self imposed duties, assure me that the British colours will be confided to trustworthy hands.

'Take them! & remember that it behoves you to guard and defend them jealously, & by ready attention to your duties, by the strictest obedience to your superior officers, & by cheerful submission to discipline, to raise & sustain the character of your corps & preserve unsullied the honour of your colours.'

To the Queen, Charlotte wrote of a visit to wounded soldiers in a Calcutta hospital putting her in mind of 'former visits with Your Majesty to the wounded men' from the Crimea. She knew approval would be given to pains having been taken to keep soldiers, arriving by sea and not immediately going north, 'from committing all sorts of imprudences as they are always inclined to do on first landing after a weary voyage'. Believing it would entertain the Queen she told her how 'the sailors & Highlanders have more effect on the natives than any soldiers ever seen. A . . . native . . . had some expressive name I do not remember for sailors & said they were 4 ft high & 4 ft broad & carried 9 pounders & 12 pounders in their arms as a coolie does a parcel. Highlanders count still as fiends kept in cages & let out to fight';[6] they were also suffering sadly from mosquito bites on their legs.

From Windsor came distressing news, not only in the death at Claremont of the Queen's first cousin, but also in the melancholy anticipation of the Princess Royal's marriage. The inevitable photographs were not forgotten.

Windsor Castle
November 25th 1857

Dear Lady Canning,

I thank you much for your kind and interesting letter of the 9th October received by last mail & which was so cheering with respect to Lucknow . . .

We have been all plunged into *deep* affliction by the most sudden & unexpected death of my dearly beloved cousin Victoria (Dsse de Nemours). She was safely confined on the 28th October with a very fine little girl (after having had none for eleven years!) & went on perfectly well; I visited her on the 7th when she was still according [to] French fashion—*in* her bed;—she continued quite well when on the 10th November in the morning—while her hair was being combed—she suddenly called out to her Nurse 'Mlle Bordet—mon Dieu!'—her head fell on the Nurse's arm, & her pure spirit had already left that beautiful form which charmed every one! The poor Duke who was below reading to his Mother—rushed upstairs on hearing she had fainted and when he came up her hand was cold! To describe the agony of her distracted husband—to whom she was every thing,— & the scene which presented itself when we went to Claremont (the Prince went there the same day) the day after,— & I stood by the bed, where three days before I saw her well,— & where she lay lifeless yet beautiful in the ghastliness of death, her long beautiful tresses falling over her shoulders— & her poor Husband sobbing & asking me to continue my friendship & affection for her to him, would be difficult!

Dear Lady Canning it has been a terrible blow to *me*, she was like my own sister, we bore the same name, married the same year—loved each other tenderly— & since *48* saw each other so often. No one can replace her & she was *so* so dear, *so* good—one of those pure virtuous—unobtrusive characters who make a Home peaceful, cheerful & happy! What the unhappy Exiles are to do without her—I cannot imagine. My dearest Prince has been terribly over set by this event; he also loved her quite as his Sister having none of his own, besides, & they were so much together when children. The gloom it has cast over our family & the sensation it has made is very great— & *this* four days later than which forty years ago Princess Charlotte died at Claremont! The cause of her death was the coagulation of blood in the pulmonary artery—a very rare occurence—but which a violent cold or feverish attack might equally have rendered fatal. In France the greatest sympathy has been shown. I have written you *all* these melancholy details—knowing that they will interest you & knowing that you will be so truly shocked at the sudden removal of one so lovely & so good!

Prince Frederic William came here on the 17th but leaves us again on the 3rd December—then to return towards the end of January to carry off our poor Child—who I feel is still *so* young to leave her *very* happy Home! The poor King of Prussia is in a very sad state—better in health but his mind still sadly impaired.

I send you dear Lady Canning, a photograph after a very pretty picture Winterhalter did of me & dear Victoria in *52* for the Prince, as also a little group done at Balmoral of Lord Aberdeen (who was very ill about 3 or 4 weeks ago but is better again I am thankful to say) . . .

Ever

Your's affectionately V R

We have just received the Telegraphic news saying Lucknow is reinforced— & provisioned & that it is safe!—a great blessing!

A month later the Queen followed this up with a further letter rejoicing in the relief of Lucknow while manifesting her dejection at her child's approaching marriage.

Thank God! Lucknow is *saved*, & the poor, unhappy Ladies, Women, Children & sick at last after so many months agonies of doubt—safe! I cannot tell you how truly thankful we all are, & how rejoiced it should have been known just *before* Christmas! . . . Our poor Victoria is wretchedly low at taking leave of *all* she loves & cares for— & of every fête & anniversary being the *last* she shall spend here as a happy innocent Child! She feels that she leaves a *very very* happy Home & I am sure she will feel *very* sad & lonely at first—tho' she is excessively attached to Prince Frederic & he to her. On the 25th January the Marriage takes place & on the 2nd February she is to leave her happy Home!

Referring to the death of the Duchesse de Nemours, Charlotte could sympathize over the loss of 'the friend & companion of young & happy days', remembering so especially 'Her Royal Highness in her brilliant beauty when every one at Claremont had suffered so much from unwholesome water'. Of the Princess Royal's marriage, how readily she could enter into the feelings of the Queen and Prince, for indeed it would be a trying time.[7] Havelock's death at Lucknow she wrote of with grief. 'His death was from dysentry, but he was quite worn out. He must have been happy knowing how warmly his exertions to advance upon Lucknow were appreciated',[8] and in her journal she noted: 'I knew him better almost than anyone. He was very small, & upright, & stiff, very white & grey, & really like an iron ramrod. He always dined in his sword & made his son do the same. He wore more medals than I ever saw on any one, & it was a joke that he looked as if he carried all his money on his neck.' Before the year closed she felt justified in reassuring the Queen that despite public abuse from home, Canning's policy throughout had been one, not of appeasement, but of stern justice. 'In all cases plain justice' had been the rule of the Governor-General and 'not "leniency", and the only special care taken is not to confound the innocent with the guilty',[9] adding later: 'I trust Your Majesty does not believe that I talk of 'poor dear Sepoys' & have any sort of softness or tenderness towards them. I hate injustice & I know how nobly *some* few have behaved . . .'.[10] Of some importance in the context of the rumoured ill-feeling between Canning and Sir Colin Campbell is her defence of their relationship.

The good support given to Lord Canning by Ld Palmerston in his late speech at the Mansion house has already had a very perceptible effect here, & the hearty testimony borne by the Duke of Cambridge to the friendly & cordial understanding which has from the first existed between Sir Colin & Lord Canning has been a real satisfaction to him, for tho' he could contentedly bear imputations of being a 'blunderer' or a 'vacilator' from those who were tricked by false or imperfect information, it was most painful to him to be accused of thwarting & obstructing the Commander in Chief when he was exerting himself to the uttermost to give him every assistance & support & lived with him on the most friendly terms of confidence. It was gratifying that His Royal Highness should take the first opportunity of setting at rest that mischievous & false report.[11]

Her last letter to the Queen in that calamitous year ended on a farcical note.[12]

I think I once mentioned to Your Majesty that amongst other attempts to provide carriage for the troops, some Elephants were to come by sea from Burmah. They have now arrived, 20 in one ship & 50 in another. The landing of some I saw. They were hoisted up from the mast & suspended by a bandage passed under their bodies & fastened to a hook, then a crane swung them round & lowered them to the water's edge. The great creatures sprawling in the air were more ridiculous than I can describe. Some however behaved with very good sense steadying themselves by the bulwarks & rigging, others roared & struggled, but all walked off quietly ridden by their 'mahout' [driver] as soon as they were released from their trappings. I believe there was one exception & that one walked off altogether.

Charlotte looked forward thankfully to the ending of the year. A charming and original note was struck by the domestic staff at Government House on Christmas morning, when to show how thoroughly they understood English customs hot cross buns were served for breakfast. On the first day of January—at which hot cross buns came again—Charlotte was able to write that it was 'a cheerful day. I never felt more glad of the end of any year than of the last terrible & unhappy one.'

22

Coonoor and Ooty

Several events contributed to brighten the opening of the new year. The appointment of Colonel Stuart, Char's first cousin, as Military Secretary in succession to Canning's nephew was an agreeable one, the more so as it brought her a friend and companion in Minny Stuart, his wife. 'We have another addition to the staff in a young son of Ld Stanley of Alderley' she told the Queen.[1] The 'very merry young ADC', Johnny Stanley, 'like a merry page, so civil & useful' had fallen ill in the Crimea and had been invalided home. Delicate from birth, high-spirited, given to violent likes and hates, and thinking India preferable to his hut at Aldershot, he was delighted to be sent out as an ADC, though he never greatly cared for Canning, but immediately fell a slave to Char—'say how much I have worshipped her, for I cannot well say so to her face', he wrote to his mother on leaving India three years later.[2] The descriptions of the Cannings, set down at the time by both men enables one to form an idea of how exacting had been the toll laid upon them the previous year. 'Charlotte has grown thin and aged, how could it be otherwise' wrote her cousin, 'for though never ill, she is easily fatigued and looks worn.' He thought her perfect in manner to everyone. 'At large parties she goes about and speaks to everybody in a charming way that I have never seen in any viceregal or colonial court. The Governor-General does his honours well too, but he is in general very silent. He bears up nobly, and I think has minded nothing except the lies told about him and Sir Colin Campbell.' To Johnny Stanley Canning appeared so pale and overworked that he scarcely knew him. 'Lady Canning I recognized directly, she looks much older but still handsome . . . Colonel Stuart eats a great deal & never speaks & Lord Canning never opens his mouth all day even at dinner.'[3] Meanwhile Mrs Stuart, an ardent, prosing, Christian was at loggerheads with Johnny probably through jealousy of his admiration for Lady Canning, whilst he on his part found her exceedingly tiresome: 'Mrs Stuart lays herself out to please in that particular manner one might perhaps call toadying.'[4] A heavy-weight, as seen through Johnny's eyes, puffing and blowing when out walking, requiring to be lifted over stones a foot high[5] does not seem to coincide with her own conception for she sometimes broke into song 'as if she was a merry milk maid in a field',[6] and when 'old Mrs Stuart' was singing "Peace be around thee" Johnny nearly went into a fit and had to go outside to laugh.[7] Char too had difficulty in hiding her face on one occasion—as he told his mother—'Fancy Mrs Stuart told me yesterday I was flatulent',[8] and since he reported her as having a bad head for argument one may deduce it had been often put to the test.[9] (Understandably his grandmother, Maria Josepha, Lady Stanley, and his mother, were curious to know more about Mrs Stuart and were reassured to learn from a friend that she was 'one of the most charming women that ever was & I heard the same from somebody else'.[10])

With the likelihood of rebellion settling in the north, Canning now proposed to move up-country and establish himself at Allahabad for the best part of the year and Charlotte, forbidden to accompany him, wrote to Queen Victoria[11] that she was considering two or three months in the Nilgiris (Blue Mountains), inland from Madras, as she ought to avoid a third hot season in Calcutta though she felt it to be disagreeably out of the way. Before Canning's departure she had an incident of some interest to record concerning his commission to the Andaman Islands, headed by Dr Mouat, to examine the possibility of a prison settlement.

Two doctors from the Andaman expedition dined & told us all sorts of curious things. Dr Mouat brought us a savage they caught exhausted in the water after one of their attacks in canoes. He is gentle looking &

very black & dressed in a sailor's suit of clothes. They are always accused of being cannibals but no one knows anything about them—they are more like Africans than the Malay tribes of the other islands. This man is small & has a good expression but is very ugly. He imitates sounds like a parrot & is amused at everything & very tractable. There are supposed to be only about 3000 in all those large islands & they are of the most hostile disposition. The two doctors came up to them with beads & looking glasses & were answered with showers of arrows wherever they met them.

The islands have beautiful harbours & plenty of stone & timber, they are covered with dense forest & in parts are marshy & nothing grows there but Mangrove, but generally it seems perfectly habitable. They found good nets & baskets & arrow heads of beaten nails, well made bows & rough string, not an attempt at clothing, huts & canoes rather well made & curious little hatchets. The savage saw a man on board mending a net, he seemed to think it ill done & insisted on taking it from him, undoing all the bad mending with wonderful skill & redoing it much better. Do tell Grandmama this. The thing that seemed to astonish him most was a glass of water—the clear part that he could not drink from at the sides. A looking glass of course charmed him, especially a full length one. He was very touching at the sight of the first little child shown to him & patted its face so tenderly & wanted to be let to take it. The Mama remembered the cannibal reputation & wd not allow it. He pointed in the direction of his island & held up one finger & made his friend the doctor believe he had left one little child at home.

He never makes a mistake in pointing to the island but always first looks up at the sky & points right. They hope to learn his language in teaching him English & to make him very useful. The place will do perfectly for a penal settlement but much jungle must be cleared. They brought me a most beautiful piece of madrepore, like petrified heather, it must be full 2 feet long, & of oval shape, & the most delicate pinky lilac tint, redder & brighter by candlelight—all the little cups of heather flowers. They say the corals & madrepore & fish of the brightest colours were perfectly beautiful in the shallow near the shore. There are hardly any fruits or any wild animals but pigs.

Charlotte's thoughts were in England on January 25th, the day of the Princess Royal's marriage in the Chapel Royal, St James's.

'I regret nothing more than not being near Your Majesty at such a moment & with Your Majesty's other old servants who have known & loved the Princess nearly from birth.'[12] One observer considered 'the Princess looked too young to be married and the Prince of Prussia a disagreeable German',[13] but Charlotte knew the proper note to strike: 'Your Majesty & the Prince will have gone through a sad time in those joyous celebrations leading to parting with your very dearest eldest child . . .'[14] A letter from the Queen was on its way.

Buckingham Palace
February 8th 1858

Dear Lady Canning,

I have three most kind & interesting letters to thank you for . . . which I received at a time when I was entirely engrossed with the preparations for & festivities of the marriage of our dear Child, as I may say I still am with her sad departure & very triumphant & enthusiastic journey & reception in her new Country.

Nothing ever went off better or was more impressive or touching than the marriage itself . . . The great enthusiasm & loyalty exhibited here, the feeling & affection for our dear Child has been most *gratifying* to us & to her & her Husband & Prussians in general. Victoria looked extremely well— & behaved beautifully. We spent one very happy week with the dear young people after their marriage which seems to me (as it will to you) a *dream*, & it is only *18* years ago—on the 10th—that *I* was married!

I never saw any one more *posé*, unembarrassed or happier than she was & she appeared as if she had been married a year! Nothing could be more satisfactory than to see their happiness. But alas! The departure was a dreadful day & our poor Child was quite heartbroken, at leaving us & her dear Home & Country & above all at taking leave of her beloved father—whom she worships—on board the yacht. She has left a *sad* blank here & the separation—at such a distance—is a great trial—but we hope to visit her in Germany in the course of the year. We have heard by Telegraph today of their entry into Berlin which has been very successful & brilliant.

What a blessing the relief of Lucknow & safety of those poor Women is! . . . What *our* poor Sex have had to endure, what courage & resignation they have shown! The horrors seem however to have been *very greatly* exagerated—which for all the relations is very shocking.

I trust that you will soon hear no more of those infamous attacks against Lord Canning whose conduct has been so admirable under such *very trying circumstances.*

The arrival and landing of those Elephants must have been most curious!—I trust we shall soon hear of more successes of Sir Colin's. I am always anxious for his health . . .

A further letter followed almost immediately.

Dear Lady Canning, I have only *just* time to send you this little Photograph of our *young couple* taken at Windsor the last morning which I think you will like. I shall send you another very shortly . . . I send you also a piece of Wedding Cake & of the trimmings of Victoria's Dress & a little print of her. Ever your's very affectionately, V R

With the hot weather Char left for the hill stations of Coonoor and Ootacamund, for Calcutta without her husband was a lonely place and a change of climate was essential, though the garden at Barrackpore had never looked more lovely. 'No words can describe the beauty of the Bougainvillaea, wreaths of lilac as brilliant as a lilac flame, a colour that seems full of light.' The journey with Minny Stuart, Johnny Stanley and another ADC, for companions, and her two maids, took her by sea to Madras, inland to Vellore and then by stages mostly at night to avoid the heat of the day, in 'Mrs Anson's old carriage, full length on cushions' and by *tonjons* to Bangalore, and up through glens and winding pathways banked with scarlet rhododendrons in trees, to Coonoor. The party reached their destination at the beginning of April to the heartening news of the fall of Lucknow. On March 14th Canning had made the Proclamation from Headquarters at Allahabad which provoked an outburst when it reached England and led to unforeseen repercussions. Based primarily on the confiscation of property in the Province of Oudh it was a just, if severe, punishment for the crimes of the Mutiny, but to many at home it seemed that Canning, who earlier had been blamed for leniency, was now exacting too harsh a retribution. His friends hastened to endorse his action fearing that on grounds of forfeiting the Government's confidence, Canning might resign his office.

But these events had not yet arisen to cast a shadow at Coonoor where lodgings had been taken at 'Glen View', a group of bungalows 'covered with roses in a beautiful garden with a view across the valley of hills covered with woods of evergreen . . . I have a glimpse of the burning plain, just enough to remind me of what I have left', wrote Charlotte in her letter to the Queen, admitting that it was 'a joy to be able to wear warm clothing & light a fire in the evening & sit out of doors amongst orange trees & green house flowers'.[15] This was Coonoor's oldest hotel; at some earlier date, possibly when Richard Burton was there ten years before, it had prospered, perhaps a trifle self-consciously, under the name 'Tusculum', which may not after all have been a misnomer for Charlotte was at some pains to write of the vegetation being Italian rather than tropical and of most brilliant colour. Contrarily, she compared the country to the 'Highlands on a gigantic scale', so 'Glen View' may yet have been the more appropriate. Though no longer a hotel, exteriorly it is practically unchanged. The cluster of low buildings shaded by long verandahs with little trellised columns, incongruously exhaling a gentle flavour of Regency architecture, opened into a garden on the edge of a steep hill facing south. The three detached bungalows, of which the largest was occupied by Charlotte and Rain and held the two living rooms, the one at right angles to it Mrs Stuart's and West's, the third the ADCs', present much the same appearance today as in that spring of 1858 when Charlotte made her sketches and wrote her journal with her thoughts far away at Allahabad, and Mrs Stuart was so exceptionally provoking. She was not at ease on a horse and on their daily rides was so afraid Johnny Stanley would abandon her that she would ask him to smoke, knowing well that he could not then go on and join Char. 'She gives every horse she gets on to a sore back', he observed glumly.[16]

The church at Coonoor, consecrated in 1854, was served by the Reverend Henry Taylor, military chaplain to the barracks at Jakatala (now Wellington) close by. A misunderstanding arose respecting church services, Charlotte wishing for a more equal distribution of Matins and Evensong, between town and barracks and while both she and Mr Taylor were all compliance each was bent on gaining the point. Mr Taylor, having at his command 'Orders', 'Circulars', and the 'Officer Commanding Jakatala' to resort to, seems to have won the day with a promise of morning service every Sunday, but there is a suspicion that the trump card was Charlotte's. 'A very clever sermon by that unprepossessing chaplain who preaches so well & is so disliked, and will never read the prayer for Parliament & Indian Empire, & Governor General, & Governors, & all in authority. I shall have him pulled up for this by giving a hint.' A visit to the barracks under construction afforded her a description to interest the Queen, and the many who have known it through succeeding years will not dispute its handsome proportions and commanding position, or that it would be possible to 'over praise that very fine work. It will be a delightful station for troops & 1200 men will be lodged magnificently—600 might go in at once. It could hold many more. The place seems so good, the long barrack rooms with an open verandah in front & a broad closed in verandah & a wide passage at the back. Married couples in a separate building with 2 rooms to each family. The Hospital is finished & occupied & schools are being built & everything that can be wanted.'[17] Some account of the country was not out of place.[18]

Grass & Fern (Bracken) cover the ground, but every hill side & nook has its little run of water & wood of ever green trees with great white stems & a load of creepers like curtains—& often some fine orchids besides. Grain wd grow anywhere & flocks & herds might range over all the country. The outer edge of the hill track is magnificent, full 7000 ft of steep descent to the plains—then long precipitous spurs & all of rock & magnificent wood. Coffee grows on Forest land & hill sides & these beautiful plantations yield enormous profit. I think above 6000 ft the coffee is not successfully cultivated. I see a few settlers, usually privates from regts gone home, who seem very prosperous paying a minute rent for a trifling bit of land & growing coffee & having a few beasts & living in a house of about 10 £ cost & the work of their own hands. Most of them get some other little occupation, but I think settlers as small farmers wd thrive & be happy & useful.

The labour is too cheap for white men to compete with natives, as labourers, & one cannot expect that a large white population can find sustenance in these hills, but a great many more might easily be provided for & I shd think soldiers married to half caste women wd gladly stay.

She could not foresee that before very long Coonoor, and more particularly her sister Ooty, would be the most renowned hill stations of the south, attracting settlers and those who, caught in their toils and unable to break the binding spell of this small verdant paradise of British India, retired there and remained to die. Rather the reverse. 'I think one or two speculating farmers might thrive near each hill station: feeding sheep, & selling milk, butter & poultry, & growing vegetables for their beasts, as well as to sell; but I am quite convinced there is no kind of "opening" for colonists.'

The Todas, the hill tribe of the region, interested her though she did not find the women pleasing in looks or manner. 'They live in idleness, the dressing of their long shining blue-black curls being the business & pleasure of their lives', whilst the men 'like young saints or prophets by Raphael' she pronounced truly magnificent. 'They wear only one piece of brown stuff draped in heavy folds like ancient Romans, & with their high noses many people imagine them to be a Roman colony. I of course guess them to be the Lost Tribes.' At Ootacamund, twelve miles away, where mid-way through April the party made a little junket to celebrate Lou's birthday, Char was able to see a Toda village of huts built of mud and thatch; the sleeping platform took up half the area, and the entrance having no door the inhabitants were obliged to creep in and out as if into a dog kennel.

While at Ooty for a few days, Charlotte stayed at 'Lower Walthamstow' (now Warley House), an unpretentious bungalow sheltered in luxuriant growth on a sweep of hill east of the lake. With no need for a verandah at eight thousand feet above the plains, and with its two pairs of chimney stacks rising solidly above, the cottage still wears a curiously Georgian appearance of a modest order, only slightly adapted to the wholly Eastern vegetation against which it nestles. Higher up the hill the main property 'Upper Walthamstow' was rented by Colonel Pears (chairman of the committee for the construction of the present Nilgiri Library) and his family, friends of Mrs Stuart. It was here she stayed but it was not considered sufficiently commodious for Lady Canning who was probably happier in the privacy of what she called her 'humble cottage'. Preferring Coonoor for its dramatic views and its trees and 'gorgeous foliage & tangle of creepers, sometimes like curtains of great green leaves looped up with coils of ropes', she was nevertheless greatly attracted to a certain 'Woodcot' (now Gulaihind) which she would have taken had she been at Ooty. Built on the ridge of a shallow valley with a view of Willow Bund, it is a charming white plastered house with graceful porch and, still in place, a fireplace for burning peat ornamented with a teakwood gothic surround. Its owners, Colonel (later Major-General) and Mrs Cotton, of the Madras Engineers, were estimable people. 'She is very English & came late to India & knows how to appreciate the things new to her instead of wanting what is not to be had, & her garden & collection of orchids show this', Charlotte noted with approval while sketching in the grounds. Keeping to her usual hours she drove before breakfast to the Botanical Gardens and scrutinized everything with Mr McIvor the superintendant, brought up in the Chatsworth garden under Paxton; eager as always to see and learn she admired excessively what he had done with the small allowance at his disposal. The large new variety of fuschias were worthy of special attention and the heliotropes and verbena '11 ft high & enormous circumference of bush' she considered 'as large as the largest shrub of lauristinus'.

But this was a strange interlude for her, constituting the longest absence from Canning since their marriage and as a holiday very different in every respect from their round of country-house visits in England, and though once back at Coonoor her main occupations were riding, sketching (from the point which today is known as 'Lady Canning's seat') and walking with her customary energy —enthusiastically likened by Johnny Stanley to a goat—she was impatient to be back at Calcutta within reach of letters and news. By the beginning of June the generally unfavourable reaction to Canning's Proclamation had reached her and she exclaimed at the change of opinion which 'instead of railing at "Clemency", is now calling out for an amnesty'. Hearing that Canning had had a sharp attack of fever at Allahabad she made preparations for departure. At Madras letters told her of the death of her dear grandmother Hardwicke, 'the keystone holding us all together', and while grieving for herself her sorrow was for her family. 'I felt sure I should never see that dear kind face again, so I do not put myself amongst those who can feel it as a fresh loss', but her mind must have wandered back to an earlier time when her grandmother favoured her marriage to Carlo, and to her youth at Tyttenhanger when, secure in the affection of family and Aunthood, days of happiness stretched ahead in seemingly limitless felicity.

23

First Viceroy

Charlotte had not been more than a week at Calcutta before she wrote at length to the Queen explaining her husband's policy.[1]

I trust that his measures are approved by Your Majesty and that the result of them will soon be apparent . . . Lord Canning has never yet put forth a general amnesty—his chief object has been to seize opportunity of pardoning on a large scale & over considerable districts . . . As long as any part of the province is actively contumacious & hostile, it is difficult to make a grant of pardon for the whole province with dignity, unless Sir Colin is able at the same time to show a considerable force. I believe that Ld Canning is satisfied that the time is near, when it will be politic as well as merciful to extend a free pardon to large numbers of Sepoys—indeed to all the less guilty ones. . . . I know that he is well aware that such a step will raise a howl of indignation all over India, but it is his conviction that such a step must be taken if the country is ever to have real quiet.

A letter from Buckingham Palace was already on its way (it had been preceded two months earlier by an emphatic 'The *reports* about the Princess Royal are *quite untrue*, I am thankful to say, for she is far too young to think of having Children'), and must have gratified Charlotte exceedingly.

Buckingham Palace
July 1st 1858

. . . I am quite shocked at my *long* & really unpardonable silence . . . but the fact was I *hardly* knew how to write to you at that *painful* & *distressing moment* now more than six weeks ago, when things happened which I could not prevent & which distressed me more *than I can say*. You know, dearest Lady Canning, what I always have felt about Lord

Canning, & you will believe that those feelings are unaltered . . . I only hope that Lord Canning will *not* think of leaving his post or mind what has passed for it *has* passed & there is but one feeling now about him here. People are very *strange* here, about six months ago the blood thirsting was too horrible & really quite shameful! . . . All this came from judging of things from a distance, & not understanding them & not waiting for explanations. It is very melancholy but I hope that neither of you will mind it . . .

The letter closed with a recollection of earlier days for the Queen was going to the Rhine at Coblenz: 'I shall think of you & of our journey in [18]45 & miss your ever ready & kind *pencil* which has contributed so much to our Albums.'

Delighted with the prospect of rejoining her husband at Allahabad Charlotte was not disposed to allow either the August heat or the slow four weeks transport up the Ganges to hinder her determination. It was a tedious journey in a kind of barge with the Stuarts and two ADCs accompanying her. 'We have besides a great retinue of servants—tailors, washermen, &c many of whom at night spread their beds on the upper deck: in the day we sit there a great deal under an awning. A steamer with three guns & forty English soldiers tows & defends, & a shabby native boat astern of us has the kitchen & sheep, poultry, cows, goats &c. Another small boat to land in closes the procession, or rather tail, & a long heavy one it is to drag, so no wonder we get on slowly.' She did not dislike the weeks of creeping up the river (despite 'the horror of the live nature moving about the cabin & dinner-table, especially of one pale insect as big as a bird') which may have recalled past journeys on the *Gondola*: 'I think no one but me ever thrives on an idle life on board ship, & it certainly suits me to perfection.' All her old enthusiasm returned and she was able to tell the Queen: 'The great sight of all was Benares . . . I now really feel I have seen *India*. Not a trace or touch of anything European exists there. Sounds, sights, & *smells*, are as wholly & entirely Hindoo as they could have been 200 years ago. We were carried in silver tonjons . . . The great temple with its offerings all wet with Ganges water, & its domes covered with sheets of gold is a curious & horrible sight with its nearly naked painted priests & Faquirs . . .'[2] To Aunt Caledon she confided: 'It is the best sight I have ever seen. Cairo is not to be named by it, nor even Constantinople.'

Allahabad was reached at the end of August after eight months separation from her husband; Minny Stuart, who had been 'getting more grumpy than ever', noticed the 'bright look in Char's eyes as she came in to dinner with her light step'. Canning seemed older, though to Johnny Stanley who was not impressed by 'as odious a place as can be imagined', he was not much changed but for his mouth, which had 'gone in more as he never wears his false teeth now. Ldy C is very happy now she has come back to him'.[3] But the rift had not healed as is evident from Johnny's letter to his mother written at the beginning of October. '(This is private) I do not like the way the G.G. treats Lady Canning, she is so constantly thinking only of him & how to please him & he is as sulky as possible & last night at dinner he snubbed her dreadfully for nothing & her poor face looked so pained, she tried to laugh it off but it was a very agonised laugh. I wd go a good way to save her such a scene as that for she is as proud as possibly can be with all her devotion to him.'[4] Later Johnny observed that her husband was nevertheless 'jealously alive to any possible slight that might be put upon her'; but surely this pride to which he referred again, was to one with so strong a sense of propriety instilled from birth and nurtured at Windsor, a mask assumed to disguise her hurt before others. If, as Johnny wrote, Lord Canning was 'so uncertain & often so undignified'[5] (while adding that there was much to admire), one may surmise that what appeared as arrogance was the necessity of remaining outwardly invulnerable.

The Cannings did not leave Allahabad for Calcutta until the new year. On November 1st 1858 the Queen's Proclamation had been read, granting pardon, and transferring the government of India from the East India Company to the Sovereign, simultaneously appointing her Governor-General to be India's first Viceroy. The next day Charlotte wrote to the Queen at length, speculating whether anyone but herself was struck 'with the coincidence of having accidentally chosen All Saints day for this ceremony. When I was reading over the Epistle for the day by myself it felt a strangely striking coincidence to read of the pardon & merciful message to the great multitude of many nations & tongues! May it not be an omen of good?'[6] The letter ended on a more prosaic note; shawls ordered by the Queen's command had arrived and she feared the patterns were almost too quaint. In replying, the Queen's wishes were clearly set forth: 'With respect to the *future shawls* I should wish *long as well* as square ones & also *sometimes one* or *two embroidered in gold*.'

Letters from home told of the now almost total approval of Canning's policy. 'No one can doubt that he has conducted the most difficult Government that ever man had most admirably, and indeed successfully', wrote Lady Stuart de Rothesay. At Marienbad for a cure she had called on Metternich. 'He said he had "*beaucoup suivi les affaires de l'Inde*", both from the great interest attached to the subject and his personal feeling for Canning, who, in his opinion, had acted worthily of "*le beau nom qu'il porte*"; and he judged from the cry of too much clemency having suddenly changed to too much severity, that he had exactly seized the proper medium.' Back in London with her sister Aunt Somers, at Grosvenor Place (the old Carlton House Terrace having been sold), her mother gave Char a vivid description of a 'quite an abroad morning' with Lou. 'We went to South Kensington to see the Sheepshanks pictures, and then to the Antipodes to see a G. Bellini sketch-book which Mr. Rawdon Brown expected her to look at, at the British Museum. Panizzi [the Librarian] came out to me and made the galleries resound with his admiration of Canning's writings and Canning's conduct.' Charlotte's own drawings proved something of a sensation. 'I am enchanted with the variety and beauty', wrote her mother, 'and really your labour, industry, taste and science can only recall Miss Berry's oft-repeated speech—"One cannot speak of Char in sober terms of praise".' Ruskin, a stern critic, was enraptured, and said 'they were the grandest representations of flowers he had ever seen. He said what a *subtle* use of colour you displayed: it was especially so on a sheet with a sort of trumpet-flower or bignonia, in which there were about two inches in the corner of bougainvillia. He thought that uncommon shade quite marvellous, as well as the orange tone of scarlet in the flower, and the poinsettia perfectly dazzling.'

At Calcutta in March with the hot weather starting, Charlotte could exclaim: 'Now three whole years have passed, I dare to look forward to getting back again as the pleasantest thing in the world.' A few weeks later she was stunned to hear of Lord Waterford's death out hunting in Ireland, and at almost the same time news reached them that Canning had been created an Earl; the Grand Cross of the Order of the Bath had been conferred on him the previous month, and there was later a suggestion of a further honour, for in 1861 Char was writing to her sister-in-law:[7] 'No tidings of the Garter'.* They had no notion of changing their name, Canning admitting that he was rather 'low at leaving the Viscounts, whom I have always looked upon as a more select caste than the Earls', but there was the question of a second name 'to provide for contingencies'. In 1811 George Canning and his wife had bought an estate in Lincolnshire[8] comprising Stowgate and 'Market-deeping', neither of which names was acceptable, Charlotte finding 'Stowgate' 'very hideous'.[9] Finally they decided to have no second title.

Waterford's death affected Charlotte deeply; she needed someone to whom to talk about Louisa and it is significant that it was not to Mrs Stuart that she turned. 'The very next day that the telegram about Lord Waterford came', little wild Johnny wrote to his mother: 'Lady Canning sent for me & talked to me of how miserable poor Lady W must be, tho' Mrs Stuart who was bouncing in directly the news came naturally got a snub—she said afterwards to me "Ly C is very odd about her sorrows, she does not like showing any". I said to myself "how few wd—to you"'.[10]

* On this same day (October 27) Palmerston wrote to inform Canning that the Order of the Garter was to be conferred upon him on his return to England.

Her letter to the Queen was written with touching restraint.[11]

Calcutta
May 4th 1859

Madam,

I thank Your Majesty most gratefully for . . . the promise of the Portrait of Your Majesty's little Grandson which is a treasure I am longing to receive but which has not yet arrived.

There are many things of which I wished to write to Your Majesty, but at this moment I can hardly do so, for I have felt so overwhelmed by a very sad piece of news in our family . . . There seems no hope for doubting its truth and that Waterford has been killed out hunting.

My poor sister's sorrow must be dreadful at this cruel sudden blow. She was the most fond and devoted wife and was so perfectly happy. I know she will be patient & resigned in her grief, but her whole life will be blighted from henceforth, and it is sad to think she will never be again the bright happy creature I have known. Waterford's frank noble character was most endearing in his family & I feel his loss very deeply. He was so strong & full of life that he was the last whom one expected never to see again.

I have been so grieved at this that I feel I cannot attempt to write at length, or on other subjects, to Your Majesty, but I cannot allow a mail to pass without attempting to express the gratification with which I heard of Your Majesty's gracious favour to Ld Canning being announced in Parliament by Ld Derby. Honours which are such valued tokens of Your Majesty's public approval of his services as to make them greatly prized by us, tho' not more prized than Your Majesty's continual personal kindness.

Shortly afterwards she was able to thank the Queen for the 'facsimile of the drawing of the baby Prince Frederick William . . . It reminds me very much of Your Majesty's children at that very early age when I have seen nearly all of them, excepting the Princess Royal and Princess Beatrice. It must be a good artist' (and is there here a suspicion of some hesitancy in striking the right note in regard to the future Kaiser?) 'to give so much what they call "individuality" to such a very young face.'[12]

The Queen wrote with genuine concern at Charlotte's loss.

Buckingham Palace
April 3rd 1859

. . . It is with a truly sorrowing heart that I write to condole with you on the terrible misfortune which has befallen your dear excellent Sister! *What* a blow, what a shock will this be to *you*, who loved that Sister with such tenderness! I have been so shocked, & my thoughts constantly turn to that lonely, beautiful Widow, who has seen *all* she loved *best* in this world—*carried home* at night a lifeless corse! Dearest Lady Canning, we *do* feel *so* much for *her*, so much for you—who will learn these woeful tidings so far away— & cannot be a comfort to *her* in her *deep* grief! But you are both so truly pious & good that *you* will find support in *Him* who never forsakes the sorely tried & beloved ones!

Later the Queen wrote again; in her reply Charlotte expressed her gratitude for unfailing support during the critical years, and for the honour recently bestowed upon her husband.

Buckingham Palace
July 4th 1859

. . . It has been a great pleasure to me to confer at length on Lord Canning a public mark of my esteem and for the high sense I entertain of his services during the most trying time. You & he know that *I always* felt entire confidence in him & was deeply grieved at the manner in which he was treated. But I trust you have both forgotten those painful moments & are assured of the truth being known & felt & appreciated as it ought.

Barrackpore[13]
August 22nd 1859

Madam,

Your Majesty's most kind letter of the 4th of July has given me sincere pleasure & I offer my most grateful thanks for it, and for the words in which Your Majesty speaks of the pleasure it gave Your Majesty to confer upon Lord Canning the honour he has received.

He may well be proud of such distinction bestowed by Your Majesty's gracious hands in token of approval of his conduct and services, and it will be with heartfelt gratitude that Your Majesty's constant favour & support will ever be remembered by him and shown in his zealous & devoted service; and for myself I cannot find words to express how deep I have ever felt the inestimable value of Your Majesty's confidence in him & full justice towards him at all times, & indeed the knowledge of this was a comfort & support at very trying emergencies.

The Cannings were now at Barrackpore where the Viceroy found relaxation in driving his phaeton and Charlotte's enjoyment of her garden is very evident. The better part of the day was spent under the great banyan tree and she wrote proudly of a high bamboo fence covered with convolvulus which when in flower was like a blue wall. It was in this year, 1859, and perhaps now in the quiet of this August spent in the garden she had created, that the Cannings drew close to one another again. The Stuarts had left for England in July. Colonel Stuart had known his cousin since childhood and spoke of her with insight born of affection and understanding. He regretted leaving her, and while fully alive to her husband's 'grandeur of character', confessed that 'her lines have not fallen in pleasant places here'. With admiration he wrote of 'those small, delicate, and exquisitely beautiful features: that most lovely, bright, and intellectual countenance, sometimes radiant, more often sad; always one of the most expressive that ever was seen'. It was left to his wife to remark that it was impossible not to be aware 'how much climate and anxiety have aged and altered her'. To another friend who had known her in England she seemed at this time '*so beautiful* still . . . But there was more than *beauty* in her countenance'. Her conversation she accounted 'so chaste and high-minded, revealing such purity of mind and high intent of purpose and aim, yet so simple and gentle',[14] that one is reminded of Fanny Kemble resorting to this same expression when describing her many years earlier: 'the sort of chastity that characterised her whole person and appearance'.[15] If, as seems to be the case, these last two years of her life were 'happier to both than they had been for many many past ones', she never at any time referred to the burden of sorrow she had carried for close on fifteen years. 'Much of her married life had not been at all happy but no suffering had embittered her—no disappointment had lowered her aims, nor had she ever departed from the path of perfect devotion to her husband', recorded this same friend.[16]

24

To the Borders of Tibet

In the autumn of 1859 the Cannings started on a long camp journey north, to Simla and beyond to Peshawar, stopping at Cawnpore, Lucknow, Agra, Delhi, Ambala and Lahore. Charlotte found these marches exhausting. The camp (in Emily Eden's day) consisted of about 12,000 persons with their tents, usually setting out at five in the morning, or earlier, so as to gain about twelve miles before the sun made further movement unpractical; furniture, elephants, horses, camels, and baggage were on the move at the same time. The large dining tent (and Char exclaimed at the ease with which it was possible to order dinner for fifty people instantaneously) and the Durbar tent were set up in the cities; the Cannings' tents probably consisted of three rooms each, with a covered passage leading from one tent to the other. By the time they reached Agra in late November it was cold and Charlotte could not pretend that she found the travelling agreeable. 'Much of it is quite detestable, with cold and wind and dust. The cold is worse than the heat and if it is to go on crescendo, I cannot tell how we are to bear it. A tent is not pleasant with the walls shaking, the dust coming in, and draughts kept out with the greatest difficulty. I like seeing new places and can bear anything, but cannot the least see the delights of camp-life.' She was nevertheless punctual in reporting to the Queen, who in turn was not remiss in rewarding Charlotte with the usual abundance of family likenesses.

Osborne
December 9th 1859

Dear Lady Canning,

I was just going to write to you, to thank you for *three* kind & interesting letters . . . when your long & most interesting letter from Cawnpore of the 2nd November reached me this morning. How *very, very* interesting *all* you have seen is, how very insignificant *every* thing that you or we have ever seen must be in comparison! To see India & above all to *show* personally my *great anxiety* for the welfare of my Indian *subjects*, would be a *great* pleasure for me for I *do* feel so anxious that *kindness* & a *deep* regard for their feelings & susceptibilities, & strict & impartial justice, coupled with requisite firmness should not only usher in the *commencement* of a *new order* of things but that the Indians should be accustomed to *look* upon *these* as principles of their Queen and her Government!

Most painfully interesting must it be to have seen the scenes of so much suffering and of such bravery and endurance! The heat however wd kill me for I can't stand any warm climate so that even if I *could* go as far as India, the sea voyage & the heat would effectually deter me from undertaking to go there! The camp life must be very fatiguing—but very striking.

We had a most delightful time at dear Balmoral & made endless long expeditions. We found dear Mama, who remained at Norris Castle (which she took for three months) wonderfully well on our return . . .

I send you by this mail the last new Prints of our Children which have been done after the Pictures Winterhalter did of them this year & which are very like. Alice's does not quite render the delicacy of the original Picture however. Our fine full length Pictures are to be engraved . . . I will shortly send you some more Photographs of ourselves & Children.

Like Emily Eden before her (the sister of a previous Governor-General) who had found the Taj at Agra 'quite as beautiful, even more so, than we expected after all we have heard, and as we have never heard of anything else that just shows how entirely beautiful it must be',[1] so too Charlotte was not disappointed. Pushing on towards Delhi, Char awoke one night to find her tent on fire, but acting promptly she was able to save life and serious damage though her own tent was burnt to the ground with almost all its contents. An officer seeing her in the moonlight in a blue flannel dressing-gown—her only piece of clothing saved—and with her hair streaming, called out in amazement: 'Lady Canning, is that you?' Writing home she reported having lost her drawing bag, a great deal of good lace—though 'My old wedding Mechlin lace passed through the fire unhurt in the middle of a mass of linen which was not burnt through'—and some rings of handsome rubies and emeralds; her pearls which had belonged to her great grandmother Baroness Mountstuart were injured and other jewels were more or less black, but safe. The rings were later recovered when offered for sale by a private soldier to a Calcutta jeweller, indicating that they had been stolen from her tent; they were again stolen the following year from her bedroom at Government House but this time were never recovered.[2] On hearing of Charlotte's escape and recalling Louisa's accident in Ireland soon after her marriage, Lady Stuart was moved to write: 'You and Lou have been both especially saved in great pain and peril, and I feel whatever was lost, *my jewels have been preserved*. I am glad that so were most of yours, and I do feel superstitiously pleased that the wedding lace passed through the fiery ordeal!' The maids, Rain and West, woke and fled in their quilts. 'They behaved quite well' was Charlotte's only comment. Her writing boxes were lost, and, though escaping destruction, the Indian journals and letters from Queen Victoria, were in some cases so severely burnt that they remain illegible.

Details of the incident were sent to the Queen.

Governor General's Camp, Umballa[3]
Jan 17th 1860

... We had full 12 days at Agra and after hearing of the wonder & beauty of Taj, till the subject was wearisome we felt compelled to admit that it was quite impossible to be disappointed ... I believe I have seen all the great works of the Moors in Europe and none approaches this ... it is no exaggeration to say that I have had it detailed to me many hundred times in the last 4 years. I quite feel a scruple mentioning this much used topic to Your Majesty.... It was on the night we rejoined the camp . . . that I had the misfortune of so nearly burning down the camp by my stove. Your Majesty will probably have heard of this alarming adventure. The cold had been so great that I had been delighted to find my tent so well prepared for me & trusted that experienced people had arranged this new stove safely. I believe the pipe heated a canvas screen it passed thro', & when I happened to open my eyes about 2 hours after I went to bed the fire had just begun to run up to the top of the tent.

I instantly told the English sentry to give the alarm & the bugles round the whole camp. The whole tent was in a blaze in a minute & I only dragged out my portfolio of drawings but even that was somehow much burnt & I lost all but the dressing gown I had wrapped myself up in. Happily in camp a great deal is always sent on overnight & to be found at the next encampment. I ran to wake Ld Canning and to tell him I was safe, but the fire went fast & his writing tent was burnt & two passages before the fire was stopped by the Seik sentries cutting the tent ropes with their Tulwars [swords] & throwing them down.

It was all so quick that I had no time to be frightened & happily as I knew I was safe, & no one else in danger, I had no anxiety. Every one came to help & condole & Ld Clyde arrived with an enormous dressing gown an admiring compatriot tailor had sent to him in the Crimea & in this I remained enveloped. I happily remembered that I had a great many jewels in an imperial and they were rescued just in time & before the fire had penetrated to them, but I grieve to say Your Majesty's picture is a good deal scorched & discoloured & I fear will not recover, but it has gone to Calcutta to be cleaned.

On the threshold of 1860, in camp at Delhi, Charlotte's thoughts turned to her family. 'How I like to think we can now say "Next year" for getting back to you all. It is difficult to believe we have really been more than four years away even now', and from camp on the Sutledge, hoping to accompany Canning as far as Peshawar and seeing the 'uttermost point of India', she closed her letter to Aunt Caledon: '. . . how often I am longing to be at Tyttenhanger again'. From Lahore and on to Peshawar, the cumbersome procession of men and animals continued its way, with Char in high spirits though the last five days in a camel-drawn carriage were very tiring, but she was keenly aware of the importance attaching to the frontier town, 'this strange country and the actual boundary of India, & the very door of it, which is really the case at the entrance to the Khyber Pass'. This would be a good end to her travels and she felt she could then return home and enjoy sitting still for ever more.

Queen Victoria was gratifyingly interested.

Buckingham Palace
June 11th 1860

Dear Lady Canning,

I have again been far too long silent . . . What splendid & interesting tours & excursions you have made, & what have you not seen! Indeed, there is *nothing* in this world in the shape of scenery, or *sights* which *can* astonish you any more! Those Durbars, & Seikh Chiefs must be such very interesting sights to see. Agra must be *very* striking. I saw *some* of your *beautiful* drawings about three months ago which Lady Caledon brought me to see—I *hope* to see many more.

We were indeed much grieved to hear of your alarm of fire which might have been *most* serious; it was bad enough as it was. You must let me replace *my picture* . . .

You will probably have heard that my good, excellent Brother-in-law, Prince Hohenlohe, died on the 12th April. He had for long been sadly out of health but had shown such strength & such tenacity of life that we had hopes to the last. My dear Sister is pretty well again now . . . We were for three days at Windsor last week, and had dreadful weather for Ascot—altogether the wet & the storms we have had since the second of May have been terrible. I hope however it is *now* improving.

With the Prince's and Alice's kind remembrance & our's to Lord Canning

Believe me always,

Your's affectionately V R

I hope soon to send you a fresh collection of Photographs.

By April the Cannings were on their way to Simla making a detour by pony and *tonjon* to Kangra and the tea-planting district, with elephants as escorts; the temples, forts, snowy heights and woods of ilex and scarlet rhododendron, were all grist to Charlotte's pencil. Unfortunately she made no graphic record of their excursion on a river and down rapids, seated on a board placed astride inflated bullock skins, while men used their feet as paddles. On camp marches she wore a serge dress and jacket with a white muslin bodice, while for 'travelling gowns' she asked her mother to send her '2 or 3 foulard washing silks'—preferably tiny chintz flowers on a dark ground, the other to be light grey with a spot—for nothing kept so tidy and clean or crumpled less.

Writing from Barnes Court, Simla—a place she thought vastly overated—Char informed her mother that, Canning being called back to Calcutta, she was making an expedition to Chini on the borders of Tibet and then returning to Landour, another hill station situated on one of the outer ranges of the Himalayas. West would of course accompany her, but Rain, preferring a Mr Fitz-Squires, had married him at Simla, a loss Char would feel keenly after twelve years service.

The expedition, a notable one for a woman at that period, was described in a letter to the Queen, its length being accounted for in the final paragraph.

Landour near Mussooree[4]
June 28th 1860

Madam,

I think Your Majesty may like to hear from me after a wild journey I have just made in the Himalayas & I think I must give some explanation for embarking in such an undertaking. When Lord Canning found his presence so necessary at Calcutta that he must travel down at the worst season of the year, I could not prevail upon him to let me go with him, & he insisted upon my remaining in the hills until the extreme heat had passed & the rains began to fall, & here I am still, awaiting the news of rain fallen in the plains but I hope in a few days to be able to begin my journey to Calcutta.

Your Majesty will easily believe that I did not much like being left behind, so I think it was a good deal to comfort me that he strongly encouraged me to travel into the interior of the hills & see all I could of the highest mountains, all as far as Thibet, and to go to places I had not a chance of seeing in his company, as he must always be within reach of telegraphs & rapid posts.

I have consequently had a month's travelling, & have been well repaid by all I have seen. I had the smallest possible camp & had with me two of Lord Canning's Aides de Camp, & Ld William Hay who is Commissioner of the Hill States, & my maid & servants. Everything had to be carried by coolies, & with every possible economy of baggage we made a long procession winding over the hill sides with all the stores & provisions & sheep & poultry & all the necessaries of life required in these wilds. For a week I travelled along the Thibet road made by Ld Dalhousie. I went up the Sutledge valley as far as Chini, the place where Ld Dalhousie once went for three months to avoid the rains. No wonder they do not arrive there, for it is defended from them by a range of Peaks 21000 feet high. There is a moderate slope for a few miles about this place & it is rich with cultivation & Apricot trees & lower down with vineyards overhanging the Sutledge . . . Some walnut groves of gigantic trees & cedars with a background of pinnacles of rock & snow, being full 15000 feet above, would have made a picture & I shall always regret having failed to attempt it.

To cross & recross the Sutledge I had to pass over the different sorts of bridges in use in these hills. The one kind made of trunks of trees reaching as far as possible, rising at an angle from the side & joined by two very long trees across the centre space; & to recross I was reminded of the Dee at Abergeldie for the *Jhoola* is on the same [swinging basket] principle.* It is however better in one respect for the passenger sits alone & is pulled across by ropes & suspended from 6 or 8 ropes over which a semicircle of wood runs from which the seat is fastened. I thought it decidedly less alarming than sitting in front of the Gardener on the 'cradle' of Abergeldie. I happily never came upon a third style of bridge over which the traveller has to *walk* on a rope . . .

My camp was pitched at the edge of the snow in a dreary spot about 13000 feet high & next morning at peep of day we began to ascend. There were full 7 miles of snow to cross & we had dark glass 'goggles' & veils to protect the sight & gave all the scraps of muslins & veils that could be collected to the servants & coolies, but no one suffered. Sometimes the whole party is blinded by the glare & unable to see for a day or two & precautions are very necessary . . . The highest part of the pass is 15480 feet. I had rather wished to go a little further up the sides to accomplish the exact height of Mt Blanc which could be easily done, but one has not breath for much activity at that height & I felt

* In September 1848 on the first visit to Balmoral, Char made a sketch looking up the Dee towards Abergeldie from near the bridge (Windsor Castle).

some compassion on my bearers who had carried me up so well. We used constantly to meet flocks of sheep & goats with little sacks laden with grain & goods of different kinds; a great number of these reached the summit of the Pass as we were sitting there busy in not very successful experiments of boiling water with a thermometer to see it boil at barely 180°, but our provision of spirits of wine fell short before the boiling point had been very distinctly reached.

The scenery in the descent . . . was very striking.* My camp was that day well clear of the snow in birch woods with very fine purple rhododendrons (the common scarlet kind grows much lower) and under enormous cliffs of rock just at the beginning of forests of fir. We had some disagreeable snow drifts to cross next day & used caution to avoid sliding down into snowy caverns & roaring streams *under the snow*. Most of the interest of the journey was over when we passed out of the highest range . . . & the last camps were cruelly hot, 97° in the tents. It was a sort of race against the rains which were liable to begin any day after the 20th so I was glad to reach this place by that day having made 27 marches—about 320 miles— & many of them very long ones & only four halts of a day each.

I do not think settlers will ever be seen in any part of the country I have passed thro'. There never can be useful roads . . . In the country near Chini many women carry the loads and I was prepared to feel distressed at the sight, but I found them so merry & chattering & so perfectly competent to scramble up the almost perpendicular roads without loosing breath, that one's compassion vanished. They had a curious dress with enormous plaits of sheep's wool at the back of their heads . . . Their blanket is draped like a statue & held together with an enormous brass brooch like the old Irish pattern.

The poor people of the village always brought milk & honey, or butter & walnuts. I saw very few of the Thibet people & regretted being unable to visit one of the Lama convents but I hardly liked to prolong my journey. Sometimes a Lama man or woman in her yellow dress appeared carrying a load with the other coolies. I saw [evidence of] Buddism by the little temples with sort of urns painted, one white, one grey, & one yellow; or piles of engraved stones in the highways . . .

* Charlotte confided to her mother that she could not resist 'a "honey-pot" descent, which was not in the least improper, as I put on all my warmest clothing, & had an old Balmoral cloth riding-habit & a pair of strong dark cloth trousers: & the descent was rapid & delightful'.

In one village I came upon large praying machines in wooden buildings like dog kennels. A prayer is written many times over inside & the roller revolves & is set spinning & praying by every passer by.

The Tartar type of face is rarely seen on this side of the border. I saw a Tartar colony near Simla & the women dressed with the peculiar band of red cloth studded with rough turquoises from the forehead to the back of the head. The hill people I met had handsome faces with almost unusually acquiline noses.

. . . I am inhabiting [Maharajah] Duleep Sing's* house, called the Castle; it has a beautiful view over the large station of Mussooree & looks up to the Landour hill where are invalid soldiers. I am inclined to think this place almost prettier than Simla, only the cedars are wanting & it is much too crowded & public in its walks to be a pleasant residence. I mean to stay a few days . . . at the first of this range of hills to see the Tea plantations & I hope very soon to join my boat at Allahabad & to reach Calcutta the middle of July.

I trust this will find Your Majesty preparing for the annual journey to Balmoral. I believe I may venture to send this long story without apologies for I am sure no account of this portion of Your Majesty's dominions has ever been sent directly, or is ever likely to be sent, by one of Your Majesty's female subjects who has just visited it.

I beg Your Majesty to present my remembrances to His Royal Highness & I am Madam

Your Majesty's

Devoted humble servant

C. Canning

Back in Calcutta in July after twelve days travelling down from the hills accompanied by Colonel Yule, the public works secretary, and experiencing heat of 103°, she had been met at Allahabad by Johnny Stanley and her tug-steamer; the remainder of the journey was down the Ganges and the last eight hours on a newly-opened railway. She had been away a year. Rather to her dismay Canning had grown a short beard; in the abstract she thought it becoming, but it rendered him old and sad-looking and not the man she had married twenty-five years earlier.

Soon after her return she had a parcel to despatch to Queen Victoria.

* Deposed in 1859 and sent to England where he lived to the end of his life.

Government House, Calcutta[5]
August 9th 1860

I have ventured to send a parcel to Your Majesty by this steamer. It contains some cloaks of cashmir embroidered at Delhi; and I shall be very happy if they are thought worthy of the acceptance of Your Majesty and the Princesses. The Black cloak I had worked for Your Majesty, the white one for Princess Alice, and the three smaller ones of scarlet for Princess Helena, Princess Louisa & Princess Beatrice. There are also some skins of different sorts of the Himalayan Pheasants which I hope will serve to make into trimmings for Riding hats. I could not have them cut and arranged here so I have ventured to send them in a rough state, but hope that Your Majesty and Their Royal Highnesses will use them & like them.

The Queen's acknowledgment followed a few months later.

Windsor Castle
December 17th 1860

Dear Lady Canning,

It is a very long time since I wrote & I must *ask* you to excuse my silence—but we have had a very active life this summer & autumn— & since many events of *interest* to take up much time. The *most* prominent of these, is our dear Alice's engagement to Prince Louis of Hesse, whom *you* saw as a beautiful *boy* at Mayence in *45*, with his Parents Prince & Princess Charles at his late grandfather's Prince William of Prussia's House; (he was then Governor). Prince Louis is the Nephew & heir presumptive to the Reigning Grand Duke of Hesse Darmstadt, & a *most* charming, excellent, highspirited young man, whom we love already as our Son. He was here last June with his brother & after they left we heard what a deep impression Alice had made upon him & likewise saw that *he* much pleased *her*. We invited him to come here again to us this winter, & he arrived on the 24th ult:— & on the *30th* the engagement took place & gives us the greatest satisfaction as we feel sure our beloved Child's future is *safe* in *such* hands,—besides we feel that we shall be able to see much more of her than of Victoria. I never saw two young people *happier* or *more devoted* to each other. It is a touching & a happy sight for our *hearts* to behold— & I pray God may help & protect them!

We had a charming expedition to Coburg & spent a very happy tho' very quiet time there, for we arrived alas! *just* the *day after* my dear

Mother-in-law (who had been very ill for some months but seemed a little better just before we started)—died,—which you will easily understand threw a *great* gloom over our arrival. Then the Prince had a frightful accident being run away with & having to jump out of the carriage. Thank God! except at the time, there was no further cause for alarm, as beyond some bruises the Prince was not shaken at all & none the worse . . .

We are most grateful for the beautiful cloaks you sent us, & the beautiful pheasant's Feathers. Your mountain expedition was indeed intensely interesting but *I* think much of it sounded very dangerous.

I believe that the young Maharajah Duleep Singh whom you knew already in England & in whom you know we take so warm an interest—is going to India by this very Mail. I recommend him very particularly to you & Lord Canning, & even more to *you*, as he is *much* open to the beneficial influence of a *lady* who will show him real kindness & interest. He is an excellent, well principled young man—*singularly truthful* & straightforward, & with most gentlemanly feelings—but very helpless—undecided & indolent, as all Indians are,—but very intelligent. The kind influence of a *superior* female mind has always been of the greatest comfort & use to this poor Boy who is very forlorn,—the more so perhaps from having become a Christian. His intention is to return to England after a short stay in India, & if possible to bring his Mother back with him. How far this may be feasible I dont know. I am however sure that both Lord Canning & yourself will do all that is kind by him & cannot fail to take interest in & like him.

Before concluding I cannot omit saying that Alice's marriage will not probably take place till she is *19*.

Now with the Prince's kind remembrance & our's to Lord Canning,

Ever

Yours affectionately V R

You will deeply grieve to hear of the death of our dear, honoured & valued Lord Aberdeen! He had been declining for a year & a half & been infirm for three years. He is an irreparable loss! . . .

Meanwhile soon after her return to Calcutta in the summer, Charlotte had been faced with the unwelcome news of a delay in their return to England. 'It is a terrible disappointment', she wrote, 'but there is much doing & to be done. Canning cannot go away

& leave all in new hands.' She had been counting up the months to their departure, but 'next March will *not* see us home. Do tell me all you can about our friends; everything is only too precious that comes from England', and with a great surge of longing exclaimed: 'I do *long* to get home.' In November the Cannings started on a further camp journey taking them to Central India for three months. There the jungle country appealed to Charlotte, and in the 'good cultivation & enormous groves of trees' she found something to compare with England; the miniature valleys she likened to the Roman Campagna.

25

The Last Journey

'I hope by this time next year (if we are alive) we shall be arriving in England', Charlotte wrote from Calcutta in the middle of March 1861. Once again her hope of returning in early autumn had been deferred, but January 1862 was fixed for their departure ... 'If we are alive' ... Canning wrote more forcefully that nothing would induce him to stay 'beyond the last day of my sixth year—*i.e.* February 28, 1862', and in a later letter: 'In a few weeks we shall be beginning to pack off our long sea goods. It is pleasant to look at the barouche and to think it will soon be undergoing renovation in Chandos Street'.* Charlotte, who had no vanity, conjectured how old and grey they would seem to their friends, for though only forty-four she felt very old in Calcutta 'where there are not three women older than myself', and looked forward to 'becoming young again next year' in England. In every letter now there was eagerness to see again her mother and Lou, and the Aunthood. 'Six years and a half away make a great hole in one's life', she wrote to Aunt Caledon. 'But happily we shall find fewer changes amongst our own belongings with the two great exceptions of Grandmama, whom I could never expect to see again, & poor Waterford—perhaps the most unexpected of all.'

Johnny Stanley's time in India was also coming to a close. With a pang he realised 'what an enormous *blank* it will make in my insignificant existence not having her to speak to & look at. When you get this', he told his mother, 'you might write to Lady C (I shall be near home then) & say how much I have worshipped her,

* Barker & Co., coach makers, 66 Chandos Street, Covent Garden.

for I cannot well say so to her face'.[1] In a later letter he admitted that 'Ld C will not break his heart, no more shall I, when we say goodbye, yet I have served him honestly & to the best of my powers although I have never taken to him. I wish he had a firmer mouth', he added with engaging candour, 'it does so spoil his face.'[2] When he heard of Charlotte's death he wrote down an account of his leave-taking, touching in its simplicity and devotion.[3]

> The night before I left Calcutta I bought a little gold cross which was made to open & when I went to dear Lady Canning's room to say goodbye to her I asked her (I have often wondered since how I had the courage) if she would put a little bit of hair in it for me to keep as a remembrance of her. I did not wait for her to answer but kissed her hand & ran away. Half an hour after she sent it back with what I had so much wished for & a few very kind words at parting.
>
> It is very sad getting my letters returned from Calcutta & in reading through there is so much I had not said before & shld have liked her to know.

Charlotte still looked forward to two delightful expeditions ahead of her: to Burma, entailing a sea voyage with Canning across the Bay of Bengal to take place late in the year, for what has been described as 'a piece of administrative tidying';[4] and more immediately to Darjeeling, a journey of six days on the road and only two nights in a bed, while Canning went ahead to Allahabad to prepare for the investiture of some Indian heads of states with the Queen's new Order, the 'Star of India'. This was to take place on November 1st, the anniversary of the assumption by the Crown of the government of India, and for which event Char would join him. Before setting out for Darjeeling she went for a short rest to Barrackpore—the last before being brought back there to a timeless rest—and she admitted to being quite low at leaving it for she had done so much to the garden in the way of flowers, groves, and thickets, even to a double hedge of poinsettias ready in a month or two to blossom into a wall of scarlet. But no regret was equal to the refrain which now ran through all her letters: 'I can think of nothing but the joy of getting home.' On

August 26th a large party was held at Government House, Calcutta. Charlotte in white, wearing a diamond coronet and a spray of ivy entwined in her dark hair, now showing signs of grey, was long remembered for her grace and charm that evening, radiating a gaiety which sprang from an inward happiness. It was the last time Calcutta society was to see her. 'I look upon the hard trial of India as almost over, for I have but one more week of Calcutta in its heat', she wrote at the end of September, 'for next Monday I go off with my maid & two young captains to Darjeeling. I hope it does not shock you to think of such independence, but I am very old now, & can go anywhere with anybody.' Before her departure she received a letter from Queen Victoria mourning the death of her mother in the early spring.

Osborne
August 2nd 1861

Dearest Lady Canning,

I was till quite *lately* under the impression that I *had* written to you since the *sad* & *irreparable* loss I have sustained, & I am quite distressed to perceive by referring to my Book in which I note down my correspondence—that this was *not* the case.

Your very kind & feeling letter . . . touched me *deeply*. Such *universal sympathy* in my *overwhelming* grief, *such love* & respect for the memory of that *dearly* beloved mother were seldom seen, & I *have* felt it *gratefully—deeply*. But oh! dear Lady Canning, to lose a *Mother* & *such* a Mother, from whom except for a *very* few months I had *never* been parted, whom I heard from & wrote to, almost daily—*whose* love for me & mine *exceeded* everything, whose sympathy in "weel & woe", whose interest in *every* little trifle concerning our family—was so great—is *dreadful*! *What* I have gone thro' & suffered in spite of the love & affection of *all* those *so dear* & near me—only *those* who *have* lost a *loving* Mother *can* tell!

My *health* has *never* really suffered at all, but my nerves (never of the strongest) were *very* much shaken (A wicked report was *set* about that dear Mama had become a Cath: & *I* was gone out of my mind! Which I trust never reached you)— & are so in fact *still*. It was *such* a shock for tho' she had certainly been suffering (chiefly from *acute* neuralgic pains in her back) *all* the winter, her *general* health was good;

& *even* when her last illness (which only lasted a fortnight) *began*, she never was near as *ill* as she *had* been two years ago—when she recovered so wonderfully, & had been improving satisfactorily for the last few days.

To be sent for therefore to her already unconscious—was dreadful—tho' it was the greatest blessing that she was spared the pang of separation & the end was *so* peaceful—*so* painless! The dear pure spirit fled, her dear hand in mine, & there was no pressure—no contraction—nothing. But—it is a fearful thing—to see a beloved Being die, to watch the ebbing of life,—to feel you *cannot keep* it! I lived as in a dream for some weeks— & only after a time did I *feel* the shock it had given me. I remained very quiet, & *weak*, I could have remained entirely in the country—but *duty* required a return to Town, which (with the exception of a few days—passing thro') took place on the 1st of June.

But London is a dreadful place for a *sore* heart! I held two Drawing rooms & saw *few* (very few people) to dinner, but otherwise *of course*, remained quite in private. But it is very hard in my position to be *obliged* to do anything of that kind when one's *heart* longs for seclusion.

All Anniversaries are *dreadful*! *All* birthdays, *most painful*— & on my own poor birthday the *day* of all others which (except twice) for *forty one* years she ever celebrated with such peculiar *joy* & love, as a day *too sad* to think of! Then *again* returning here in July—*when* dearest Mama always came here & spent some days before we went to Scotland—I felt *so* wretched! The *blank* seems only to increase as time goes on— & you keep *hoping* & believing *against* your *reason* that the dear *One must* return!

When I am *happiest*—I am saddest as I long to tell it *her*— & constantly feel a chill come over my heart—to warn me that from *here* she is gone for *ever*! My *sole* comfort has been in the certainty of Her happiness—Her *nearness* tho' unseen & of the blessed reunion hereafter!

. . . We have had many Visitors in our seclusion, my beloved Uncle Leopold kindly came *for my* birthday & remained five weeks. Our future son-in-law Louis of Hesse spent six weeks with us (he had the Measles here & gave it our three youngest children who got well over it tho' poor Leopold was very ill)—then the Archduke Maximilian & my dear Cousin Charlotte have just been here for three days— & tonight we expect Prince Louis' Mother & Sister for three days— & last of *all* (which is rather a fatigue & exertion as *he* is quite a stranger) the King of Sweden for one day!

Then comes a very trying Visit—we go to Frogmore on the 16th to visit on the 17th (dearest Mama's birthday) the Mausoleum *there*, which was *not* finished in March & where the beloved Remains have been placed only on the 1st instant. On the 21st we go to Ireland (a private visit) on our way to Scotland where I hope to recruit in quiet & good, pure air, my shaken nerves, & where I expect the comfort of having my dearest Sister with me.

I have *written* you a Volume & yet I feel as if I had not told you *half* I wished. I have *so much* to thank God for! *Such* a Husband—such affectionate Children, that I will not murmur at *what* I have lost—but *such* a loss *cannot* be replaced— & when the only One *above you* is gone, you feel at once older by many years! . . .

Now dear Lady Canning let me end this letter (on the 6th) with many kind messages to Lord Canning.

Ever yours affectionately V R

. . . I add a number of Photos: of ourselves taken last year & this year. I have been reading your kind letter again & feel I have not said half enough in answer, for *every* word you say on my heavy loss is *so* true! My beloved Prince did indeed feel it as a son, for oh! *how* she did love him & *what* unbounded confidence she had in him!—she would have been so glad to see you again & your letters always interested her so much! May *you long* be spared a sorrow like mine.

In her reply[5] Charlotte, referring obliquely to the report of the Duchess of Kent having become a Roman Catholic and the Queen gone out of her mind, ventured to suggest that 'Foolish narrow minded persons who are in wonder & amazement at the signs of strong natural affection in a sphere much above their own, do fall to manufacturing extraordinary explanations of all appearances of grief, but they are so unworthy of notice that one only feels contempt for anything so stupid'. Hoping to strike a more cheerful note she enlarged on the Queen's forthcoming visit to Balmoral, 'pleasant and wholesome now in every way', though prudently qualifying the remark with a sympathetic adjustment: 'tho' not exempt from the memories which for long must be vivid everywhere'. She ended by telling of her projected expedition, coupled for the first time with any hint of weakness.

I look forward with much pleasure to this excursion for I have sometimes felt rather worn out after so much heat and I am going to a spot with the highest mountains in the world immediately before one in full view. Lord Canning is unable to give himself this real treat & I am to hurry back to join him at Allahabad for the investitures on the 1st of November which I would not miss on any account.

We still hope to pass a few days in Burmah before Lord Canning has to return here to spend the last two months . . . I cannot but look with great delight to returning home after so long an absence and the time now feels very near.

On the same day she wrote to her sister-in-law, Lady Clanricarde,[6] of the long and very sad letter she had received from Queen Victoria.

Like all her letters as simple & true as a child's. It quite convinces me of what I always felt sure that even if she ever felt angry with Albert for not telling her of her mother's danger (& this does not appear) she has borne him no *rancune* for it. She mentions him as affectionately as ever & even shews that some little thing I had said abt his being such a real son to the Dss of Kent & so loved by her, had been *the* thing in my letter which had pleased her. She alludes to the wicked reports of her Mother having turned R Cath & of herself having gone out of her mind.

In Charlotte's judgement this was explained by the fact that the Queen had not the hard head and strong sense she was credited with, but that 'in some ways' she had real softness and feeling, and '*very* weak nerves'.

Just as everybody would say she was never sea sick, so it was always thought nothing shook or 'upset' her. Great care abt little trifles, like her father in a much less degree, has always excited, only it used to be not much known except by those quite about her. I believe the Prince of Wales as a little child seemed to inherit it too.

This tendency, though more inconvenient in a man, did not strike Charlotte as unduly disquieting since those unconnected with the court were always honoured to render assistance, and delighted 'in all the little things wanted to be got & done—openings &

shuttings of doors & windows & getting cushions, shawls, &c &c, & detailed orders on dress'.

Soon after Charlotte's arrival in India in 1856 she had told the Queen of the 'beauty & merits of a hill station, Darjeeling' of which she had been hearing. 'The highest mountain in the world *was* to have been seen from it but a higher still 60 miles further has been discovered of past 29000 ft. It was said to be without a name & the Geographers threatened to call it after the surveyor, Mt Everest, but nearer neighbours easily produced the local name & a very good one, 'The Abode of God' 'Deodhanga', & another which I forget also competes so we may hope the surveyor's will be dropped.'[7] Now, in 1861, Charlotte was to see the wonder of Mt Everest for herself.

Her journey and stay at Darjeeling are well documented in her letters to Canning—the only ones to him that survive. Written in the last weeks of her life they irradiate her love and eagerness to please and vividly reflect her impatience to be again in England. Weighing on her mind was his going on ahead alone to Allahabad. 'Goodbye Treasure', she ended her first letter on October 1st while still on her way up to the hills, 'I have such a compunction at thinking of you toiling away when I am voluntarily away on a holiday. It sits heavy on my conscience. Your own Char.' The next day she admitted to a '*dazzle* of a headache', but 'Goodbye darling treasure. . . .' When nearly at Darjeeling she exclaimed: 'It seems an age since I went away. Goodbye darling, I have written rather in haste in a very great noise of coolies. The woods are quite magnificent more like the Nilgheries, but I have never seen such expanse of clothed hills. Goodbye darling, CC.' At last on October 7th, riding her white pony, Charlotte arrived in Darjeeling. During a difficult journey West, probably by now thoroughly spoilt and certainly disagreeable, behaved provokingly —she had already refused to accompany her mistress to Burma— but Char's interest lay in everything around her. 'The forests never cease & give me an idea of damp as I never saw, but then it is such wonderful luxuriance—quite unlike all else tho' perhaps I saw forests as fine before, yet never anything like this extent of them—it is as if the whole country round Simla was clothed with enormous trees & creepers & underwood, & tied together with cables of creeper, not much in flower now.' She was sleeping badly but delighted in the cold air and warm fires at night. 'I have your very darling letter. Goodbye treasure, your own Char.' Constant rain did not spoil her enjoyment. 'Nothing is to be compared to it, not even Chini. Children look bursting with health & I suppose it is like the west of Scotland, people get used to the rain— & mist. My grievance is still not sleeping. I have often slept badly but never as badly as now & I do not know now when I shall ever sleep again.' An expedition to the frontier of Sikkim was afoot for the next day and Charlotte wanted badly to go into the interior and see the lama monasteries. Three days later an account of the excursion was forgotten in the disappointment—side by side with what one detects as relief—of hearing from Canning that she was not to join him. Rightly he judged that she should avoid the exertion of further travel to Allahabad, so soon to be followed by a journey to Burma. The same letter brought gratifying news: 'As Lord Canning will soon be returning to England, the Queen is anxious to offer him the Rangership of the Park at Blackheath, and the house which dear Lord Aberdeen had for some years . . .'[8] There is some indication that Thatched Lodge, Richmond, where Granny Stuart had lived may have been once proposed, but this intoxicating communication stimulated Char to every kind of speculation.

Darjeeling
Oct 17th 1861

Darling Carlo. I have just got your letter about the Allahabad journey & now I feel really very much ashamed of being so poor spirited, & of being away from my post after always following like the faithful little dog. I think it really looks as if it would be rather a relief to you that I did not come. It is even now *pouring* with rain & on such a day as this I *could not* get away. Then as to this place doing me good in health, I dont think it does, for I sleep shockingly, but then again I have a little bowel disarrangement, and tho' I am sure I *could* have got thro' it all quite well, I believe it is wiser to give it up. I don't know that I could have done much for you usefully, but I do feel being away as if I *did not care* for it all, very much.

I am quite pleased at the Queen's offer of Blackheath. Strange to say I like it very much indeed—almost better than the old Lodge. It is not so pretty but I think there is more ground and in every way it will be very nice to have. One can have plenty of plants & *potager* & laundry, & the old park & common are charming—there is no sort of view but one can make it nice, & it will answer so well to store away things & one can have charming dinners of friends & fresh whitebait for them. I like it so very much, & a garden for plenty of flowers one can have there as well as anywhere else & perhaps a farm too & at least a poultry yard & cows, for we can surely turn them out in Greenwich park. It is such a very new idea. Stuffed birds, curiosities, all sorts of rubbish can go there and be quite a resource. I only remember of garden a green paddock with a shrubbery single walk all round, but of course that could be made available for flowers & fruit & there may be a kitchen garden. I am afraid you have not written for ages to the Queen, it is very nice of her to do you this little personal civility herself, & so graciously. Goodbye darling, Your own Char.

Two days later she was able to reassure Canning that a few drops of Chlorodyne had set her 'interior derangement to rights', but her thoughts were ranging over Blackheath and 'every hour I remember something which makes it more convenient for storing away all our things. There is so much more space than at the Lodge that it will answer for hothouse, & dairy, & poultry. All our large china & stuffed birds &c will do so well there & the carpets. The dairy I specially like the thought of. I suppose too there are good stables'. Mount Everest, Sikkim, opportunities for sketching—these were scarcely referred to; the attractions of a dairy were paramount. 'The very day before I knew of Blackheath I had been thinking was there any use in carrying home a nice little bamboo milk can that would go charmingly in a dairy, & I was so wishing for a dairy where one could put a few rough odd things of that kind.' She remembered the house as dark and rather gloomy but this could be remedied by cutting down some trees; a few purple cocks in the paddock were envisaged, and hens and a pheasant or two. On October 25th there was a mention of 'looking again into Sikkim' but Blackheath was a more welcome prospect. 'I am so fond of my Bleackheath Villa in my mind's eye, especially the orchid house & dairy, & we must have some Cochin fowls. Nothing was ever so convenient.' When not preoccupied with the house there was a carriage to consider.

Now as to Blackheath & the Sociable. The old pattern never would do, for it had no sort of top or head and one could not go out in it on doubtful or showery days. I am for keeping the Barouche. We shall certainly want a Brougham and that would do for *light* going backwards and forwards, wouldn't it? We shall be very *chilly*—for Blackheath shall we not want some very light kind of Basket carriage or poney chaise? I don't figure to myself a Sociable but if you do, & can imagine the head & some sort of comfort & that it would do to drive about London, then do as you like about it, only the old pattern was not convenient in bad weather. Would the Burmah ponies go in a basket carriage?

I am quite sure the house is a *rez-de-chaussée* but still I think it is three storey high and has brick bow windows. I only remember a dullish drawing room & dining room. We must go to the expense of taking out a sash or two for large panes of glass or even throwing out a bow or somehow getting light. My idea of the outside is like a Hanover Square brick house. I suppose low rooms & good chimney pieces but I really remember it very little.* Goodbye treasure, Your Char.

If the repairs of the Barouche cost a very great deal, don't mind my wish to keep it & let it stay & be sold here.

At the beginning of November Charlotte left Darjeeling to be at Calcutta to welcome home her husband on the 10th. Her route lay through swamp ground infested with malaria and on her arrival on the 8th it was very obvious to an observer that she had caught jungle-fever. As she turned in from the road through the

* Today the two-storeyed Ranger's House is exceptionally light. Built in the early eighteenth century it presents a handsome appearance; wings with bow windows were added fifty years later. A doll's house in relation to Government House, it nevertheless has a fine drawing-room with coffered ceiling, and a staircase with twisted banisters. The garden steps now lead directly on to a public walk in Greenwich Park.

great gates of Government House, her eyes may have lingered for a moment on St John's Church where her monument, designed with all the ingenuity of a pious sister's love, would one day stand in the north verandah. She had enough strength to write a short note to Canning to reach him on the road down from Allahabad.

Government House, Calcutta
Nov 8th 1861

Darling Carlo. Here I am safe at my journey's end but so very shaken & tired that I don't think I could have got to Allahabad without knocking up & having fever. I think I ache more than I ought & shall treat it as fever & take a calomel & opium pill & be quite well before you come.

We must get bamboo milk pails in Burmah for I have only one & I believe they are bigger there.

Goodbye treasure, Your own Char

Throughout eight days of illness Canning scarcely left her side; when he was obliged to, her eyes constantly turned to the door lightening with a radiant smile at his return. On November 18th in the early morning the chequered life of sunshine and cloud was perfected. She had come home at last.

Canning's account of her death was written with all the reserve of a man to his Sovereign.

Barrackpore[9]
Nov 22nd 1861

Lord Canning presents his humble duty to Your Majesty. Your Majesty will have heard by the last mail of the heavy blow which has fallen upon Lord Canning. The kindness of Your Majesty to Lady Canning has been so invariable and so great that he feels it to be right that Your Majesty should receive a sure account of her last illness with as little delay as possible.

Lady Canning had been, as Your Majesty is aware, in the Himalayas near Sikkim for some weeks, and had left the Hills on the 4th of November to meet Lord Canning in Calcutta previously to their embarking for Burmah. She reached Calcutta on the 8th, and Lord Canning arrived 36 hours after her. He found her complaining a little of headache & fatigue, and a little feverish . . . but she was up and at breakfast as usual and afterwards showed to Lord Canning with all her usual interest the Drawings she had been doing and the curiosities she had collected. She was however indisposed to much exertion. The next day she lay on the sofa, but was not, apparently, worse. On the day following she was not allowed to leave her bed—and she never rose again from it. This was Tuesday the 12th, and from that day the fever increased strongly . . . She was perfectly conscious and able to talk (though not much disposed to do so) till Thursday. On that day the mind began to wander, but only occasionally . . . The doctors declared that it would be a struggle of strength between the disease and the constitution and this was too evidently the truth. On Saturday morning however the fever did abate, and quinine and strengthening food were given freely. The good symptoms continued through that day and part of the night, and Lord Canning was full of hope . . .

But early on Sunday morning the disease returned,—more terribly than ever. What little strength had been regained was soon lost . . . Weakness increased visibly . . . and there was more restlessness and quickness of breathing. This state of things continued through Sunday until about midnight . . . At ½ past 2 o'clock on Monday morning she died quite calmly in Lord Canning's arms. There was never any pain;—probably, at last, no consciousness;—but the same gentle, patient, unrepining look which from the beginning had never left her face for an instant.

The Funeral is over. It took place quite privately at sunrise on the 19th. There is no burial place for the Governor General or his Family, and the Cemeteries at Calcutta are odious in many ways. Lord Canning has therefore set a portion of the garden at Barrackpore (15 miles from Calcutta) apart for the purpose. It is a beautiful spot;—looking upon that reach of the grand river which she was so fond of drawing,—shaded from the glare of the sun by high trees,—and amongst the bright shrubs and flowers in which she had so much pleasure.

Your Majesty will be glad, but not surprised to know of the deep respect which has been paid to her memory . . . The Coffin was conveyed to Barrackpore by the Artillery, and was borne through the garden by English Soldiers.

Lord Canning feels sure that Your Majesty will not consider these details as an intrusion . . . She loved Your Majesty dearly, and Lord Canning is certain that he is doing what would have been her wish in thus venturing to write to Your Majesty.

In the last connected conversation which he had with her, just before the illness became really threatening, she said that she must write again to The Queen, 'for I don't want her to think that it was out of laziness that I was not at Allahabad'. The fact is that she had always intended to be present at the Investiture . . . but Lord Canning, hearing of the bad state of the roads owing to the heavy & unseasonable rains, and knowing how fatiguing an additional journey of nearly 900 miles would be, had entreated her to abandon the intention, and to stay longer in the Hills and then go straight to Calcutta.

Whether all might have gone differently if the first plan had been held to, God alone knows. His will has been done.

Lord Canning . . . begs Your Majesty to accept the assurance of his dutiful devotion, and of his earnest prayer for the protection and happiness of Your Majesty and The Prince, and of all that are dear to Your Majesty.

When this letter reached the Queen the Prince's life had also closed but no like reticence marked her reply.

Osborne[10]
10th January 1862

Lord Canning little thought when he wrote his kind and touching letter of the 22nd November, that it would only reach the Queen when *she* was *smitten* and *bowed* down to the earth by an event similar to the one which he describes—and, strange to say, by a disease greatly analogous to the one which took from him *all* that he loved best. In the case of her adored, precious, perfect, and great husband, her dear lord and master, to whom this Nation owed more than it ever can truly know, however, the fever went on most favourably till the day previous to the awful calamity . . . To lose one's partner in life is, as Lord Canning knows, like losing *half* of one's *body* and *soul*, torn forcibly away—and dear Lady Canning was such a dear, worthy, devoted wife! But to the Queen—to a poor helpless woman—it is not that only . . . To the Queen it is like *death* in life! Great and small—*nothing* was done without his loving advice and help—and she feels *alone* in the wide world, with many helpless children (except the Princess Royal) to look to her—and the whole nation to look to her—*now* when she can barely struggle with her wretched existence! Her misery—her utter despair—she *cannot* describe! Her *only* support—the *only* ray of comfort she gets for a *moment*, is in the *firm conviction* and certainty of his nearness, his undying love, and of their eternal reunion! Only she prays always, and pines for the latter with an anxiety she cannot describe. Like dear Lady Canning, the Queen's darling is to rest in a garden—at Frogmore . . .

Though ill, the Queen was able to tell her precious angel of Lord Canning's bereavement, and he was deeply grieved, recurring to it several times, and saying, "What a loss! She was such a distinguished person!"

May God comfort and support Lord Canning, and may he think in his sorrow of his widowed and broken-hearted Sovereign—bowed to the earth with the greatest of human sufferings and misfortunes.

Epilogue

A recent traveller in India paused beside Lady Canning's grave on the anniversary of her death, laying tuberoses and field flowers hastily gathered, and a sprig of evergreen brought from a place she had loved in England. Today the domain of the military, Barrackpore—house, garden, and park—can not have altered much since her death. The Indian Commandant wearing medal ribbons and the escort of soldiers accompanying him drew themselves to respectful attention. Leaning forward to read the inscription, sight for a moment was blurred by the courtesy of their action.

'... *Honours and praises written on a tomb are at best but vainglory; but that her charity, humility, meekness, and watchful faith in her Saviour will, for that Saviour's sake, be accepted of God, and be to her a glory everlasting, is the firm trust of those who knew her best, and most dearly loved her in life, and who cherish the memory of her, departed.*'

Her husband, it was said, had prepared this epitaph the day after her burial, and three years later Sir Gilbert Scott had executed a white marble monument from a design by her sister. But the inlaid cross of Italian mosaic surmounting a towering headstone had suffered from monsoon rains and this simpler copy in Indian marble was later erected in its stead, the original being placed in St John's at Calcutta. Of this one had read. How also Lord Canning on looking through her diaries had seemed to break down altogether; how he had then realised for the first time the depth of her suffering and how devoted and self-sacrificing and loyal had been her love for him all her life. It was too late to make amends.[1] Stricken in spirit and destroyed in health he had sailed home to England, dying there seven months after his wife. She had left no will; he had not altered his. All that had belonged to her was sold, some of her trinkets, amongst them two rings she had always worn, were bought by Queen Victoria, to pass on to Lady Stuart de Rothesay who had received nothing.[2]

Glancing again at the grave the traveller read of Canning's burial in Westminster Abbey, and the recollection of the marble images of the three Canning statesmen in the north-east transept of London's great Valhalla seemed not incongruous under that wide Indian sky. Of the three, Stratford de Redcliffe, the 'third great Canning' and the last to die, is placed slightly apart, while father and son, Prime Minister and first Viceroy of India, stand together in lasting fame.

Yet outwardly Lady Canning's grave was not a lonely one. Perhaps some stirring of memory, some understanding of what Canning in his liberal policy had aimed at for India, some knowledge of how his wife had been loved, had disposed Authority to unite their monuments. Until the 1960s the bronze equestrian statue of Earl Canning had stood proudly in sight of Government House, Calcutta. Now as he sits his horse within the burial enclosure at Barrackpore, his lowered eyes gazing enigmatically over the broad sweep of water—that same river which had witnessed their arrival in India so many years ago—he seems to keep sentinel over his wife sleeping undisturbed in Indian soil.

With these thoughts crowding the mind the traveller, turning to leave, caught sight of a further inscription on the white marble, glittering now in the heat of midday, and stooped to read:

'I will ransom them from the grave, I will redeem them from death.'

Reference Notes

LIST OF ABBREVIATIONS

RA	Royal Archives, Windsor Castle
Journal	Queen Victoria's Journal, Royal Archives
Eleanor Stanley	*Twenty Years at Court: Hon. Eleanor Stanley*, ed. Mrs S. Erskine, 1916
Granville	*Letters of Harriet, Countess Granville*, ed. F. Leveson-Gower, 1894
I.O.L.	India Office Library and Records
Letters	*Letters of Queen Victoria, 1837–61*, ed. A. C. Benson and Viscount Esher, 1907
Malmesbury	*Memoirs of an Ex-Minister*, Earl of Malmesbury, 1884
P.R.O.	Public Record Office
Stanley	*The Stanleys of Alderley*, ed. N. Mitford, 1939

CHARLOTTE STUART, *pp. 7–19*

1 *George IV, Regent and King*, C. Hibbert, 1973, 121. The sheet of paper used by Princess Elizabeth lacks any pretensions to elegance and is plain in the extreme.
2 *Granville*, i, 105
3 *Journals & Correspondence of Miss Berry*, ed. T. Lewis, 1866, iii, 74
4 *Ibid.*, 197
5 *The Jerningham Letters*, ed. E. Castle, 1896, ii, 92–3
6 *Granville*, i, 106
7 *Ibid.*, i, 114
8 *Ibid.*, i, 96
9 *Ibid.*, i, 118
10 *The Story of my Life*, A. Hare, 1896, iii, 14
11 *Granville*, ii, 23–4
12 *Greville Memoirs*, ed. L. Strachey and R. Fulford, i, 219
13 *Letters of Lady Louisa Stuart*, ed. J. A. Home, 1903, 38
14 *Granville*, ii, 76, 78
15 *Ibid.*, ii, 89
16 *Ibid.*, ii, 91

17 P.R.O. Crest 2/533/256, 144
18 P.R.O. Crest 2/533/452
19 P.R.O. Crest 2/534/1687
20 *Highcliffe and the Stuarts*, V. Stuart-Wortley, 1927, 303, 304, 306
21 P.R.O. Crest 2/534/4795
22 Private information
23 Malmesbury, i, 273
24 *Highcliffe and the Stuarts*, 321
25 *Granville*, i, 216

DEATH AND AGUE, *pp. 20–32*
1 Newcastle MSS., St Deiniol's Library, Hawarden, Flintshire
2 Correspondence of W. E. Gladstone and his wife, St Deiniol's Library
3 *Chronique de la Duchesse de Dino*, ed. Princesse Radziwill, 1909, i, 40
4 *Granville*, ii, 224–5
5 *Ibid.*, ii, 232, 233
6 Malmesbury, i, 79
7 *Granville*, ii, 233
8 *Ibid.*, ii, 233
9 *The Spas of Germany, France and Italy*, T. M. Madden, 1867, 94–5

TO VENICE BY 'GONDOLA', *pp. 33–44*
1 Malmesbury, i, 191
2 *Elizabeth, Lady Holland to her Son*, ed. Earl of Ilchester, 1946, 175
3 Unpublished diary of Mary Richardson
4 *Russian Journal of Lady Londonderry*, ed. W. A. L. Seaman and J. R. Sewell, 1973, 5–6

LORD WATERFORD'S COURTSHIP, *pp. 45–58*
1 *Elizabeth, Lady Holland*, 191
2 *Letters*, i, 409
3 *Ibid.*, i, 442
4 P.R.O. Fo65/273
5 *A Memoir of Baron Bunsen*, Baroness Bunsen, 1868, i, 625
6 *Ibid.*, ii, 13
7 *Ibid.*, ii, 15
8 *Ibid.*, ii, 1, 3, 172. Seven years later Lady Stuart de Rothesay had a brush with her tenant over the rent, though Charlotte seems not to have taken entirely her mother's point of view. In 1849 the Bunsens removed in two days to No 9, where they gained a greater amount of space and light. 'What a dreadful hurry skurry his evacuation will be. I think as I was going away from Mme Bunsen the other day', Char wrote, 'she muttered something about "With all their fondness for the house everything came to an end

at last." I did not hear distinctly for my back was turned & I was involved in the dark labyrinth of doors & did not know whether it was a pious speech or a little moral & she said "f*u*ndness" & I heard it "f*u*nds", I thought it was something about the furniture being old & wanting repair & only on repeating the sounds to myself I made out what I have written.'

9 *Diary of Philipp von Neumann*, ed. E. Beresford Chancellor, 1928, ii, 161
10 Malmesbury, i, 105–6
11 *Greville Memoirs*, iv, 181
12 *Russian Journal of Lady Londonderry*, 109
13 *The Lieven–Palmerston Correspondence*, ed. Lord Sudeley, 1943, 140, 215
14 *Elizabeth, Lady Holland*, 219
15 *Lieven-Palmerston*, 221
16 *Catherine Gladstone*, M. Drew, 1919, 45
17 *Baron Bunsen*, ii, 7
18 *Reminiscences of Lady Dorothy Nevill*, ed. R. Nevill, 1919, 54
19 *von Neumann*, ii, 183–4
20 *Murray's Handbook for Northern Europe*, 1849, ii, 397
21 P.R.O. F065/279
22 P.R.O. F065/281
23 *Duchesse de Dino*, iii, 195
24 *Lord William Russell and his wife*, G. Blakiston, 1972, 463

AN HONOURABLE DISTINCTION, *pp. 59–65*

1 Journal, June 1842
2 RA S15/21
3 *Correspondence of Sarah Spencer, Lady Lyttelton*, ed. Mrs H. Wyndham, 1912, 330
4 *von Neumann*, ii, 188
5 *Elizabeth, Lady Holland*, 191
6 *Lieven-Palmerston*, 235, 239

A COMMISSION FROM THE QUEEN, *pp. 66–75*

1 *Lieven-Palmerston*, 239
2 *Reminiscences of Court & Diplomatic Life*, Georgiana, Baroness Bloomfield, 1883, i, 53
3 Journal, Dec 20 1842

QUEEN VICTORIA'S RUSSIAN TORQUOISES, *pp. 76–85*

1 *The Victorian Country House*, M. Girouard, 1971, 131
2 *Duke of Argyll, Autobiography & Memoirs*, 1906, 155
3 *Elizabeth, Lady Holland*, 218
4 Malmesbury, i, 160

Reference Notes

ON BOARD THE ROYAL YACHT, *pp. 86–93*

1 *Letters*, i, 608

A VISIT TO KING LEOPOLD, *pp. 107–118*

1 Eleanor Stanley, 45
2 Journal, Sept 13 1843
3 Journal, Sept 15 1843
4 *Charlotte Brontë*, W. Gérin, 1967, 243. Charlotte Brontë also noted that the Queen was 'laughing and talking gaily'.

REPORTS FROM ST PETERSBURG AND WINDSOR, *pp. 119–128*

1 Eleanor Stanley, 39
2 *Ibid.*, 59, 67
3 P.R.O. Fo65/298
4 P.R.O. Fo65/298
5 P.R.O. Fo65/298
6 P.R.O. Fo65/298

ROSENAU AND GOTHA, *pp. 149–165*

1 *Reminiscences*, Baroness Bloomfield, i, 108
2 *Illustrated London News*, Nov 2 1844, 275
3 *Letters*, ii, 32
4 *Illustrated London News*, Aug 30 1845, 136
5 *Life of the Prince Consort*, T. Martin, 1875, i, 281
6 *Ibid.*,
7 *Ibid.*, i, 285
8 *Ibid.*, i, 289–90
9 *Ibid.*, i, 287
10 *Coburg State Archives*, LA AI 28b 17A III Nr. 54; ebd. 17L III Nr. 93
11 RA Z279/38
12 Journal, Sept 11 1845
13 Journal, Sept 12 1845

TINTED STATUE OF THE QUEEN, *pp. 166–173*

1 I.O.L., MSS. EUR D661
2 *Society, Politics and Diplomacy*, F. W. H. Cavendish, 1913, 181
3 Eleanor Stanley, 125
4 RA M50/50
5 RA M50/50
6 Malmesbury, i, 186, 188

FAMILY BETROTHALS, *pp. 174–183*

1 *Victoria R.I.*, E. Longford, 1964, 576n

2 Journal, May 4 1849
3 Journal, June 17 1849
4 Journal, June 20 1849
5 RA Add. MSS. C4
6 Eleanor Stanley, 176
7 *Ibid.*, 168
8 Journal, Nov 21 1849
9 *Society, Politics and Diplomacy*, 181, and Index
10 *Letters, Remains and Memoirs of the Duke of Somerset*, ed. W. H. Mallock and G. Ramsden, 1893, 281

MISS NIGHTINGALE, *pp. 184–192*
1 *Reminiscences*, Baroness Bloomfield, i, 219
2 RA S15/37
3 RA S15/38
4 Eleanor Stanley, 219
5 *Letters*, ii, 542
6 *Florence Nightingale*, C. Woodham-Smith, 1950, 110

LORD CANNING'S APPOINTMENT, *pp. 193–200*
1 Malmesbury, ii, 82
2 I.O.L., MSS. EUR D661
3 *Life & Letters of Lady Dorothy Nevill*, ed. R. Nevill, 1919, 187
4 Journal, Nov 22, 24, 1855
5 RA Z502/1
6 *'Clemency' Canning*, M. Maclagan, 1962, 23
7 RA Z502/1

GOVERNMENT HOUSE, *pp. 203–214*
1 RA Z502/3
2 RA Z502/4
3 RA Z502/7
4 RA Z502/5
5 RA Z502/5
6 RA Z502/5

'IN COURTLY STYLE', *pp. 215–224*
1 *Young America abroad in Europe, Asia and Australia*, G. F. Train, 1857, 182–5
2 RA Z502/4
3 RA Z502/4
4 RA Z502/5
5 *The Life & Letters of Lady Dorothy Nevill*, 185

6 *Unconventional Memories*, ed. R. Nevill, 1923, 40
7 '*Clemency*' *Canning*, 133
8 British Museum, ADD MSS. 47469, and '*Clemency*' *Canning*, 56

INDIA, 1857, *pp. 225–240*

1 RA Z502/9
2 RA Z502/10
3 *Physician and Friend*, Dr A. Grant, 1902, 172
4 *Life of Second Earl Granville*, Lord Edmond Fitzmaurice, 1905, i, 274
5 Malmesbury, ii, 75
6 *British Government in India*, Lord Curzon of Kedleston, 1925, ii, 227
7 RA Z502/11
8 *Queen Victoria's Little Wars*, B. Farwell, 1973, 101
9 *Red Year*, M. Edwardes, 1973, 73
10 RA Z502/13
11 RA Z502/14
12 RA Z502/15
13 '*Clemency*' *Canning*, 105
14 RA Z502/14
15 RA Z502/21
16 RA Z502/18

THE QUEEN'S CONFIDENCE IN CANNING, *pp. 241–251*

1 RA Z502/20
2 *Society, Politics and Diplomacy*, 313
3 RA Z502/30
4 RA Z502/37
5 RA Z502/21
6 RA Z502/23
7 RA Z502/30
8 RA Z502/26
9 RA Z502/27
10 RA Z502/31
11 RA Z502/27
12 RA Z502/27

COONOOR AND OOTY, *pp. 252–261*

1 RA Z502/31
2 *Stanley*, 311
3 *Ibid.*, 200, 213
4 *Ibid.*, 203
5 *Ibid.*, 214
6 *Ibid.*, 232

7 *Ibid.*, 216
8 *Ibid.*, 232
9 *Ibid.*, 213
10 *Ibid.*, 222
11 RA Z502/31
12 RA Z502/31
13 *Society, Politics and Diplomacy*, 317
14 RA Z502/35
15 RA Z502/41
16 *Stanley*, 212
17 RA Z502/47
18 RA Z502/47

FIRST VICEROY, *pp. 262–269*
1 RA Z502/49
2 RA Z502/50
3 *Stanley*, 220
4 *Stanley*, 223
5 *Stanley*, 225
6 RA Z502/51
7 British Museum, ADD MSS 47469
8 *George Canning*, W. Hinde, 1973, 243
9 British Museum, ADD MSS 47469
10 *Stanley*, 251
11 RA Z502/57
12 RA Z502/58
13 RA Z502/61
14 I.O.L., MSS.EUR D661
15 *Records of Later Life*, F. Kemble, 1882, 348
16 I.O.L., MSS.EUR D661

TO THE BORDERS OF TIBET, *pp. 270–281*
1 '*Up the Country*', Hon. Emily Eden, 1866, 208
2 I.O.L., MSS.EUR D661
3 RA Z502/64
4 RA Z502/66
5 RA Z502/67

THE LAST JOURNEY, *pp. 282–295*
1 *Stanley*, 311
2 *Ibid.*, 312
3 *Ibid.*, 330

4 *'Clemency' Canning*, 290
5 RA Z502/69
6 British Museum ADD MSS 47469
7 RA Z502/5
8 *'Clemency' Canning*, 302
9 RA N26/6
10 *Letters*, iii, 608–9

EPILOGUE

1 I.O.L., MSS.EUR D661
2 Journal, March 23 1863

Index

Index

Index

Index

Index

Index

Index

Index